A CHURCH AT WAR

A CHURCH AT WAR

ANGLICANS AND HOMOSEXUALITY

STEPHEN BATES

I.B. TAURIS

LONDON · NEW YORK

Published in 2004 by I.B.Tauris & Co. Ltd
6 Salem Road, London W2 4BU
175 Fifth Avenue, New York, NY 10010
www.ibtauris.com

In the United States of America and Canada distributed by Palgrave Macmillan, a division
of St Martin's Press, 175 Fifth Avenue, New York, NY 10010

ISBN: 1 85043 480 8
EAN: 978 1 85043 480 1

A full CIP record for this book is available from the British Library
A full CIP record for this book is available from the Library of Congress

Library of Congress catalog card: available

Typeset in Goudy Old Style by A. & D. Worthington, Newmarket, Suffolk
Printed and bound in Great Britain by TJ International Ltd, Padstow, Cornwall

CONTENTS

To my Evangelical wife, Alice,
and my Evangelical children, Helena, Timothy
and Philip, with much love.

PREFACE

This is a work of journalism rather than theological and historical scholarship. It is written for Anglicans and others interested in the church and its fate, in an attempt to explain how and why it has come to its present pass, threatened by the most serious split in its modern history over an issue that many people within its portals and beyond regard as being of at best secondary importance to its overall mission or to the concerns of the overwhelming majority of its members.

As a member of the small but dauntless band of national newspaper religious affairs correspondents, I have had a front-row seat to watch the Anglican Communion's struggle and have formed what some would say was too decided a view of the merits of the contest. This would have surprised me a year ago before the fight started in earnest. If my views have altered, it is because I have watched the contest being fought in a way that does little credit to many of its participants.

I hope this book will be read by those in the church who have been left bemused, confused and distressed by what has been going on. This includes many Evangelicals who have struggled both to comprehend the row and to continue to bear witness to Christ by living good and holy lives. If they feel under-represented or overlooked in what follows, it is because many of their self-appointed leaders have been actuated by altogether more partisan, political, motives than theirs.

I have covered a great many specialist areas as a journalist, for a number of national newspapers, but only in religious affairs have I ever been asked about my own beliefs, so I had better come clean from the start. I am a Roman Catholic by birth and upbringing, so an outsider in this particular debate, but my father was a devoted communicant member of the Church of England throughout his 89 years. I am married to a committed Anglican Charismatic Evangelical and, furthermore, in defiance of the Catholic way, my children are being brought up in the Evangelical tradition too because my wife is a better Christian than I am. So I am by no means as hostile to Evangelicalism as some may suppose.

I owe a great many thanks to those who have helped me: firstly to Alex Wright, my editor at I.B. Tauris, whose idea the project was and who has been a great source of support for it; secondly, to my loyal and patient agents, Michael Sissons and Jim Gill at PFD; and thirdly, to the members of the *Guardian* Home News Desk, Ed Pilkington, Andrew Culf, Simon Rogers, Gary Finn and Colin Blackstock, for their interest in the story and their encouragement to me to pursue it for the *Guardian* both in England and the USA. I must also thank my colleagues among the corps of religious affairs writers, particularly Jonathan Petre of the *Daily Telegraph*, Chris Morgan of the *Sunday Times*, Steve Doughty of the *Daily Mail*, Andrew Brown and Paul Handley of the *Church Times*, Ruth Gledhill of *The Times* and Jane Little of the BBC, all of whom have protected me from error and often guided my thoughts in refreshing directions.

In the US I was greatly helped by Mark Pinsky of the *Orlando Sentinel*, George Conger of the *Church of England Newspaper*, Jim Solheim and Jan Nunley of the US Episcopal Church, Mike Barwell of the diocese in New Hampshire and, as always, Nick Ulanov, Princeton theology graduate, Episcopalian, Rhodes Scholar and truest of American friends.

I also wish to thank all those from all sides of the current debate and both sides of the Atlantic who gave me interviews and whose words and thoughts appear in this book. Their names are listed at the end. In particular, I have profited hugely from the advice and encouragement of Canon Martyn Percy of the Lincoln Theological Centre at Manchester University, Christopher Rowland, Dean Ireland's Professor of the Exegesis of Holy Scripture at Oxford University, and the Rev. Giles Fraser, vicar of Putney and lecturer in philosophy at Wadham College Oxford, all of whom have read and commented on parts of the text. Only two people I approached felt unable to see me: John Stott and Canon Jeffrey John. I was particularly grateful to the Most Rev. Rowan Williams, the Archbishop of Canterbury, for agreeing to discuss the book and offer his perspective. Most of the rest of those I spoke to are credited in the text but some wished, for obvious reasons, to remain anonymous: I hope they nonetheless feel their thoughts and opinions have not been misrepresented.

Stephen Bates
Tunbridge Wells
Kent
March 2004

1

THE SORROW
AND THE PITY

'Pope Gregory, the memorable Pope, said (in Latin), "What are those?" and on being told that they were Angels, made the memorable joke – "Non Angli, sed Angeli" (not Angels but Anglicans) and commanded one of his Saints called St Augustine to go and convert the rest.' (W.C. Sellar and R.J. Yeatman, 1066 And All That)

You can choose any one of a number of dates for the foundation of the Church of England and hence its international offshoot, the Anglican Communion. Perhaps it can be traced back to the summer of 1526 when King Henry VIII first began to wonder whether his marriage to Catherine of Aragon might be quite legal, especially as she was unable to bear him a son and heir.

Or possibly it came a little later, in the 1530s, as the breach with Rome widened. But probably we should stick with the final, statutory, establishment in 1571 of the Thirty-Nine Articles of belief, which are still theoretically the doctrines of the Church of England to this day. What men believed 430 years ago about the 'sweet and unspeakable comfort' of predestination and the wickedness of the Roman Catholic Mass are still what their successors are supposed to believe today. Article 32 endorses the right of priests to marry and Article 26 establishes that the unworthiness of ministers does not invalidate the sacraments received from their hands.[1]

The date for the break-up of this great Communion is more problematic. In years to come it may be traced to 2 November 2003, a dark, drizzly autumn Sunday, and the consecration of an openly homosexual bishop in the arena of an ice hockey stadium in a small New England college town. For that was the day on which parts of the Communion decided they could no longer live one with another. This book is an attempt to trace the reasons for the split.

Across the globe more than 77 million people call themselves Anglicans, a significant number of Christian believers certainly – compared with 30 million Baptists and 25 million Methodists – but one that pales in comparison with the world's 1 billion Catholics, to say nothing of its 800 million Hindus and 250 million Buddhists.

In England it remains the state-established religion, though as much in the breach as the observance. It is a significant and ceremonial part of the fabric of the nation, the repository of much of its history and custodian of a large proportion of its oldest and noblest buildings. It has a presence in every village, suburb and inner city, and claims the allegiance of maybe 26 million people – a sizeable proportion of that 77 million – though only 835,000 or so of them make it through its church doors on any given Sunday. Half of its dioceses are running deficits, half of its clergy are retired and receiving increasingly costly pensions. In 1993 its pensions bill was £69 million; in 2003 that had risen to £101 million. In the same period the amount it spent on mission had sunk from £57 million to £26 million.

The Royal Family remain devout adherents and the Queen is supreme governor of the Church of England. Even here though the behaviour of her heir is not exactly in conformity with the highest traditions of the church that he will one day nominally lead, though it would probably swallow its pride and marry him to Camilla Parker Bowles, with whom he had an adulterous relationship, should it ever be asked to do so. But it is a good job Prince Charles is not gay; otherwise the church would be in much more of a fluster than it already is.

Meanwhile it basks in its established status, largely content to have its regulations, prayers and orders of service endorsed by parliament and its senior appointees finally chosen by a prime minister who may, or may not, even be one of its members. It is a deal the church accepts in return for the privilege of leading the nation's prayers on formal occasions, crowning its head of state from time to time, attempting to influence its moral conduct and periodically its laws, and generally trying to set a good example to the country.

In the United States too the Episcopal Church, whose white steeples rise picturesquely above many a main street and suburban freeway, has a role out of proportion to its following. It is the church of the white establishment if not the established church, a mere 2.3 million members strong, a tenth the number of the American Baptists, a thirtieth that of the Catholics. It is also the church of many black congregations and of Native Americans, a legacy of its history of social concern.

President George W. Bush himself is a Methodist although he was brought up an Episcopalian. His change of allegiance may indicate something about the church's declining status, or the changing imperatives of political candidates, though 40 members of Congress are Episcopalians, but it does not invalidate the church's historic and venerable place in the country's hinterland.

Increasing numbers of the Anglican family walk and cycle to worship in the thatched huts of Equatorial Africa and the corrugated sheds of the West Indies. This is the new Anglican constituency, where the church is said to be burgeoning - 17 million in Nigeria alone, nearly a quarter of the worldwide Communion - which is why its leaders are patronized and deferred to by Anglicanism's traditional white leadership. Nineteenth- and twentieth-century missionaries did their work so well that some unjokingly suggest that the developing world should send some missionaries back to re-convert the West.

From its roots in the English Reformation, the Anglican Communion now has a presence in 164 countries, many but by no means all of them former British colonies. It spread first from England in the seventeenth century to the shores of North America, then to the other colonies: Canada, Australia, New Zealand and South Africa, then, later in the nineteenth century, across the Dark Continent and the further-flung reaches of the Empire, even to the smallest dots on the Pacific Ocean.

The church is divided into 38 regional and autonomous provinces encompassing 500 dioceses, 30,000 parishes and 64,000 individual congregations. Some such provinces represent mighty hordes of worshippers in a single country, others scattered and tiny populations spread across a continent amid a sea of other faiths.

Some of these churches call themselves Anglicans, others Episcopalians and their worship embraces a range of traditions and styles from the most stern and sombre low-church Calvinism to the most exotic high-church camp, from joyous singing and dancing in the aisles and the expostulation of extempore prayers to a rigid adherence to the seventeenth-century formularies of the Book of Common Prayer. There is scarcely one form of worship within the Communion whose adherents do not vaguely disapprove of, or feel uncomfortable with, those of another. And yet they all call themselves Anglicans and until now have not questioned the right of others, who worship the Lord so differently, to belong too.

Heaven forbid that this should be a curial church, ruled by a single figure, or a small cabal, of immense spiritual and disciplinary authority. Anglicanism is a communion of eclectic variety, which often finds it hard to define its common features - Anglicans being those who call themselves Anglicans in the words of one former archbishop of Canterbury – and whose ties are those of affection and common loyalty. It is a faith with a hierarchical structure, with bishops and above them archbishops in authority, but with no overarching international supremacy such as that of the pope.

Since the 1880s, when the need for some set of common principles was recognized and agreed upon, the so-called Chicago and Lambeth Quadrilaterals have established the basics of Anglican faith. There are only four: belief in the Holy Scriptures as 'containing all things necessary to Salvation'; in the Apostles' Creed as the sufficient statement of Christian faith; in the two sacraments ordained by Christ – Baptism and the Eucharist – and in the historic Episcopate.

The Archbishop of Canterbury, the head of the mother church, is nominally the head of the worldwide Communion, but he cannot interfere in the workings of another province or impose his will upon the rest. Although he calls archbishops together every other year or so and all the world's bishops – nearly 800 of them at the last count – to Canterbury once a decade, each province is self-supporting and self-financing. True, the wealthier provinces, pre-eminently the Americans, help out their poorer brethren but that produces no obligation or even influence, as we shall see. This largely amorphous and informal communion has been successful for a century, founded on compromise, tolerance and common affection. But now, perhaps, no more.

For there is a small worm in the worldwide apple. The Word has spread across the world but whether those hearing it continue to recognize one another as members of one Christian family remains to be seen, for their leaders are busily declaring anathemas on each other.

One archbishop declares that the members of another national church must have been taken over by Satan, others that heresy is being taught. 'The devil has clearly entered the church. God cannot be mocked,' pronounced the Archbishop of Kenya before the hymn singing had even died down in New Hampshire.[2] Deviation is in the air. Schism is openly discussed, or at least something mysterious called 'impaired communion'. The word 'truth' is bandied about without consequence. Some query whether others belonging to the same denomination can even count themselves as Christian. In some parts of this historically broad, tolerant and liberal church, the duly consecrated ministers of another country, or those that have touched them, are no longer recognized.

The Archbishop of Canterbury, the head of the worldwide Communion, speaks of a huge crisis. But some among his own flock in England cannot even bring themselves to kneel at prayer in the same room as him.

Others maintain that he will not be welcome in their churches. He himself says he cannot recognize an elected bishop in the USA and withdraws his support from a bishop he has himself approved in England. A growing number in the Western church will not share their wealth or recognize their bishops. They cannot agree on doctrine, authority or even the meaning of Scripture. Things fall apart; the centre cannot hold and, as W.B. Yeats goes on to say, the best lack all conviction, while the worst are full of passionate intensity.

How has it come to this? Those in the pews may not yet recognize it, but their old church is breaking up. And extraordinarily it is doing so not over the sort of debate that used to divide the church: the divinity of Christ, say, or the nature of his humanity – the subject of controversy at the Council of Nicaea in AD325 – or over the transforming nature of infant baptism, but on an issue, homosexuality, which affects only a small minority of the church's adherents and which is at best, unless you have an obsession with the subject, only of secondary, even peripheral Scriptural importance.

It is an issue that receives only a scattering of mentions in the Bible and none from its most authoritative recorded figure, Jesus Christ himself. It is neither fundamental to belief, unlike, say, the Resurrection or the Trinity, nor central to the lives of the majority of worshippers. The church's views on the matter affect neither most of the non-church attending population, nor a majority of secular gays. But it is the sore that cannot be healed.

The Church of England's position on homosexuality is inconsistent and confused. It derives from a committee-compiled document called *Issues in Human Sexuality*, published as a discussion paper in 1991 but since adopted by some of the church's Evangelical constituency, whenever convenient, as settled doctrine and beyond debate. It says that while under certain circumstances the church should accept lay couples in same-sex relationships, such behaviour is unacceptable for ordained ministers. This is reinforced, strengthened and partially contradicted by the resolution adopted at the 1998 Lambeth Conference of all the bishops of the worldwide Communion that all homosexual practice was incompatible with Scripture. This was carried by a large majority following an acrimonious debate and, although resolutions of the Conference have never been regarded as mandatory on the member churches of the Communion before, it has ever since been taken to be the immutable policy of the whole Anglican body by those who wish it to be so. It is into these ambiguities of doctrine, teaching and discipline that dissent has crept like freezing water breaking open a rock.

The immediate crisis arose, as such situations often do, from a series of accidents of timing in different parts of the world. An archbishop of Canterbury was chosen in the summer of 2002, thought by some to be overly sympathetic to gays. A diocese in the west of Canada that had been contemplating introducing a formal blessing ceremony for same-sex couples for some years – as other dioceses had done informally – decided to go ahead with them. A gay but celibate canon was appointed to a minor English bishopric and then forced by the same unsound archbishop, an old friend of his, to withdraw. And a small diocese in New Hampshire chose as its next bishop a pastor it had known for many years, who happened to be not only gay and divorced but living with his male partner.

Each of these crises was stirred up into a row that threatened within a few weeks to engulf the worldwide Anglican Church in the summer of 2003. They confirmed the worst suspicions of some conservatives that their church was being taken over by revolutionary heretics, subsumed in a wicked and ungodly tide of liberalism. And they alarmed liberals, fearful that their church was being subverted by homophobic bigots, about to cast them out because of the surging demand by a reactionary faction for conformity.

In England, Evangelical opponents of the appointment of Jeffrey John, the chosen gay Bishop of Reading, argued that their view should prevail because theirs was the majority opinion in the Church of England. In America the opponents of Gene Robinson, the elected gay Bishop of New Hampshire, argued that their views were not being respected because they were the persecuted minority of an Episcopal Church governed by liberals. Both called in heavy artillery from the developing world for the first time to bolster their case.

Although the immediate causes of the division were in themselves small, they were symptomatic of a widening breach. The battleground had been long anticipated and prepared for, so that only a spark was needed to set it ablaze. Both sides ceased talking to each other because they believed they had nothing more to say. It was, as one participant, the South Carolina theologian Kendall Harmon, has noted, as if they were playing tennis on separate courts, serving the ball over the net but with no one on the other side to return it.

The outbreak of hostilities was all the more remarkable and pathetic because it directly concerned such a small group of people – at most 5 per cent of the general population, though perhaps a rather higher proportion of Christians. Church-going gays are a group who are generally rather conformist, usually intelligent, often artistic and more affluent than their fellow, married, congregants. They tend to be single or engaged in loving relationships, and, in the circumstances, surprisingly keen to be members of a church that is highly critical of their behaviour.

And they are quite likely to be in need of help and guidance, filled with guilt and racked with alienation, probably because of what that same church says about them. In short they are the very sort of people you might think a Christian church with an inclusive message might wish to encourage. They are, after all, like everyone else, male and female, young and old, white and black, made in the image of a living God. And sinners, like everyone else.

A great many of those gays who are Christians have also been attracted to ordination. The reasons for this are unclear, but may, apart from the obvious reasons of faith, belief and commitment and a desire to serve and help humanity, be to do with the companionship that churches offer lonely men, the transcendent rituals and ceremonials they inspire, the opportunity to live in male company and even the chances for dressing up that they provide. These clergy have undergone sacrifices and dedicated their lives to God and the service of the church. Statistical certainty is not available in such matters, though gossip suggests that in some English dioceses as many as a fifth or even a quarter of the clergy are gay. The Lesbian and Gay Christian Movement thinks the overall figure may be as high as 20 per cent. Gays certainly know that parts of the diocese of London are more welcoming than, say, Chelmsford, or that Portsmouth has a more relaxed attitude than Rochester or Winchester.

Across the denominations, the American former president of a Catholic seminary caused consternation a year or two back when he suggested that perhaps half of those in training for the priesthood in the USA were gay.[3] The Vatican of course has an even sterner line on homosexuality than other Christian organizations, believing it to be intrinsically a disordered condition and a moral evil. Other faiths and other religions also condemn the practice. Few have a good word to say for it, whether they take their guidance from the Bible or not. And yet gay clergy are still drawn to the ministry.

Often these gay clerics have chosen to work in cities, in tough parishes, where their relationships are more easily hidden, parishioners are more tolerant or less censorious, and where men with families fear to tread. No one really suggests they should not be priests, just that they should deny themselves any kind of intimate affection or sexual contact. Some of them are even bishops – though we often have to wait for their obituaries to learn of their sexual orientation. It is even possible – indeed statistically likely – that some have become archbishops.

The knowledge that there are homosexuals within the ministry appears to come as a surprise to some of the more innocent of their opponents, who have maintained a level of shocked outrage at the appointment of men known to be gay to bishoprics in the Church of England and US Episcopal Church, as if such a thing had never been heard of before. They seem to prefer such things to be not thought of, but hidden.

This is not a new phenomenon. Henry VIII, after all, used the homosexuality of monks as one of his excuses for the dissolution of the monasteries. And which clergyman now would emulate the Edwardian Norfolk rector, the Rev. Edwin Emmanuel Bradford, unblushingly publishing as recently as 1918 the verse:

> Our yearning tenderness for boys like these
> Has more in it of Christ than Socrates?

The Times, incidentally, pronounced his poems 'cheery and wholesome'.[4]

The Church of England accepts that homosexuals can be Christians and may become priests. Those parts of the world that ordain women Anglicans accept this for lesbians too. Where it draws a distinction, and where it gets its knickers most conspicuously caught in a twist, is between orientation and practice. If you are unfortunate enough to be a homosexual - and, in a relatively recent advance, the church now accepts this is a condition you may not be able to avoid, because it is in your genes or part of your nature - then sexual expression is forbidden to you, as it is to everyone outside the confines of heterosexual marriage.

Essentially, though, the injunction is worse than that because, whereas a heterosexual at least has the possibility of sexual fulfilment by getting married - indeed the church rejoices if unmarried partners choose to wed and it does not ask too many questions about what they have been up to previously - for a homosexual this ceremony is forever and in all circumstances forbidden. There is of course no injunction against a homosexual marrying a person of the opposite sex, however, no matter what convulsions, dissatisfactions and unhappiness in a relationship this may ultimately cause.

One drawback of all this concern with practice is that it inevitably leads to prurience. If a church acknowledges that you can be gay but cannot allow what you get up to in your bedroom, then it is bound to find itself sooner or later ogling through the keyhole to check up on you.

Of course not all Anglicans are like this, but a surprising number of those who are concerned with the issue of homosexuality are. This absorption with function creates a censoriousness that breeds either hypocrisy or obsession - two shortcomings that the outside secular world has long come to associate with the church's behaviour, much to its annoyance. Or, as Michael Scott-Joynt, the Bishop of Winchester, told the Church of England's General Synod in York in July 2003: 'My experience of the church is that the notion that we are obsessed with sex is simply false.'[5]

Well, you could have fooled the outside world about that. For the church finds itself for the first time in 2,000 years seriously out of step with society on a matter of morals. This is a recent development, of the last few decades in the Western industrialized world, where suddenly the writ of Christian morality is not necessarily absolute in secular law.

The church finds itself inveighing against a lawful practice conducted by people in private, who it insists it wishes to welcome into its churches and who it says it hopes to love and cherish like any others. It has even gone so far as to equivocate about whether the practice is any longer a sin or whether it is condemnable in all circumstances and by whoever is committing it. If it can be acceptable for lay people and discreet gay priests to remain in the ministry, why does a homosexual bishop split the church?

Even at the parochial level this leads to earnest debates. If a gay couple attend church, how should they be welcomed? At what point should they be told to mend their ways and move apart? At what stage over the rattling tea cups after the Sunday service should this delicate matter be broached? When does doctrine supersede good manners? Evangelicals discuss this often.

This is an uncomfortable position, appearing to graduate sin according to the sinner. But it is also a recognition of social realities in Western societies. The Archbishop of Canterbury has himself appreciated this: 'We have a special relationship with the cultural life of our country and we must not fall out of step with this if we are not to become absurd and incredible,' says Rowan Williams.

For if the Church of England is unwelcoming of a minority of the country's citizens, can it really claim to make itself available to all, as Establishment demands? If it seeks to be a proselytizer – albeit a singularly ineffective one in recent years – can it afford to present itself as so unwelcoming to those of whose conduct it disapproves? One of several ironies of the current debate has been that it is Evangelicals, those most committed to spreading the Christian message, who have been most concerned with the wickedness of homosexuality and hence with conveying a censorious image to the outside world.

All this is part of a wider equivocation, especially within Anglicanism, over sexual mores. Although it believes that the only place for sex is within heterosexual marriage, every weekend the church accepts and marries people who have lived together, and even adulterers and philanderers, almost entirely without demur. It anxiously examines statistics on what proportion of the weddings in the country it conducts, in order to keep an eye on its market share.

The Church of England now – thanks to a committee chaired by the Bishop of Winchester – accepts that the divorced are not necessarily promiscuous fornicators and can be remarried in church. It would like them to be. And it long ago accepted the idea of contraception and hence that sex can be for recreational as well as procreative purposes. The church does not believe therefore, as the Catholic Church believes, that the only purpose of sex is the conception of babies.

Yet the church condemns homosexual practice on the inflexible basis of a Biblical writ that it has not hesitated to reinterpret or even repudiate in other circumstances in the past. It is only 150 years since the Good Book was being cited, in remarkably similar arguments, to justify slavery, but very few would attempt to do that now.

And now suddenly the Anglican Communion has such a difficulty with homosexuality that it cannot bear to live with itself, to such an extent that, after ignoring it as an issue for many years, it suddenly finds it is an imperative threat to its very existence, a line in the sand that cannot be crossed, a boundary that cannot be breached.

This has been exacerbated by the very worldwide growth of Anglicanism that has been one of its chief recent accomplishments. But where hitherto its broadmindedness, its provincial autonomy within a common communion and its tolerance of difference has been its strength, that is now held by the opponents of homosexuality to be a grave and undermining weakness as they seek a uniformity of belief and practice, the imposition of a common rule of behaviour.

It is a serious question whether a church built on the basis of Episcopal authority and provincial autonomy can continue, as if it was one harmonious body, to accommodate congregations from many dissimilar parts of the world, where different attitudes and traditions prevail. Is it possible to encompass the attitudes of the African savannah, of Lagos and Lahore and those of Plano, Texas, Concord, New Hampshire, Vancouver, British Columbia and Reading, Berkshire?

These points of the compass may be vastly different but one thing brings them closer together – the Internet, which enables the exchange of views, signatures and outrage within seconds. No time for tempers to cool or news to soften. This technology brings a network together in a way that letters never could and with an immediacy that missionary societies would never have dreamt of when they set out to convert the heathen in the nineteenth century.

It is an irony that this advance should be used as a means of squashing a diversity of practice, and that the morality it vows to impose should be that of the developing world, a morality which in the case of Nigeria tolerates polygamy, child sacrifice and the stoning to death of adulterous women (but not their male partners) seemingly without demur but cannot contemplate how a loving relationship between couples of the same sex could be allowed. Not, of course, that homosexuality is a problem in Nigeria – we have the authority of its archbishop in saying so. He cannot conceive that such a thing exists there.

Such is the pass to which modern Anglicanism has come in a few years, a fearful intolerance which drags it out of step with the very Western societies it wishes to convert and alienates those it claims to hope to proselytize because of the picture of itself it presents to the world, a dogmatic certainty which yet fears the judgement of others outside its flock who might be ill-intentioned towards it in dusty, distant corners of the world. It is an undignified posture, like a bishop doing the splits, and it cannot be sustained.

But ultimately this is not so much about homosexuality. The answer to this crisis cannot lie in some recently discovered sexual proclivity. It is much more than that. It is about control and authority. And at its heart are base issues of power and politics.

2

THE WORD
MADE FLESH

'Mr Doctor, this loose gown becomes you mighty well; I wonder your notions be so narrow.' (Elizabeth I to a Puritan divine in Oxford, 1566)

John Stott, the high priest of Evangelical Anglicanism, announced in the 1970s: 'We Evangelicals are Bible people.' It is worth starting the journey to the roots of the homosexual dispute with the Evangelical community because it is here that the debate originated and has been voiced most rancorously. That is not to say that other groups within the Anglican community have not been concerned with the issue. Nor is it to suggest that Evangelicals are all of one mind. But it is among them that resistance to any change in the Biblical injunctions has been strongest, that the outrage has been most intense over any accommodation with homosexuals, the organization of protest most deliberate and the threat of schism most clearly and repeatedly expressed. These have been the shock troops in the battle for the church's soul.

Stott, now in his 80s, a lifelong bachelor, former rector of All Souls Church, Langham Place in London, a chaplain to the Queen and director of the London Institute for Contemporary Christianity, is such a central figure in the movement that I had hoped to interview him about Evangelicalism and its part in the rift. But sadly it was not to be. Although he was just back from an international lecture tour and a few weeks later certainly looked hale and hearty enough when I came across him signing his latest books for devotees at an Evangelical congress, he did not wish to speak. 'His brain does not work as fast as it did and he really tries to avoid these impromptu questions,' his devoted secretary told me.

The 'Evangelical Pope', as he is sometimes irreverently called (or 'Stotty' to his intimates), the second most influential Anglican of the twentieth century after Archbishop William Temple, according to former Archbishop Robert Runcie, has been such a dynamic force within Evangelicalism that his endorsement a decade ago of the ordination of women helped to undermine the campaign by the more militant parts of the Evangelical movement against it. There has been no such equivocation on homosexuality.

Indeed, Stott has written a pamphlet, *Same Sex Partnerships? A Christian Perspective*,[1] which affirms that there should be understanding, respect and support for persons with a homosexual disposition but then refers to them as perverts and inverts. It proceeds squarely with the line that: 'modern, loving, homosexual partnerships are incompatible with God's created order' and adds there can be no 'liberation' from God's created norms because true liberation can only be found in accepting them. Homosexuality is a deviation, a fallen disorder. This is a standard Evangelical position, though how understanding, respect and support - conditions implying a degree of toleration - can coexist with an uncompromising opposition to homosexual practice is sometimes hard to discern. The only remedy for homosexuals is a life of celibacy.

Stott argued for Evangelicals, as a cadre of believers, to work within the Anglican tradition in the 1960s and he remains hugely influential, not just in Britain but around the world as a prolific writer and serious prose-lytizer. The Langham Trust, set up under his aegis, spreads the message to the developing world by offering scholarships to likely ordinands and future church leaders to study in Britain, provided they sign up to Evangelical Christianity. The mission has been particularly successful in Central and West Africa and it is unsurprising that the archbishops most outspoken in their opposition to gays recently have come from there.

Central to traditional Evangelicalism is its emphasis on an understanding of the Bible as the revealed Word of God, its insistence on personal conversion, its fervent belief in the redeeming power of Christ's sacrifice on the cross and its insistence on taking its message to the world, so that everyone else can experience the ecstasy of conversion as well.

This has been a powerful message for many years, fuelling periodic revivals and convulsions in the Church of England since the eighteenth century and providing a turbulent and sometimes fractious but devout backdrop to its life. In the last half century particularly - coincidentally the period of the ministry of Stott and a number of other inspirational leaders - Evangelicalism has been a rising force within a numerically declining church, consciously spreading its influence beyond the boundaries of the Nonconformist churches which it also dominates.

In the 1950s fewer than 10 per cent of Church of England worshippers classed themselves as Evangelicals. Now the figure is said to be about 40 per cent and 60 per cent of ordinands in training are classed as Evangelicals too, based on the allegiances of the theological training colleges they attend – a steady rise in recent decades.[2] More than a quarter of the church's bishops now profess themselves to be Evangelicals.

Evangelicalism is not, as outsiders sometimes think, uniformly conservative in politics or morals. Indeed it has always had a powerful social conscience, from the time of the great Evangelical political and social reformers of the nineteenth century, to the present day. John Stott's writings reveal a lively concern with environmental and social justice issues. Nevertheless in the last 15 years or so, it is the conservatives who have made the running and have driven forward Evangelicalism's politicization within the broader church.

The movement's core themes play powerfully into the homosexual debate because Evangelicals believe in the power of conversion to God's ways as revealed in his inerrant though interpretable Word in the Bible. In such circumstances it appears obvious that homosexuals can be persuaded to change their ways or at least remain celibate if they want to become a proper Christian. Anything less shows a moral weakness, a perversity of mind and character, a commitment to sin and an inherent un-Godliness.

Any form of sex outside marriage is wrong because the Bible says so and a homosexual in a same-sex partnership should get out of it and repent his ways if he wants salvation. A heterosexual can escape to fulfil his sexuality through marriage, but a homosexual can achieve salvation only through abstinence. Some Evangelicals persist in believing that those of a homosexual orientation can be 'cured' of it through medical help, although many psychiatrists are doubtful about this. The Bishop of Chester, Peter Forster, who is a chemistry graduate, told his local paper in November 2003: 'Some people who are primarily homosexual can reorientate themselves. I would suggest they consider that as an option, but I would not set myself up as a medical specialist on the subject – that is, in the area of psychiatric health.' After complaints that he was being homophobic and an investigation by the local Cheshire police, he received a ticking off from the chief constable.[3]

Evangelicalism is not a homogeneous faith for, like any campaigning organization with strongly held views, it is subject to splits. Although concern over the issue is not confined to a narrow section of Evangelicals, or indeed to Evangelicals alone, it is conservative groups that have become more aggressive and assertive in pursuit of their view of the Bible. Homosexuality has naturally become the issue on which these groups have chosen with a ferocity bordering on obsession to assert their position. Or, as they would say, it has become the issue that has presented itself to them and on which they trust to stand and fight.

The reasons for this are indeed based on a conviction that this is what the Bible says – a fact so obvious that many of them scarcely feel any need to debate it openly or examine the text in further detail. As an additional justification, they refer to 2,000 years of church tradition. Both of these assertions may satisfy followers and, even if they are not strictly or entirely accurate, they are clearly sincerely meant.

But it would be naïve to suppose that there is not also a degree of calculation here, particularly among the group's leaders. Homosexuality is seen as an issue on which followers can be united and energized in a way that was not the case over the ordination of women priests in the Church of England a decade ago, though that was clearly also an issue of Biblical authority, just as strictly delineated in Holy Scripture. While many have accepted the fact of female ordination without accepting the principle that a woman can be in headship of any organization – either in a church or in a marriage – the same can absolutely not be said for homosexuality.

✠ ✠ ✠ ✠ ✠

Follow me on a visit to some prominent Church of England Evangelicals. It was a tour undertaken in the weeks leading up to the first gathering of the National Evangelical Anglican Congress for 16 years, which took place in Blackpool in September 2003. This was going to be an opportunity to demonstrate Evangelicalism's vibrancy and unity, and indeed the organizers went out of their way to discourage a diversity of opinion. The very first page of the conference's study book spoke of the dangers of 'militant secularism, militant Islam, militant materialism and militant liberalism', all alike in recognizing no geographical borders. The message was clear: Evangelicals had to be all of one mind to face the threats confronting them and their beliefs.[4]

My first stop was with Wallace (Wally) Benn, the Suffragan Bishop of Lewes, a council member and pillar of the pressure group Reform. Rotund, bearded in the vestigial modern style – more undergrowth than stubble – quietly spoken with a soft Irish burr, he welcomed me into the bishop's lodge which is actually a modern executive mock-Tudor villa in a tree-lined street in the suburbs of Eastbourne.

It hardly seemed a hotbed of Fundamentalism. Golf clubs were stacked in one corner of the study, model cars lined the bookshelves and on the door was posted the facetious notice: 'I trust in the Lord but I still have to study.'

Thirty years ago it would not have been considered fashionable to consider yourself an Evangelical, he said, but now:

> An amazing thing has happened. Over the last 50 years we have grown phenomenally. I think in uncertain days people want to hear a certain sound, the gospel of Jesus Christ and the teaching of the New Testament. Its simplicity and power is very attractive. It is in every generation and every culture and it remains so today.

> When you look at surveys, it's not Jesus Christ that people are impatient with, it's the church. Any movement emphasizing back-to-basics - perhaps that has unfortunate connotations - back-to-bedrock teaching is bound to have an attractiveness.

This is a common theme of Evangelicals. It has been for 250 years, but particularly so now within the Reform movement. It is the church that has let the people down by not teaching the right message. This sounds odd coming from a man who is, after all, a bishop, dressed in a purple shirt. But if only the message can somehow be got out, the people will respond.

> I think there are things we need to do as a church, to build bridges to a world that has moved away from where the church is. Churches which build bridges and are enthusiastic about the Lord find themselves successful. Churches which stay still or have lost their enthusiasm about the message find themselves emptying.

> Some of the implications of believing the Bible are becoming clear and some people do not like that in a post-modern society, don't like people being definite in their beliefs. People in the Christian church have not been clear enough about that. Pluralism should mean freedom for everybody.

> I am very concerned about where the Anglican Communion will go. I think there is a battle on for the soul of our church. We believe in a tolerant church, committed to the Scriptures but we believe in boundaries.

> There are reasons for holding the things we have held for 2,000 years. I think some liberals are trying it on. I think there is a calculated movement in some quarters. The church is built upon the foundation of the prophets. That foundation remains the same and we move away from it at our peril.

> I think homosexuality is the presenting issue of a much deeper problem, which is how faithful to the teaching of the Bible will the church be? It teaches us God's perspective on how he made us and how we are meant to relate to one another sexually. Jesus offers forgiveness and a new way of life. If the Gospel says believe in Christ, if I change what it says, I change the Bible. Homosexuality has become the key. I wish it wasn't, but it has become the issue we are presented with.

It is all about Christian leadership. It is not about homosexuality, it's about homosexual practice. I have the utmost respect for those who are homosexual in orientation and believe that faithfulness to Christ means abstinence or celibacy.

There could be no room for compromise. It was not enough for those holding a different view of the nature of homosexuality to say they would uphold the church's current position. They must believe it too. No room for doubt, or debate. No space therefore for the discussion and reflection that church leaders are supposed to be seeking.

If any province goes its own way in consecrating practising homosexuals or authorizing same-sex unions, it should be expelled. If that does not happen, orthodox Christians will simply realign themselves with the Anglican Communion. If provinces are not disciplined I think the Anglican Communion will disintegrate and there will be a fracturing worldwide. It is individualism gone mad. If you disregard the teaching of the Bible, you need to think again about what autonomy means.

I think the teaching of the Bible and therefore of our Creator is pro-family; therefore other ideas undermine God's idea of the family and are viewed by the Bible with disapproval. We ought to seriously consider that we are living in a society which is witnessing the disintegration of the family, which ought to make us think: are we really so sure we have got it so right now and that the Bible is wrong? The views held in the media are not representative of where people are generally. There is a progressive liberal elite.

Even at the *Daily Telegraph*, I ventured, mindful of its editorial stance during the Reading affair? 'Well yes,' the Bishop answered.

It is the radical liberal agenda that is always plotting. It is Machiavellian. I am really, honestly, not interested in party things in the church. Evangelicalism is at its worst when it is a party, at its best when it is a movement. We do our worst when we are plotting, but Jesus does say be as wise as serpents. It is not wrong to be co-belligerents if we are stopping the church being pulled away from its moorings. We have to save it, to save what we think is right.

The only reason I am a Christian is because I believe Jesus changes lives. If I am obsessed with anything it is that. That is what bugs me. It is not about sexual issues – that is just our presenting issue. It is keeping our church faithful to our Lord and to the Apostolic revelation.

Several times Bishop Benn told me he was not homophobic. He said he wished the word could be banned. He wouldn't hear it said. He said he had homosexual friends. They were of course celibate.

Later as we stood in the bishop's garden, overlooking the local hospital, he asked me what Gene Robinson was like. I said he is an archetypal vicar, a small man. 'Really, *really?*' he said, intrigued. 'He looks so much taller in the pictures.' I was momentarily reminded of the nineteenth-century tracts that advised how you could spot a homosexual by his appearance – large bottom, limp wrists, taller than average stature (for some reason).

Talking over tea and biscuits in the lounge, happily provided by Mrs Benn who had been waiting in the kitchen, the Bishop shook his head: 'If Jeffrey John was a heterosexual and holds the views he does, he still wouldn't be fit to be a bishop. There's an irreducible core of belief and if you stop believing that ... well, I don't know how you can go on. I don't know what I'd do.'

As I was leaving, I told the Bishop, who was clearly fishing to find out where I was coming from in my beliefs, that I was a Catholic but my wife was an Evangelical. 'Really?' he said. 'Well maybe she will convert you one day.' And as he shook my hand he added: 'Give my best wishes to your Evangelical wife.' Not me. Just her.

✠ ✠ ✠ ✠ ✠

Christina Rees, a fair-haired, earth-motherly figure greeted me as I navigated the end of the steep track to the family smallholding on the top of a rise at the edge of a pretty, ancient village on the boundaries of Hertfordshire, Cambridgeshire and Essex. Negotiating the broody hens, peacocks and lolloping elderly dogs, we sat outside in the autumn sunshine looking towards an apple orchard.

Christina used to be one of the most senior lay Anglicans in the Church of England, serving on the Archbishops' Council, the church's executive body. Feisty, articulate and determined, especially on women's issues, she got some backs up, including those of fellow Evangelicals, suspicious of her feminism – a difficult issue for them. Her directness, the legacy of an upbringing in the USA, may also have unnerved them. She lost her place on the council in 2001 after lobbying against her by Evangelicals belonging to an internal caucus on the council known as the 1990 Group. 'Archbishop George Carey wrote me a letter afterwards saying he thought I would be the last person to lose my place. I don't know whether he knew or not. Some people in the group took against me and lobbied the Synod's new members to get someone else elected.'

Christina also walked out of the Church of England Evangelical Council in October 2002 in opposition to its stance on the appointment of Rowan Williams:

> I went knowing it would be a difficult meeting. There had been letters in the press, Church Society and Reform going to see him, trying to force him to as-

sent to the policy on homosexuality adopted after the 1998 Lambeth Conference of bishops. He told them he had assented to everything required of him
as a bishop but they still had it in for him. Now they wanted him to confirm
his orthodoxy.

There were 30 or 40 people in the room and one man leapt to his feet and
said: 'Rowan Williams is unorthodox on the creeds and the Christian faith.' I
could see how it was going. I leapt up too and said: 'Am I to understand that I
am the only person in the room who is delighted that Rowan Williams is to
be the next Archbishop of Canterbury?' There was a huge shout of yes. So I
said: 'Is there nothing about Rowan Williams that makes you glad that he is
our new archbishop?' And they answered no.

The chairman, Paul Gardner, the Archdeacon of Exeter, then took a vote on
the motion and everyone supported it except me. 'I guess that's unanimous
then,' he said. I realized that when my face and vote were ignored, I had
ceased to be useful, so I walked out. Several people came after me, crying. I
was quite tearful too because I had never done anything like that before. My
temperament is to be a peacemaker. I stayed up all night writing my letter of
resignation. The next day they toned down the resolution slightly and asked
me to sign it, but I refused. I said I could no longer remain a member with the
current leadership in charge.

The only reason I still call myself an Evangelical is because of the Evangelical
understanding of when you become a Christian – you bring the good news of
God to others. There is the witness of accepting Jesus as saviour as well as going along and wanting to be associated with the local churches.

The majority Evangelical position is pro-Rowan Williams, pro-sticking with
the Anglican Communion and working through our disagreements. There are
a lot of Evangelicals who are against Rowan's views on homosexuality and
take a more conservative line and there are a lot of Evangelicals who are questioning the issue. It's not clear in the Bible. The comments on homosexuality
in St Paul are surrounded by views that the West has long discarded. Paul is
against sodomy but does not address the issue of same-sex relationships. He'd
probably never heard of lesbianism.

People now believe that if you complain loudly enough you will get your own
bishop. I think it has all been highly organized by the conservatives. What
characterizes them as people is knowing they are always right. That is the danger, that is what threatens Anglicanism. Christians should have the modesty
to assume that they don't know everything. There is a spiritual arrogance that
ignores the fact that maybe God has been working in this process. I believe
they think that God only kicks in when the fundamentalists go into action.

The most important thing is that nowhere in the life and ministry of Jesus
Christ does he ever mention the issue of homosexuality, not one word. If conservative Evangelicals want to make the gay issue a line in the sand they are

doing something our Lord did not. They are elevating the issue into a Christian orthodoxy and that is very misguided. If you look into the core message it is one of overwhelming unconditional love of God. God wants all of creation to be reconciled to Him. That message is rather more important. Jesus was ridiculed for associating with down and outs and outcasts and reserved most of his ridicule for the hierarchy: woe unto you, you hypocrites. That was said to the religious hierarchy of his day. I really think we should ask ourselves, who would Jesus be spending time with now and what would he be saying?

I think we are missing the point to get all hung up on gay sex. One in two heterosexual couples in England get divorced. If you are talking about love and faithfulness and making things stick, maybe we have something to learn from gays.

Christians are divorcing left, right and centre, leaving children damaged. Suicide is the most common cause of death among young men. Why do young men want to kill themselves? Why is mental illness so prevalent among young women? These are things the decadent West needs to address. That's much more relevant than what a tiny minority get up to in their beds. At worst, we should support them instead of hounding them.

Homosexuality is almost a disability, something that people have to cope with in life. The church's attitude must be such an added burden. What if the church said it would help them instead? If it really says they have to abstain from sex, what is it doing for single people? We don't have a logical attitude. Instead of trying to pinpoint things we don't like, why not ask how to build a happy, overarching society? Conservatives want everyone to be wholesome, but how do you teach wholesomeness? Instead we are making certain issues the new criteria for soundness.

I think it is very political. Conservative Evangelicals want to govern the institutions of the church and all its boards and councils. That is their avowed aim. They want to end up running the whole church, to make theirs the dominant view. The vast majority of the Church of England support Rowan and would like moderation and respect, without any resort to bullyboy tactics. Withholding funds as some Evangelical parishes threaten to do is not a valid way of leading views.

Cultural imperialism is now coming from the developing world. Just as it was wrong for Victorian missionaries to cover up nudity among Africans in the nineteenth century, we are now being told that we are wrong and that we have to live in a certain way. That doesn't make it right. We have learned to treat other cultures with respect but what is clear is that when some Anglicans speak out on the issue now, it comes with a threat.

I think it is about how men see themselves. It is about a cultural understanding of manhood and masculinity. It is anathema to men to think of not being very heterosexual. In Africa there is no concept of homosexual orientation as

there is in the West. Things which threaten the patriarchy will not be tolerated. Some countries do not recognize homosexuality. And there's a deep
double standard in the Anglican church in Africa: an ordained man found in
an adulterous relationship will be forced to resign then be quietly reinstated –
that does not apply to women: they are out forever.

✠ ✠ ✠ ✠ ✠

David Banting is Wally Benn's successor as the vicar of St Peter's Parish
Church, Harold Wood, an Essex suburb on the outskirts of London. He
is also the current chairman of the conservative pressure group Reform.

The church has long been a bastion of the group, through a succession
of vicars. St Peter's itself is an unlovely, 1930s brick-built building with a
dumpy tower just down from the local railway station, built amid a sea of
pebbledash and mock-Tudor semis in a borough with the surprisingly
tentative name of Havering. There's no havering about the church
though: a poster outside with a single glaring eye warned: 'Big Brother:
Jesus Christ Won't Vote Against You.'

The inside of the building is plain, with a low altar marked with a
wooden cross and an open Bible in front of the legend, inscribed on the
wall behind: 'Come Unto Me All Ye That Labour and Are Heavy Laden
and I Will Give You Rest'. Extraneous decoration, choir stalls and altar
rails have been removed and the area in front of the altar is open, with
just a circle of institutional chairs with red padded seats, a drum kit, an
electric organ and a large overhead projector screen. A dull pink fitted
institutional carpet covers nave, aisles, altar steps and chancel. We might
almost be in the conference suite of a provincial hotel. The functional
lectern has a shiny green banner reading 'In Christ Alone'.

Surprisingly, high up on an internal window, I spotted my old college's
coat of arms with its motto: 'Manners Makyth Man'. William of Wyke-
ham, the magnificent fourteenth-century Bishop of Winchester, who rose
from obscurity to become one of the richest men in England, to introduce
perpendicular architecture and endow an Oxford college and a great
school, would hardly recognize this place as a church at all. New College,
Oxford, is still the patron of the living, but Jane Shaw, the current chaplain and dean of divinity, would not be allowed in here to take a service
because she is a woman and, incidentally, theologically liberal. She could
accordingly have no leadership role.

David Banting, a thin, sallow man who in another life could have
passed for a Puritan, said: 'Some people would not be allowed to preach.
My criteria would be: are they orthodox, are they going to feed the flock or
are they going to short change them and confuse them? If someone has a

revisionist agenda I would not be happy with them preaching here. ... We don't want to unsettle the faithful.'

Banting said one of the things he learned from networking with Muslims in his former parish in Oldham was that they cannot understand a church where people can question the faith. 'I learned not to be frightened of clear Christian convictions. There was huge common ground on social and moral issues with the Muslims. We had solidarity.'

He said his parochial church council demands of visiting speakers that they affirm that benchmark on homosexuality, Lambeth 1:10. Otherwise they can't come, not even the Archbishop of Canterbury. Banting asked the new Bishop of Barking whether he could affirm his support for the resolution and he said he would, so he was welcome. It was the PCC that required this, he insisted, as if he as vicar had no influence over their decision:

> We would love to give people the benefit of the doubt but the issue is Scripture. We want people here to be committed to the authority and essence of Scripture. If people are not governed by the word or speech of God or Lambeth 1:10 it would be difficult for us to welcome them here.

> The new Bishop of Barking is himself more than orthodox. He quietly confirmed so it was lovely to welcome him here. I don't like being in this sort of world but it is the world we have now entered. ... There is a realignment happening. If Lambeth is not going to give an orthodox lead then we have to look elsewhere, like Nigeria. There will be a realignment between those who believe in Revelation and are seeking to live by it and those basically who do not have time for the Bible and don't see it as part of God's revelation.

> There is a struggle, a battle, for understanding and obedience. Just as it was a battle for me to remain abstinent in my 20s. I didn't get married until I was 28 but I believe God has given us the precious gift of sex, to take place only in marriage. I was a virgin when I married. I honour people who are themselves of a gay orientation who say that it is not appropriate for them to express that orientation. Equally, many people who are heterosexual find marriage has not been given. The prerequisite of being married is to have won the battle for abstinence. It is a battle for self-discipline and self-control. If God has not called them to marriage, they have to live abstinent lives.

> I would say to a gay couple, that is not the way of God. I would go back to Genesis. God has made male and female to come together in marriage. That seemed to be the only sexual relationship He would contemplate for human beings.

> There must be a real need and validity for the ongoing discussion and debate, but equally the Gospel itself does not change. This is the faith once and for all delivered. We have 2,000 years of church history on that. It is a core doctrine,

a core morality and this is not an area of valid debate. People say the Bible also bans eating seafood, so you can't have a prawn cocktail, but look at the verses around the homosexual one: it bans incest and bestiality and I don't see anyone standing up for that. ... God knew about food hygiene but He was also teaching us about holiness.

I asked Banting about the practices in his church:

I don't wear vestments, except at a funeral, due to people's sensitivities. We don't want to put up unnecessary barriers here. We don't use the Authorized Version. We wouldn't use it for its language, for God's sake. I would never hitch my wagon to any one translation.

I would never intrude into an area of considerable intimacy and sensitivity but the gay lobby is just so aggressive and relentless. They just will not let it rest. It is all culturally bound up. This is an issue that has come up in graphic detail. The evidence of the medical province is clear. The human body was not meant for this. It is horrid and messy.

We are in need of a second Reformation, but it will happen only by a fresh understanding of God's Word. The Scripture is essentially clear. Even a ploughboy can understand it. If the liberals are starting from their own experience they are making God in their own image. The danger for the Christian church always comes from within, whether by persecution or apathy. It's false teaching which leads inevitably to false behaviour. You need sound doctrine and teaching to suit the congregation's itching ears.

I want diversity, but only so long as there is a core morality. We need to be saved and rescued and set back on the road to heaven; we cannot only be rescued on our own conditions. If there is flagrant and deliberate sin, you would have to say you have no place in the teaching role of the church.

I don't hear the other side talking in terms of the remote possibility of being wrong. They think public opinion is on their side, But we are moving into a world where the church is going to have to be counter-cultural, more so than it has been for a thousand years. But we are used to that; that is the challenge of Christian living. At the moment we are in danger of listening far more to the face of culture than to the Word of God.

People have lost trust. What sort of lead is a bishop going to give? Where do you stand? The climate has changed. Some of us Evangelicals have got tougher.

✠ ✠ ✠ ✠ ✠

One who has is William Taylor, the vicar of St Helen's Bishopsgate in the City of London, who declared himself out of communion with Rowan Williams before he had even had a chance to take up his post. Taylor, a former junior Green Jackets officer who still has the military bearing – and dress – of an ex-subaltern, decided that Williams just did not measure up and so shipped him out.

Taylor strikes me as typical of a certain sort of Reform cleric, both in his assured social standing – many seem to be ex-public schoolboys – and in his air of absolute certainty. There is no alternative here.

Following his telephone call to the Archbishop, the vicar's perusal of his writings and discussions with his congregation and fellow clergy, the parish made the symbolic gesture of removing its stipends from the dona-tion made to the diocese of London and the Church of England and is paying its clergy directly itself. Sixty other clergy in the diocese are said to be doing the same. When the wealthiest parishes in a cash-strapped church start doing – or even just threatening – to withhold funds, the authorities shiver. It is a curious form of UDI for the quaint, ancient, newly renovated church where Shakespeare once worshipped but which is now dwarfed by the surrounding City skyscrapers. But it is possibly one that St Helen's with its wealthy City congregation in the most prosperous square mile in the country can well afford to make.

Mr Taylor told me in a businesslike way:

> All we did was short-circuit the system while continuing to pay our share of diocesan costs, but we will pay our own clergy ourselves. It is simply a gesture of concern with the appointment of a man whose teaching we cannot support. No other parishes have suffered. We support parishes in the East End.

Taylor said that he wanted to keep certain views on the future 'within the church circle':

> When we heard Rowan Williams was in the running, some time before the announcement, I got hold of his writing and studied it very carefully and be-gan to see that some of his views seemed to run in the face of what the Bible says.

> We engaged in quite a bit of consultation with him and his chaplain over two or three months. I had a very long conversation with him over the telephone and I asked him whether he still held the views that he had published, and he was very clear, saying that he was not in a position to step back from those views. It was apparent that he was going to make a promise in public to up-hold the Church of England's received teaching and Scripture as authoritative whereas in private he did not agree and he was not prepared to change his mind.

Many people might find it extraordinary that an incoming Archbishop of Canterbury should courteously submit himself to cross-examination about his views from a vicar, so that the clergyman could ascertain whether it was appropriate to endorse him or not, but Rowan Williams did this several times, meeting with Reform and even inviting the stern-faced members of the Church Society to lunch with him. It did him no good. They continued to insult him publicly, insisting that they were merely being 'robust' in their rudeness. 'If I were Rowan I wouldn't have been so damn Christian towards them,' Richard Chartres, the Bishop of London, later told me – but then he is allowed to preach at St Helen's, Bishopsgate, having passed Taylor's theological acceptability test.

Taylor went on:

> Many people struggle with their sexuality and Rowan was saying it did not matter and I felt we need to put some clear distance between us. As a church leader one has a responsibility to uphold Jesus' teaching. ... He was very gracious, very warm. I was very glad that we were able to have an open discussion.

Actually Rowan Williams has never said people's sexuality does not matter. Taylor has either misread his remarks or, as seems possible, was looking for an excuse to reject the Archbishop.

> There is a responsibility on church leaders to uphold truth against error. I think you will find the mainstream of the Church of England is very worried about the views he has expressed. At the time we might have been considered presumptuous but there are now much wider expressions of opinion.

> If you find someone taking a different line to what the Bible teaches and is not prepared to change his mind I think we have to make it clear, especially with St Helen's being such a public place, especially when we have many hundreds of young heterosexual people who have battled with temptation and a number of homosexual people who do not want to be told that if they practice a sexual relationship that can be recognized as if it was a marriage. It is the first time we have ever had an archbishop who is prepared to say that because of what I understand revelation to mean I will not uphold the Scripture.

I do find this view worrying, that those upholding different opinions must not only recant but wholeheartedly embrace the views that people like Taylor are demanding and may not even argue a different case. This seems to take us back to the burnings of the Reformation. How can previously expressed views be expunged from the record? And, *for* the record, Dr Williams has never refused to uphold Scripture.

Taylor is another cleric with difficulties over women's ordination, though he was rather more reticent on that issue than on gays, since the council of Reform is still making up its mind how to respond to the fact that women are now ordained:

> Twenty per cent of our teaching staff are women, we have as many women in ministry as any other church. They are trained. I would have no problem with

having ordained women on the staff here [long pause]. But we probably would
not have women taking services.

Then, thinking he had not made himself quite clear, he added:

I don't want to sound defensive. We believe the role of leadership within
God's people is to be exercised by men but ... some of the best possible teachers at St Helen's are girls – women – and I will even ring up one of our well-
trained girls quite often and they have been a big help. Very frequently.

Taylor paused to think a bit further and then said:

I don't think I would give Rowan pulpit space. What is going on when we
gather together to hear God speak through the Bible is so important that we
need to be clear that the person teaching is going to teach under the authority
of Scripture. It's a matter of teaching truth, not political decisions.

✠ ✠ ✠ ✠ ✠

Across London and light years away, Sandy Millar, vicar of Holy Trinity,
Brompton, dressed in a double-breasted blazer, shirt and tie, led me out
into the vicarage garden in the back of the church's compound on a
sumptuous autumn day. There was silence, birds were singing and the
flowers were still in full bloom. The Brompton Road, the traffic of South
Kensington and Harrods were only yards away, but here all was peace.

Sandy, another socially assured but this time rather more avuncular
figure, is, of course, the Alpha vicar. He and his curate, Nicky Gumbel, a
former barrister who saw the light, were the men who devised the phe-
nomenally successful Alpha course a decade ago and so found the holy
grail of modern Christianity.

The course, an introductory guide to their Evangelical brand of faith,
has been implemented in churches, schools, universities and even prisons
across the land, taken up internationally and also adopted by other faiths
such as Catholicism. Thousands have attended, many have been converted, some continue going to church. It is a franchise as much as a faith.
The secret of its proselytizing success is its non-judgementalism and lack of
dogmatism – at least in the course's early stages – and the open-hearted
welcome it offers to all. Attendees settle down to a meal and then some
gentle questioning about what this thing called Religion is all about.
Critics such as harder-line Evangelicals say it is simplistic, an ersatz form of
Christianity, but it is hard to argue with success. This is a more friendly
face of Christianity than that displayed by some of those I had been
meeting.

Millar settled into his garden chair, smiled benignly and said:

I honestly think there is a hunger for spirituality today and the issue is how we meet that. The traditional view of the church is big black Bibles claiming powers that are irrelevant and probably questionably true and that is so wrong. What we need to do is provide a site where they will not be made to feel guilty, or made to look awkward and ill at ease. We want it to be fun ... suppers, a meal is at the heart of the Christian faith. We don't make the people who come feel guilty. People don't want to be boomed at by Victorian preachers, six feet above their heads. Alpha allows us to discover what we really do think and that's the key. It's providing an opportunity to explore for themselves.

That in itself would be anathema to David Banting or William Taylor ('No, we don't do Alpha at St Helen's.') But there are currently 7,500 Alpha courses running in this country alone, 74 per cent of universities running courses (and 350 student leaders attending a conference the day I was there), across age groups – though 75 per cent of attendees are under 35, most being in their 20s. The Salvation Army, Roman Catholics and Church of England parishes of every description and across all social divisions are among those running courses – so much for unsettling the flock. The drop-out rate is apparently only 25 per cent.

Sandy grew impatient, however, when I questioned him about divisions in the church or different views. There was a spark of irritation. His is an inclusive church. It was clearly an unwelcome subject to consider: 'I think the great thing is talking about mission. Everyone is welcome but we don't want the message to be mixed. There are a lot of gay people doing Alpha. ... Alpha can appeal to everyone of good will.'

There is apparently even a Beverley Hills gay Alpha course in California: 'Hmpph. I would not encourage that, we want Alpha to be open to everyone.' But sexual identity is one of the seven most commonly asked Alpha questions. 'Well, we offer them Christ.'

I would love to think we could discuss the issues of the church not quite so publicly. ... It's very hard to hear two messages at once. Some people want to divert the mission of the church. We are giving the impression that not just the church, but that God is negative and judgemental. We are not saying: how do we get across a positive message, how do we concentrate on getting the true Christian message across and that the object of the exercise is to experience the love of God and transform society?

But Millar was getting visibly annoyed:

The tone in your voice illustrates your scepticism. There are half a million books on the inerrancy of Scripture. Jesus did not come to judge; he came to save the world. Alpha is a tool that can help. Unity of the church is close to the heart of God. The unity of the spirit is now stronger than it has ever been.

At that point Nicky Gumbel arrived and Millar retreated with relief. They were not going to the forthcoming Evangelical Congress - too busy running courses and then there were two trips to the USA, and to Australia and New Zealand, Germany and Singapore coming up. Gumbel said:

> Many of those who come are totally outside the church, they have had no Christian upbringing or they have some sort of background, they have been baptized, maybe even confirmed, but they have just drifted. Many have never gone to church voluntarily in their lives. I think people are genuinely more open than at any time in my life. They are so enthusiastic, so excited. ... These students are passionate about social action.

He gestured at the dozens of young people scattered on the grass outside the church.

Alpha does not address the gay issue specifically, except at one point when one of the talks covers Christian lifestyle:

> We talk about the Christian view of marriage, one man, one woman, commitment - that is the particular context for sex. That is the only reference. We welcome absolutely everybody to the church regardless of lifestyle, regardless of sexuality. The course is not designed just for Mother Teresa, it is designed for atheists as well, that's the whole point.

> What they do is entirely a matter for them. We are not there to tell people what they should do. We are there to proclaim the Good News about Jesus. Most of the couples who come to the course are not married. ... We never confront them, that is not how it works. People have to work out their own lives. We don't say you must get married. Sometimes people get married, sometimes they don't. The whole point is that it is not judgemental. Everyone knows what we believe: the Good News of Jesus, experience the love of God, which is life-transforming, an experience that makes people say they want to do things differently. It changes people.

> We work for unity. Anything that brings disunity is a sadness for us. It is a stumbling block for people outside. While you are arguing, people are not interested. If you cannot even agree amongst yourselves, why should they be interested? I hate reading about divisions because that is going to put off so many people outside the church. Lots of people might feel called to church politics but I don't feel it is my calling.

Outside, Gumbel shook his head and said of those who could not accept the new Archbishop: 'I just don't think they can have met Rowan. They couldn't talk like that if they'd seen him. We love having him here. It is all just so sad.'

I had assumed that Sandy Millar's irritation was caused by not wishing to be tied down to too censorious a stance lest it detract from the friendly,

open-to-all-franchise message of the Alpha courses. Alpha had been criti-
cized for keeping its head down and not making its position clear during
the gay dispute. Other Evangelicals, knowing I was visiting Holy Trinity
Brompton, had been keen to know what Sandy and Nicky thought and
what they were saying.

A couple of months after my visit Millar finally broke cover in a sermon at Holy Trinity, preached on the day Gene Robinson was
consecrated in New Hampshire. It came with both barrels, firmly on the
African side. Christians, he said, had to stand alone as God's minority: 'I
am not attacking anybody because we're not fighting flesh and blood but a
new demonic ideology that is attacking the very fabric of the church. ...
This is a wake-up call on an alarm clock without a snooze button. It's no
good banging it on the head and hoping you can leave it for another ten
years.'[5]

Pausing only to criticize Gene Robinson, Sandy Millar insisted the
church was inclusive, but people had to repent and could not stay as they
were. The overwhelming majority of Anglicans across the world stood
opposed to changes in the church's traditional teaching and practice: 'The
African section of the Anglican Communion has been amongst the most
vocal in speaking clearly against the convention in the United States. They
need encouragement and support.'

He quoted not Nigeria's Archbishop Akinola with his message about
homosexuals being worse than beasts (not a very Alpha-ish thing to say)
but mentioned instead Archbishop Malango of Central Africa who had
compared the situation in the USA with seeing one's neighbour's house
on fire:

> And if [my neighbour] says to me: 'I like my house to be on fire', what do I
> do? Well, I go and rescue the children first of all and then I put out the fire
> before it spreads to my house as well. And that of course is what is beginning
> to happen. Some say that it is not loving to speak like this. But it is loving.
> The Africans speak from a sense of community. They are passionate about
> evangelization and show a deep concern for the precious lives at stake – the
> children, young people and people outside the church – over whom this battle
> is raging.

✠ ✠ ✠ ✠ ✠

Chris Green, deputy director of Oak Hill College in north London, the
most conservative of the Evangelical training colleges, and one of the
organizers of the Evangelical Congress – he was to arrange a room at the
conference for that handful of delegates who could not abide being in the

same room as their Archbishop of Canterbury - admitted that, yes, on
reflection the language used by Evangelicals had become more extreme.

> I am not sure that aggressive is the right word, I would say determination
> maybe. I think it is a generational thing. The people who are now in their 40s,
> who 15 years ago were just beginning to come into positions of leadership,
> have a different class background. Maybe they are less gentlemanly. We tend
> to be much blunter. Maybe it's the Australian influence. The public face is
> harder. There's more determination in public maybe than there was.

> There are more headlines now, more standing up to bishops, and we are sud-
> denly newsworthy. Reform is the largest Evangelical organization in the
> country. Now there is a variety of tribes whereas in the 1960s there wasn't.

> The future? It depends very much how Rowan plays it. This is not an Evan-
> gelical issue - it is much broader than that. Reform was in existence a long
> time before he came along. This row was both predictable and preventable, if
> Jeffrey John had not been chosen and things had not started to unravel in the
> USA. Rowan should have nipped things in the bud.

An Evangelical suffragan bishop from an inner city diocese said to me a
few days later: 'Oak Hill has been taken over by hardliners. They have
forced out those who disagree with them. They tell me there's only one
woman in there now training for ordination, though they do let ordinands' wives in for Bible study. We wouldn't recruit an Oak Hill graduate
into our diocese now. They have no idea of parish ministry, no idea of
Anglicanism and no idea about how to relate to people in the outside
world.'

✠ ✠ ✠ ✠ ✠

Well aware that many Evangelical parishes would not share Green's highly
politicized, vaguely menacing view and are indeed just puzzled by a row
they find difficult to comprehend going on just above their heads, when I
got to Blackpool for the Evangelical Congress which he was helping to
organize and in which similar views were to be heard without dissent, I
headed for an 'ordinary' parish. It was a necessary corrective to my uneasy
sense of queasiness and paranoia.

St Thomas's parish church, a large 1930s building built of the charac-
teristic Lancashire dark-red stone, sits at the end of a long straight road
leading back inland from the lights of the town's illuminations, within
sight of the tower but so far away from the seafront that the parish contains not a single guesthouse within its boundaries. This is the glummest
side of Blackpool: Victorian terraces, seedy secondhand shops and what
passes locally for tower blocks of flats. There's unemployment, single-

parent families, crime and isolation. Not inner-city deprivation perhaps, but a sort of arid desolation nevertheless. Periodically they find used condoms and syringes in the street outside the church.

Inside, however, the building was cheery and bright, stained glass windows and multi-coloured banners with improving slogans such as: 'Lord pour out your Holy Spirit upon us. Let it shine.' The worship here is traditional, Evangelical, verging towards the Charismatic and they get 400 to services. The altar was still in place in the heart of the chancel instead of pushed against the back wall and, although there was the obligatory overhead projector screen, it certainly seemed more welcoming than some other churches I had recently visited.

George Fisher, vicar of the parish for the past 11 years and his newly arrived, enthusiastic young curate, Pat Nesbitt, were debating whether to attend the Congress at all. They were worried by the politics. George, who had made a special study of homosexuality during a sabbatical, had been on holiday and was anxious to make his calls around the parish. Pat was just baffled by the muffled message the church was sending out when in his view it should have been joyfully proclaiming the Word of God.

George said:

I don't believe homosexuality is the gravest sin in the world. If only we could all be more like Jesus when he attended to the woman taken in adultery – you know, go away and sin no more. This is a political struggle going on over our heads. Most churches just want to get on with helping people.

Pat chimed in:

I am so upset about what is happening in the church today. I can't believe God wants this. We should all be working together. People have a hunger for God but not for the church. At funerals people have started talking about the church ripping itself apart. They would reject the institution but not God's love. They won't go to a church that's just fighting. That's not going to impress them at all.

When I asked them whether they would welcome Rowan Williams into the parish, if he wanted to stop off on his way to lead prayers at the Congress the following day, they looked at me incredulously. Why ever would they not? It would be an honour.

✠ ✠ ✠ ✠ ✠

Roy Clements knows a thing or two about Evangelicalism. He was for many years one of the most charismatic speakers on the circuit, a member of the Evangelical Alliance's council of management, minister for 20 years through the 1980s and 1990s at the Eden Baptist chapel in Cambridge,

preaching to local congregations of 500 on a Sunday, travelling the world
on the Evangelical circuit, his tapes hugely appreciated, his books selling
well. He could have been the next John Stott. But he had a nagging problem: he gradually realized that, though married and with children, he was
himself gay.

He kept quiet about it for nearly two decades, celibate in a homosexual
sense, telling no one, not even his wife. He sat in on meetings at which
the gay issue was discussed, strategies adopted, increasingly thinking that
he disagreed with everything being said. Clements knew, however, that his
discretion could not last: congregations in the USA were increasingly
demanding loyalty oaths from speakers, requiring them to swear their
opposition to homosexuality, and he knew that such demands would
come to Britain too - as they now have in Mr Banting's church. He knew
that he could not swear a lie.

He wanted to wait until his children were grown up, wanted to slide
out gently by negotiating himself an academic post. But eventually, one
night in 1999, the secret came out. Immediately he had to leave his
charge. His marriage dissolved. His books and tapes were unceremoni-
ously and immediately withdrawn from church bookshops.

His departure made a small downpage story in the *Baptist Times*, because the then editor did not think it was worth any more than that, the
sudden departure of the denomination's best-known speaker scarcely
meriting mention.

The piece did not find room for much, did not mention the H word,
saying merely that his departure was related 'to his celibate friendship with
another man'. But it did include quotes from Viscount Brentford, chairman of the Evangelical Alliance's executive committee, offering scant
thanks for Clements' previous ministry, but saying: 'The council want to
affirm Roy for the work and ministry he has undertaken. He has shown
integrity in his decision to resign from the Evangelical Alliance and other
Evangelical bodies. We are praying for Roy and his family and would
strongly urge that they now be given time, space, support and prayers.'[6]

The article also quoted Joel Edwards, the EA's general director - a
frequent 'Thought for the Day' broadcaster, *Any Questions* panellist and
all-round spokesman for Evangelicalism - as saying: 'I hope now that the
church could stand by Roy and his family over the coming weeks and
months, giving them the love and compassion they need.'

After his soundbite, however, neither the loving and compassionate
Mr Edwards nor any other member of the Evangelical community has ever
been in touch with Clements.

We met at Gloucester Road tube station and went into the neighbouring arcade for coffee. Clements was tall, lean and stooped, his grey hair
shorter and spikier than in his preaching days. He wore a summer shirt,
not tucked in to his chinos, the image of the university lecturer he now
was. He spoke quietly but fluently and with a weary intensity.

I think there is a strand in the Evangelical leadership that has been aching for
a gunfight at the OK Corral for a long while. They have been frustrated because 20 years ago they were too weak. There was a period when the
Evangelical Alliance was regarded as too liberal and tepid, but the influx of
the Charismatics in the 1980s increased the number of Evangelical churches,
particularly in the south east. There was a middle-class influx and they had a
lot of financial clout. The liberals were in decline. None of this would have
happened without the numerical change in the balance of power.

It dawned on the Evangelicals that they now had a solid power base sufficient
to challenge the liberals for appointments in the Church of England. I think a
number of them began to look for an opportunity. They would have done better to challenge on a purely doctrinal issue but the first real chance they had
to take on the liberals was over women's ordination. Unfortunately the Evangelicals were not united on that issue. A lot of their ministers after all have
wives. John Stott said there were a lot of able women in Evangelical churches.
They could not muster enough support.

Homosexuality is a much safer issue. You are alienating a far smaller group.
Those gays who remain are tightly in the closet, there is not a lot of opposition within Evangelicalism. You can call on a particular, older, age group and
not seem so dictatorial. There are parts of the culture in which homophobia is
acceptable. I don't think they are particularly inflaming anti-gay prejudice but
I think they are passive about capitalizing on latent homophobia.

Evangelicals have not absorbed the idea that homosexuality is an identity, not
a practice. They believe it is a sin, just like murder. There is no doubt that
they are out of touch with modern British culture. They are in their own
backwater and they interpret that as being in a counter-culture with the world.
They would always be suspicious of the outside. There is a tradition of denial
which says that because the secular world does not support them, that just
confirms that they are right. Their interpretation of homosexuality is that
there is an agenda that has been pushed by liberal sexual lobbyists and that
secular attitudes are not set in concrete but are just a fairly recent aberration,
imposed under cultural pressure, which can be resisted and reversed.

They believe there can only be a spiritual revival in the UK if the Church of
England is reformed from within and becomes more Bible-centred. They look
back to the Puritans and the Wesleyan Charismatic revival and believe the
church can only prevail if it is pure – their interpretation is that the Church
of England has been corrupted by error and moral compromise for so long

that now they have to complete what was begun in the Reformation in the sixteenth and seventeenth centuries. In that, homosexuality is an opportunist issue. They needed it to crystallize opinion in their constituency. They were identifying it as the issue ten or 15 years ago. I was told then that it was the issue over which to risk schism.

They have been trying to blame the gay movement for putting the issue on the agenda and saying that that is the reason they are reacting, but it is the issue they too have chosen. Are they really saying they would have been happy for gay clergy to have remained in the closet? Did they want the old moral compromise to continue? Is that what they would prefer? I think that just shows how out of touch they are with secular culture. People are tired of things being hidden. They know that carries no integrity. It is out of touch with the psyche, it damages people as human beings. The Evangelicals are being grossly unrealistic – the church was going to have to be more open sooner or later.

I realized I was gay in the early 1980s. I was well established in Evangelical circles. I had been in denial. I believed homosexuality was something you did and I had not done any so I was not one. But it gradually dawned on me that this was not something that held water. I became aware that homosexuality was an identity. My position had changed by the early 1990s. I privately did not support the Evangelical consensus. I thought I could treat it as a secondary issue, so I just dissented privately. I would have been immediately thrown out the moment they knew. I could not afford to let anybody know. I could not be open. It was the end of my career once I held up my hand and said I am gay and don't agree with you.

I realized I was going to be in a hopelessly difficult position once loyalty oaths were being demanded. I began to look for a way out of public ministry. In the end the whistle was blown. The only fellow feeling was from other gay Christians. There were more of them about than I had ever imagined. I think it is fair to say all my Evangelical friends supported my wife. They believed I should be shipped out in order to be brought to repentance. I was in danger of Hell and they wanted to save me. When you believe that, it gives you carte blanche to do anything, to treat anybody anyhow in any way, if you believe their soul is in jeopardy.

I still call myself an Evangelical. My view of how we approach God is still rooted in the Bible; it is just that I believe the Evangelicals have been reading the Bible wrongly. They are quite skilled in using the Bible on doctrine but not on ethical issues. They are raising homosexuality to a credal level as if you are questioning the Trinity. Can you say the whole edifice of the church is in danger over this issue? We are not talking about the lewd extremes. We are talking about faithful gays and their partners. Is that really going to bring the whole thing down?

I think they want some kind of greater autonomy while hanging on to their property, which is useful to them in terms of their Evangelism. They don't want to sacrifice that. They see the Church of England as the best boat to fish from. They want to shed the oversight of liberal bishops and they will break the church. They will not step back from the political reordering because they know that another opportunity may not come along again. There will have to be some kind of partition to bring peace and there will be no more room for any kind of gay Christian except those who believe in celibacy as their only role in life. That will make it impossible to evangelize the gay community. That is a price they are willing to pay.

I see the Bible as the instrument of a personal relationship with God but they are treating it like the Qur'an. That is why they are beginning to talk like fundamentalists, but theirs is the wrong kind of certainty. In debate they don't know how to retain their convictions that secure them in their identity and yet to have an open mind to engage in discussion. Power makes people conservative you know, you want to preserve things, not to challenge them. What harm is homosexuality doing? Very little in the world compared with the sorts of policies the Evangelicals are supporting in the USA and over Iraq and Israel, policies which are actually killing people. That is what we ought to be talking about and challenging.

3

IN THE BEGINNING
WAS THE WORD

'Both read the Bible day and night,
But thou read'st black where I read white.'
(William Blake, 'The Everlasting Gospel')

The Bible forms the Alpha and the Omega of the Evangelicals', indeed many Christians', objection to homosexuality. It is the only justification for their position that offers some protection from the automatic charge of homophobia: they themselves are not being hostile to homosexuals because of prejudice, but rather because they are following the Word of God.

There are occasional attempts to widen the argument by justifying the position on grounds of a social morality or medical imperatives – alleging that gays are more promiscuous or more prone to disease because of their practices than heterosexuals. The figure of 74 per cent of gay men having multiple partners, taken from one study in which a sample of gay men was questioned, is sometimes cited, as is the assertion that only a small minority remain in faithful monogamous relationships, though of course the nature of the relationship, monogamous or not, scarcely matters to Christians if it is active, since both are sinful.

The thickness of the rectum wall, particularly in children, is also sometimes mentioned, rather suggesting that all homosexuals are also necessarily paedophiles, which is absolutely not the case at all. But these are very much add-on after-thoughts, a sort of additional medical justification rather than essential to the case. Indeed one recent article along these lines by Dr Peter Saunders, who happens to be the general secretary of the Christian Medical Fellowship, adds after medical analysis and statistics: 'God has the right both to tell us how we ought to live and to call us to account for the way that we do,' which suggests a less coolly detached professional attitude than might have been supposed.[1]

The Bible is central to this – and more importantly its hermeneutics: the interpretation and authority accorded to Scripture by both sides in the debate – because of the Evangelical view of where the Scriptures fit in their belief. Homosexuality is just part of this wider picture, a symptom rather than necessarily central to how Christians view their worship. This is especially the case in Anglicanism where there has been a long-running debate about the role of the Bible in moral decision making. The liberal or revisionist view is that the church itself has authority, using, interpreting and applying Biblical truth and taking into account social changes: God's revelation not being complete in what He says in the Bible but evolving and being re-illuminated through time and circumstance. The traditionalist view, largely taken by Evangelicals, places the Bible above the church, as the ultimate, higher authority rather than the sensibilities of the current church and its leaders.

Put this way, the homosexuality debate starts to fall into place. Providing one is sure of what the Bible says, alternative interpretations or accommodations with current social morality are irrelevant and an evasion of what God is saying. If you cleave fast to the Bible and its unchanging solutions – or at least your reading of them – then any debate is unnecessary at best and malignly intentioned at worst, an attempt to undermine the objective, unwavering truth. And that way Satan lies, preying on men's souls, imperilling their salvation and spreading falsity.

The current debate stumbles into this at the very point when Anglicanism is undergoing a struggle for its soul between those who want to insist on making the Bible central, a focus of symbolic authority, and those who believe it is only part of what needs to be taken into account in Christian belief. Until recently the latter – the so-called liberals – held sway in this debate, but over the last 15 years the Evangelicals have seized on their growing numbers and influence, in England at least, to push their agenda, with homosexuality the battering ram used to do it. In the Episcopal Church in the USA too, traditionalists argued in 2003 that they were protesting against a liberal elite that was trying to foist unsound, un-Biblical and unworkable doctrines on them.

The labels bandied about here are not particularly helpful or just, though both sides use them to demonize their enemies. Not all Evangelicals are hostile to homosexuality – nor are the conservative ritualists, the so-called high-church Anglicans, who may make common cause with Evangelicals in opposition to women's ordination, but who also include a high proportion of the church's gays. And not all liberals – a word of much greater secular political abuse in the USA than in Britain – are hostile to tradition.

As Colin Slee, the Dean of Southwark, a pugnacious and outspoken supporter of Jeffrey John and the liberal cause, argued in a sermon at the launch of the Inclusive Church group at Putney in August 2003:

> We need to relearn the vocabulary. I give you an example: I insist the cathedral clergy wear black shirts, because it is a statement of history and origin, a uniform deeply rooted in tradition and monastic antecedents; none of those sky-coloured shades indicative of a deep Mariological tendency which would shock their habitual wearers; nor the floral extravaganzas more symptomatic of a photo collage of the Chelsea Flower Show than the hard work of saving souls – and black shoes and socks; and be at the daily offices.

> Until General Synod said we could, we didn't conduct second marriages; we don't do same-sex blessings or admit children to communion before confirmation. All that makes me a 'liberal', a 'modernizer'. Then there are those who, like the Archbishop of Sydney, don't wear clerical dress, so you don't know who they are or what they represent, have liturgies which pay scant attention to canon law if at all, seek lay presidency at the Eucharist, re-baptize, are unaware that, after Alpha, the Greek alphabet continues with Beta and Gamma all the way to Omega. All that makes them 'conservative'.[2]

You get a flavour of the tenor of the debate here, as well as a warning about labels. This is a battle for Anglican supremacy, fought over its traditional roots, its plurality, autonomy and toleration, using the Bible to flatten the other side and homosexuality to force them to give way. Both sides use the Bible, but neither can agree on its meaning, or even how to read or interpret it.

So what does Scripture actually say about homosexuality? If we can establish this, then surely there is a ground-plan to establish the terms of the debate.

The essential argument is that the Bible forbids homosexuality and that, extrapolating, God has spoken directly on the matter. As Archbishop Peter Akinola wrote in a notable diatribe in the *Church Times* in July 2003:

> Homosexuality is flagrant disobedience to God, which enables people to pervert God's ordained sexual expression with the opposite sex. In this way homosexuals have missed the mark; they have shown themselves to be trespassers of God's divine laws.

> The practice of homosexuality in our understanding of scripture is the enthronement of self-will and human weakness and a rejection of God's order and will. This cannot be treated with levity; otherwise the Church, and the God she preaches, will be badly deformed and diminished. ...

> The acceptance of homosexuality and lesbianism as normal is the triumph of disobedience; the enthronement of human pride over the will of God. This

lifestyle is a terrible violation of the harmony of the eco-system of which mankind is a part. As we are rightly concerned by the depletion of the ozone layer,
so we should be concerned by the practice of homosexuality.

God instituted marriage between man and woman, among other reasons for
procreation. To set aside this divine arrangement in preference to self-centred
perversion is an assault on the sovereignty of God. Homosexuality is an abuse
of a man's body just as much as lesbianism is, ... God created two persons –
male and female. Now the world of homosexuals has created a third – a homosexual, neither male nor female, or both male and female – a strange two-
in-one human. ... Homosexuality or lesbianism or bestiality is to us a form of
slavery and redemption from it is readily available through repentance and
faith in the saving grace of our Lord Jesus Christ.[3]

We can pass lightly over the good Archbishop's apparent ignorance of
modern research in biology, human sexuality and psychology, which
nevertheless do not prevent his confident pronouncements on such
topics. And we can ignore his oversight in forgetting the church's policy,
expressed in the Lambeth Conference declaration 1:10 in 1998, which
states that homosexual people should be ministered to with sensitivity.
This is surprising since on all other occasions the declaration is a shibbo-
leth for people like Archbishop Akinola and for the Evangelical case.

But in most respects, except possibly for the virulence of the language,
the Archbishop's views would be shared by many Christians. They maintain that this has been the church's teaching for 2,000 years and so is
rooted in tradition and therefore cannot be reconsidered.

This is from Andrew Carey, son of the former Archbishop George
Carey, whose journalistic career, unhindered by his family name, has
taken him to the dizzy heights of columnist on the Evangelical weekly
Church of England Newspaper. The article was written the week before last
October's primates' meeting:

The fact is that probably for the majority of the primates and bishops worldwide the view that homosexual sexual activity is permissible for a Christian is
a clear flouting of the plain meaning of scripture. This is not just based on a
selective reading of a handful of scriptures but on an entire theology and an-
thropology arising from the creation narrative. The Old Testament and New
Testament verses only make sense in the light of the bias of scripture towards
the complementarity of men and women as the ideal of God's created order.
Any undermining of this goes against the grain of scripture.[4]

No room for doubt, or nuance then. The Bible is clear, without question.
Some say it is obvious even when it does not mention homosexuality at
all. As one American wrote to me following an article:

The Bible's position does not only come from the passages which explicitly mention it, but in the context of all the teaching that concerns relationships between men and women, and marriage in particular. ... It clearly indicates that God intends sex to be between a man and a woman in the context of a lifetime commitment.

Given that the Bible says so much about marriage and values it so highly and says that sex should only take place inside marriage and that marriage is about a man and a woman joining together, how can we possibly come to the con-clusion that the Bible condones homosexual practice as an acceptable alternative? The case for homosexual practice would be stronger if the Bible said very little about marriage but the fact that it does say a great deal about marriage and the lack of any equivalent support for same-sex relationships is something that cannot be easily explained away.

Many heterosexual women are faced with the same challenge (as gays). ... There are many more Christian women than Christian men at the moment. They are therefore faced with a decision: disobey the Bible's teaching about marrying non-Christians or remain celibate: obeying God means forgoing hav-ing sex. ... God made human beings and he knows what is best for us [and] Jesus teaches us that the pleasures of this world, whether sex, wealth, fame or power, all fade into insignificance when compared to the eternal splendour of heaven.

Well, this is a pretty good summation of the Bible believer's case, leaping from assumption to assertion to platitude and then on to something quite ruthless and authoritarian about who it is acceptable to marry and who it is not. It is quite clear too that the Bible does indeed say homosexuality is wrong, but in what contexts and circumstances and for what reasons are less clear and need teasing out.

Both sides agree that the Biblical references to homosexuality are scattered, and lesbianism is perhaps mentioned only once. But such mentions as there are can seem to be at least ambiguous in the light of modern scholarship, or certainly more nuanced than those who hold simply that the Bible condemns the practice would allow. In some cases the translations of Hebrew and Greek texts are problematic. In others it is difficult to tell exactly what the ancient author was condemning, and elsewhere it would appear that specific cultural practices are being criti-cized. In particular it would appear that the writers had no knowledge of homosexuality as an orientation as opposed to an occasional practice engaged in by heterosexuals and no concept of homosexuals settling in to a lifelong partnership. Rather, what they sometimes seem to have in mind is heterosexuals engaging in occasional bouts of homosexuality. It is also to be inferred that it is a sexual practice indulged in by unbelievers and those who are not the Chosen People.

Defenders of Biblical literalism tend to say that the tone is simply condemnatory and that their opponents are twisting the meaning of the relevant passages in a way designed solely to exculpate homosexual activity. Thus Dr Kendall Harmon, the Oxford-educated, canon theologian of the diocese of South Carolina, who is the most engaging of the US Episcopalians opposed to Gene Robinson, said to me simply: 'The special-pleading attempts have failed. The Bible is very clear in what it says.' Such sweeping assertions, however, fail to engage with the detail of the revisionist argument and so miss an opportunity for a knock-out blow at the interpretative side.

The main Christian justification for heterosexual marriage remains that set out in Genesis 1:27:

> So God created man in his *own* image, in the image of God created he him; male and female created he them.

Several thousand years after those words, or an approximation of them, were first written, 400 years after they were translated into the Authorized Version, 150 years since Darwin's theory of evolution, they remain the ur-text for a certain sort of Christian's attitude to what is 'natural' in human sexuality and what is not, what is allowed and what is not. Genesis may not refer to a marriage ceremony as such, but that is clearly what the Biblicists think the author means.

However, a recent study by the Dominican priest and Oxford University lecturer Gareth Moore has questioned even this simple analysis. In a book called *A Question of Truth* written shortly before his death in December 2002, Moore argues that the text is not so obvious and that God is not talking about marriage at all, but companionship:

> It does not show God expressing his will that we all be heterosexual. On the contrary if – despite its obvious adherence to an ideology of male superiority – it shows us anything at all, it shows that God recognises that it is not good for us to be alone and that he wants for us the partner that we can receive with joy, as Adam receives Eve.

> It shows that there is no divine blueprint; that there is only what makes glad the heart of each of us. Or rather it shows that the divine blueprint is that each of us should have the companion that delights our heart. There may be all kinds of good reasons why everybody should avoid homosexual relationships, but one is not to be found in this story.[5]

The first and perhaps most notorious apparent reference to homosexuality in the Bible is in Genesis 19, the description of the angels' visit
to Lot's house in Sodom:

> **And there came two angels to Sodom at even; ... and Lot seeing them rose
> up to meet them. ... And he said, Behold now, my lords, turn in, I pray you
> into your servant's house and tarry all night. ...**

> **But before they lay down, the men of the city, even the men of Sodom,
> compassed the house round, both old and young, all the people from every
> quarter: And they called unto Lot, and said unto him, Where *are* the men
> which came into thee this night? Bring them unto us, that we may know
> them.**

> **And Lot went out at the door unto them and shut the door after him. And
> said, I pray you, brethren, do not so wickedly. Behold now I have two
> daughters which have not known man; let me, I pray you, bring them out
> unto you and do ye to them as *is* good in your eyes.**

This strange little story has traditionally been taken to imply that the men
of Sodom wanted to rape the angels, which makes Lot's offer of his virgin
daughters to appease them – a suggestion not taken up – doubly odd. But
over the last 50 years this interpretation has begun to be challenged. In
any event, looking at the story, what was intended scarcely sounds like a
wish for an ongoing, loving, same-sex partnership. Gang rape maybe.

For there is a problem with the translation of the word 'know', the
nearest the passage comes to a sexual innuendo, though it is certainly not
clear what the men of Sodom have in mind in wanting to meet the angels.
It has been pointed out that the Hebrew word *yada* is ambiguous.[6] It
appears 943 times in the Old Testament but on only a dozen occasions
appears to refer to sexual activity, though six of those are in Genesis in the
context of heterosexual sex.

In this passage it appears that the men of Sodom are not particularly
friendly, indeed are threatening, and clearly God subsequently punishes
them – and presumably their innocent wives and children, plus any others
who did not show up at Lot's house – by destroying the city with fire and
brimstone. Apparently God could not find any righteous men in the place
at all. But what is not so clear to a modern mind is whether He was punishing them because of their hostility to strangers, their aggression, an
intention to rape the angels or because their behaviour in general was
sinful. The text is simply ambiguous.

Some modern scholars believe that the breach of the hospitality code
was indeed a heavily serious matter in an un-policed society where travel-
lers usually had to throw themselves on the kindness of strangers for their

overnight security. It could have been that Lot – himself a stranger to Sodom – breached local regulations in not seeking permission to entertain visitors, but certainly this latter suggestion appears to build supposition on conjecture in a story that is scarcely likely to be true in all its details anyway.

Elsewhere in the Bible the sin of Sodom appears to refer more generally to injustice, moral laxity or disregard for the needy. This seems to be the likelier explanation. In Matthew and Luke, Jesus does suggest Sodom's sin was inhospitality and in Ezekiel 16:48–50 God Himself apparently goes so far as to say that the iniquity of Sodom was its 'pride, fullness of bread and abundance of idleness' and that its inhabitants 'were haughty and committed abomination before me: therefore I took them away as I saw good'.

That abomination could have been sexual sin of course, but if so, it is not clear which. The suggestion of homosexuality only arose in much later writings. In the first century AD, Philo of Alexandria decided that Sodom's inhabitants – rather like those of his own city, of whom he disapproved – must have given themselves over to 'deep drinking of strong liquor and dainty feeding and forbidden forms of intercourse. Not only in their mad lust for women did they violate the marriages of their neighbours but also men mounted males without respect ... and so when they tried to beget children they were discovered to be incapable of any but a sterile seed. ... As little by little they accustomed those who were by nature men to submit to play the part of women, they saddled them with the formidable curse of a female disease.'[7] How despicable (if illogical) of them to behave like women, but it does rather beg the question how Philo knew what had been happening in Sodom so long before, or how he managed to extract this explanation from his reading of the Bible.

For many centuries thereafter sodomy was a term applied to a wide range of 'unnatural' sexual practices, not just homosexual intercourse but also bestiality and paedophilia. Whatever the reason, the city of Sodom has gone down in history as a place of particular depravity and its male inhabitants as Sodomites.

Interestingly John Stott in his pamphlet decides that, despite the ambiguity of the evidence, the sin of Sodom must be homosexuality on the grounds that the words that he says are used to describe the incident – 'wicked, vile and disgraceful' – do not seem appropriate to describe a mere breach of hospitality. That he interprets these words to have an inevitable connection with homosexuality perhaps says more for Mr Stott's attitudes to the condition than the Bible's, but in any event the references he cites in his pamphlet are simply incorrect: the words do not appear where he says they do.[8] Some of the words now held to describe homosexuality are either mistranslations or have come to have different interpretations over the years, as Mr Stott well knows.

Modern scholarship believes that Sodom, which was once on the southern side of the Dead Sea, was destroyed in an earthquake. This may well have been the original source of what was essentially a folktale about the need for hospitality towards strangers, with the collateral collaborative detail about Lot's wife being turned into a pillar of salt as an explanation for the rock formations that litter the immediate vicinity. Genesis 19 goes on to relate how Lot's two daughters retreated with him to a cave, got him drunk, then had intercourse with him and eventually produced two sons. This depraved behaviour goes uncriticized and indeed seems to be cited as an illustration of the need to keep the race pure, undefiled by foreign blood.

The recent report *Some Issues in Human Sexuality: A Guide to the Debate* – hereafter referred to as the *Guide* – published in November 2003, which represents the Church of England's latest thinking on the Scriptural references, concludes regretfully:

> If these texts ... refer to acts of homosexual rape it might seem that they have nothing at all to contribute to the modern-day debate about the ethics of homosexuality. The current debate is not about whether homosexual rape is acceptable, since everyone agrees that it is not, but about the ethical validity of consenting sexual relationships. ... However, [the texts] do serve to remind us that in the Biblical material as a whole sexual relationships that fall outside the limits that God has laid down are seen as coming under God's judgement. The question which still needs to be addressed is whether homosexual relationships *as such* are seen as coming into this category.[9]

The next references in the Old Testament to homosexuality appear much clearer. They come in Leviticus 18:22:

> **Thou shalt not lie with mankind, as with womankind: it *is* abomination.**

and Leviticus 20:13:

> **If a man also lie with mankind, as he lieth with a woman, both of them have committed an abomination: they shall surely be put to death; their blood *shall be* upon them.**

These seem plain enough. They come in the midst of stern injunctions against adultery, bestiality, incest and intercourse during a woman's period ('the fountain of her blood'). But the word translated as abomination may not be quite as strident as it now sounds: *to'ebah* was a religious term related to idolatry, meaning ritually impure or an ethnic contamination, such as eating pork or intercourse during menstruation. It is suggested that the specific references in Leviticus may in this case relate to the practice of temple prostitution.

The passages are certainly part of the Jewish Holiness Code which includes some rules that sound strange to modern ears and are not natural territory for approbation even among most Biblical literalists: polygamy is permitted, tattoos are banned, as are rare meats, clothes made from a blend of fibres, cross-bred livestock, fields sown with mixed seed, the eating of rabbits, black puddings, some seafood ('whatsoever hath no fins nor scales in the waters, that *shall be* an abomination unto you', 11:12) and the observance of Saturday as the Sabbath. If many of these instructions have been abandoned, the argument of the revisionists runs, it is perverse to maintain a special injunction against homosexuality.

Evangelicals do tackle this conundrum. A recent booklet with the intriguing title *What God Has Made Clean ... If We Can Eat Prawns, Why Is Gay Sex Wrong?* by John Richardson, a vicar in rural Essex and a writer addicted to exclamation marks, attempts to clear the matter up. It argues that although orthodox Jews are still bound by the Old Testament law, which was only intended to be observed temporarily until the coming of Christ, Christians are allowed to distinguish, conveniently, between moral laws and the rest, which can safely be ignored. In particular, Christ resolved the food laws in Mark 7:18–19, freeing mankind once more to eat prawn biryani.

Pausing magisterially to criticize Rowan Williams's grasp of theology, Mr Richardson sweeps on to argue that the difference between the Old Testament food laws and continuing condemnation of homosexual practice is that the latter violates what is natural: 'You *can* use a screwdriver to open a paint tin but that is not the natural use of a screwdriver'.[10]

Mr Richardson covers the undoubted absence of any reference to homosexuality by Christ in the New Testament by arguing that if you read the Sermon on the Mount carefully enough, the reference is undoubtedly there: 'Think not that I am come to destroy the law, or the prophets: I am not come to destroy but to fulfil. ... Whosoever therefore shall break one of these least commandments and shall teach men so, he shall be called the least in the kingdom of heaven.'

Thus, he says, despite appearances, Christ was clearly thinking of the subject: 'Certainly Christ said nothing explicitly about homosexuality, but he endorsed the Law down to the jot and tittle. The law does of course speak about homosexuality.'[11] QED.

Mr Richardson concedes that the Bible says relatively little on the subject but blames those who would change the traditional interpretation for Evangelicals' current obsession with homosexuality.

> The attention being given to it by traditionalist Christians today is a reflection of and response to those who would argue for a change in the traditional understanding, not an expression of their own agenda. Nevertheless it is also true that the New Testament is as unequivocal in its endorsement of married heterosexuality and as unequivocal in its condemnation of homosexuality as is the Old. Therefore we can still say that homosexual practice is indeed wrong 'because the Bible says so'. And the fact that we say this and nevertheless eat prawns and wear polyester-cotton shirts is no more an inconsistency on our part than Jesus eating without washing his hands or Peter eating with Gentiles was an inconsistency on their part.[12]

Even so, Richardson feels obliged to point out that there is no need to go the whole hog and condemn homosexuals to death any more, even in rural Essex:

> The New Covenant, however, being a new relationship with God is in a position to allow a different response on the basis of the gospel, while still issuing a similar condemnation of the behaviour. Thus, after listing homosexual practice amongst those things (including sexual immorality in general, but also theft, drunkenness, slander and swindling – let businessmen take note) which exclude one from the kingdom of God (which in other words still invoke the penalty of death) it can nevertheless conclude: 'And such were some of you: but ye are washed, but ye are sanctified, but ye are justified in the name of the Lord Jesus and by the Spirit of our God. (1 Corinthians 6:10).'[13]

In contrast to this somewhat tortuous reasoning to justify the bits that the vicar still thinks should be justified in his booklet, the November 2003 bishops' working-party *Guide* to the debate concludes that, while the words in Leviticus are clear enough, the question is why the rule is invoked at all. After pondering whether the writer was really worried about the waste of semen in homosexual acts, it comes down on the traditional side:

> The sexual injunctions of the holiness code ... are not arbitrary, but reflect the basic perspective set forth in the creation narratives in Genesis 1–2 that God's appointed place for sexual intercourse is within a relationship of heterosexual marriage. The various shadow prohibitions are the shadow side of this positive divine intention.[14]

Deuteronomy 23:17–18 provides the next reference:

> **There shall be no whore of the daughters of Israel, nor a sodomite of the sons of Israel. Thou shalt not bring the hire of a whore, or the price of a**

dog, into the house of the Lord thy God for any vow: for even both these *are* abomination unto the Lord thy God.

Martyn Percy argues that this is an error in translation and that *qadesh* in the original text was translated as 'sodomite' when what it really meant was 'holy one', referring to a man who engaged in ritual prostitution in the temple, though not apparently of a homosexual sort.

The bishops in the *Guide* also concede that there is no real reference to homosexuality. But they say that if there was homosexuality among the temple prostitutes it was regarded as the most acceptable form of the practice, since the prostitutes involved had been made homosexual, not become so through their own choice. This is interesting in that it appears to contradict the normal Biblical condemnation of homosexual acts, committed by people who are otherwise heterosexual. This interpretation also suggests that the bishops regard homosexual acts by heterosexuals as of lesser importance.

The *Guide* report nevertheless once again comes down on the side of a traditional interpretation, more sweeping in its implication than that permitted in the actual words of the Deuteronomy text:

> Even if we do accept that the phenomenon which is rejected is homosexual prostitution, however, the question still remains about how this is relevant to issues of homosexuality today. The answer may lie in what it tells us about the general Old Testament attitude to homosexuality.
>
> The condemnation of cultic homosexual prostitution would ... reinforce the evidence of the texts in Leviticus that the Old Testament regards all forms of same-sex relationship as unacceptable for the people of God ... it is clear that [the texts] are unequivocal in their condemnation of it.[15]

The *Guide* admits this is unusual in the literature of the time in the ancient Near East, in which the practice was well known, an integral part of temple life and no blame attached to its practice outside worship. It concludes that the stricture was a reflection of the will of God towards His people, that they should maintain a distinctive way of life.

These are the main references to homosexuality in the Old Testament, though there is also a story similar to the tale of Sodom in Judges 19, and 1 Kings also contains a reference to temple prostitution. Condemnation of same-sex acts there may be, but in a text that runs to more than a thousand pages in most versions, the mentions are relatively few and far between. Clearly it was not a subject uppermost in the minds of the ancient authors. And there is no indication that the writers had in mind committed relationships, or that their views of marriage coincided with modern practice.

Michael Vasey, the Durham theologian (who was also gay and an Evangelical), in his book *Strangers and Friends* points out that the Bible is also pervasively hostile to such varied dangers as the sea, non-Jews – indeed homosexuality is one of the many vices of Gentiles – and dogs. He wryly adds that in the latter case the English do not seem to find cultural readjustment too difficult.

As far as the New Testament is concerned, Jesus did not refer explicitly to homosexuality in anything the Gospels record him as saying, and references to the subject occur only in St Paul's letters. This may imply one man's obsession, or at least his concern with a particular ordering of life.

Thus, first, Romans 1:26–27:

> For this cause God gave them up unto vile affections: for even their women did change the natural use into that which is against nature:

> And likewise also the men, leaving the natural use of the woman, burned in their lust one toward another; men with men working that which is unseemly, and receiving in themselves that recompense of their error which was meet.

This section of the epistle concerns St Paul's attempt to describe the contemporary Gentile – and Jewish – world in order to explain why mankind needs the Gospel. The verses immediately before argue that the Gentiles – not the Chosen People – have turned away from the knowledge of God and have begun to worship idols. Because of this, God has given them up to sexual immorality, allowing them the freedom to express their own sinful desires, and in the verses following, St Paul describes other forms of vice as well (1:29–32): first a reprobate mind, then a list which extends to two more verses. These Gentiles are filled with

> all unrighteousness, fornication, wickedness, covetousness, maliciousness; full of envy, murder, debate, deceit, malignity; whisperers,

> Backbiters, haters of God, despiteful, proud, boasters, inventors of evil things, disobedient to parents,

> Without understanding, covenantbreakers, without natural affection, implacable, unmerciful:

> Who knowing the judgement of God, that they which commit such things are worthy of death ...

It is quite a list.

This is the section of the Bible that is held most clearly by a consensus of scholarly opinion – and Evangelicals – to say that same-sex activity is shameful and contrary to the natural order. It is a form of idolatry, thus part of the rebellion against God, and probably embraces lesbianism as well as male homosexuality. The fact that it is placed first on the list indicates that it is particularly scorned.

And it is particularly scorned for many modern theologians, because of the consequences for Christian tradition and Biblical authority: in Gordon Wenham's words: 'to accept homosexual acts by inverts would be to deny the doctrine of creation ... the whole biblical teaching on creation, sex, marriage, forgiveness and redemption will be fundamentally altered.'[16]

Nevertheless, not all scholars agree with this analysis. Martyn Percy argues that it may be criticizing sexual activity that is against a heterosexual person's nature or disposition, or that it could be taken to refer to orgies, or temple prostitution again. He says: 'Traditionally people have carried their beliefs about sexual orientation to this verse and interpreted the passage accordingly. The verse appears to be somewhat vague and perhaps should not be interpreted as a blanket prohibition of all same-sex activities.'[17]

Not surprisingly, this view is shared by Vasey:

A different way of attending to [the passage] is to ask what sort of homosexuality St Paul had in mind in these verses. The obvious answer is that it was the public face of homosexuality in the Roman Empire as it appeared from the perspective of a cosmopolitan Jew. ... The usual assumption of [Jewish and Stoic] writers during the Hellenistic period was that homosexual behaviour was the result of insatiable lust seeking novel and more challenging forms of self-gratification. [It] reads as if it is addressing the defiance of the 17th-century rake rather than the vulnerable but demonised gay subcultures of the 20th century. ... It is at least possible that Romans 1:26-7 should not have the sort of absolute force that it has to modern ears - ears that have often been tuned by an ignorance of gay experience, a cultural hostility to affectionate male friendship and a mythological fear of the sodomite.

This is not to suggest that this passage be ignored by gay or non-gay people today. Within the unfolding argument ... it is not about enforcing a moral code but about discerning the roots of tyrannous desire and social disintegration. Its summons to identify and repudiate the idolatries at work in our society, including our idolatry of sex - make it a vital biblical text.[18]

William Countryman in his study of New Testament religious ethics, Dirt, Greed and Sex (who says scholars can't come up with arresting titles?), suggests that although St Paul may be referring to practices that are unclean, he does not necessarily mean that they are sinful: 'he treated homosexual behaviour as an integral if unpleasingly dirty aspect of Gentile culture'. This is a controversial view, to put it mildly, since it has been pointed out that the language Paul uses is also employed elsewhere to describe sinful behaviour.

In his contribution to the discussion in *The Way Forward?*, written some time before his public celebrity, Canon Theologian Jeffrey John claims that the passage is addressed to heterosexual people engaging in homosexual acts. He points to the line about men 'leaving' their natural use of women and suggests that Paul believed homosexual activity was something that heterosexual men wilfully chose, otherwise God would not have been just in his condemnation of what they were doing and Paul himself could not have said they were behaving without excuse. This, John argues, shows that Paul's belief was false:

> There are quite clearly those whose exclusive or predominant inclination – whether for genetic reasons or reasons of upbringing – is unarguably and unchangeably towards their own sex. And, as Paul himself admits, if men and women have no choice in the matter, God would hardly be just in condemning them. ... This false assumption on his part undermines any blanket condemnation of homosexual practice on the basis of Romans 1.[19]

In the same book, Professor Anthony Thiselton of Nottingham University argues that it is unimaginable that Paul was not aware of homosexual behaviour, as a result of his extensive travels around the Middle East, but nevertheless Canon John has fun pointing out that Paul argued that other practices went against the 'natural law' too, including long hair in men and short hair in women: 'nature itself teaches us so'. He adds:

> The truth is that in questions concerning the place of women, even hardline fundamentalists have now been forced by the pressure of social change to recognise that certain biblical teachings must sometimes be weighed against other biblical principles (notably justice and charity) and must sometimes be set aside. The reason this change has come about in the case of women but not in the case of homosexuals does not relate to any systematic concern for obedience to biblical authority. It is simply that, whereas prejudice against women is now much less tolerated in society, prejudice against homosexuals is still widely approved.[20]

It seems to me that Biblical scholars come down on the side of the interpretation they naturally support in this text: Evangelicals say its meaning is quite clear, revisionists that it requires further interpretation. But there should be at least grounds for discussion about what St Paul actually meant. And once again, the inerrancy of the Bible is open to question.

The next Pauline text is 1 Corinthians 6:9–10:

Know ye not that the unrighteous shall not inherit the kingdom of God? Be not deceived: neither fornicators, nor idolaters, nor adulterers, nor effeminate, nor abusers of themselves with mankind,

Nor thieves, nor covetous, nor drunkards, nor revilers, nor extortioners, shall inherit the kingdom of God.

The word 'effeminate' is now usually taken to mean homosexual, but Percy points out that the original Greek text uses the term *malakoi arsenokoitai*, the first word meaning soft, the second apparently a male temple prostitute. He says that the early church interpreted the term to mean people of soft morals; in Luther's time it was taken to refer to masturbation and only later did it refer to homosexuals. The Revised Standard Version goes so far as to translate the words as 'sexual perverts'.

The recent *Guide* report places the reference in the context of Paul's concern about the Corinthians resorting to litigation against each other, because their actions affect the whole church and hinder their chances of inheriting the kingdom of heaven. It admits that the two Greek words either do not refer to homosexuality or that they concern a particular form of male prostitution involving pederasty: 'In either case the texts could not be seen as presenting a blanket condemnation of all forms of homosexuality.'

Nevertheless, it concludes, most scholars maintain that the traditional interpretation is correct:

We still have to reckon with the fact that St Paul obviously did see homosexual practice as a form of behaviour that would bar someone from the kingdom of God. ... St Paul is neither being idiosyncratic nor simply reflecting the cultural prejudices of the surrounding Hellenistic culture. He is instead building on the established Christian catechetical tradition of teaching concerning the nature of the Christian life. ... If [this] is right then from the earliest days of the church there was an agreed understanding of what the Christian life involved and this included a repudiation of homosexual practice.[21]

Vasey, still trying hard to wrestle the words to the ground, points out that various modern commentators have come up with different translations according to taste and decides that *arsenokoitai* refers to a general description of sex between men. However, he says, it goes beyond the evidence to read it as a condemnation of all forms of homosexuality:

It would be more natural to see it as a term for certain forms of same-sex activity that were known and disapproved of ... 'homosexual' has a hidden psychological and cultural agenda that condemns a whole class of people while excluding many men who have sex with other men. ... *arsenokoitai* can only be understood within the cultural assumptions of the time. It is likely that it carries those connotations of slavery, idolatry and social dominance that were associated with corrupt Roman society. It cannot in itself settle the question of how other homosexualities were to be judged.[22]

This sounds like special pleading to me – but the meaning of the word remains unclear.

The next text is 1 Timothy 1:9–10:

> Knowing this, that the law is not made for a righteous man, but for the lawless and disobedient, for the ungodly and for sinners, for unholy and profane, for murderers of fathers and murderers of mothers, for manslayers,
>
> For whoremongers, for them that defile themselves with mankind, for menstealers, for liars, for perjured persons, and if there be any other thing that is contrary to sound doctrine.

The term *malakoi arsenokoitai* again crops up in this passage and this time the RSV translates it as 'sodomites', whereas other authorities now cite it as men who sleep with men. The *Guide* report quotes scholars who point out that the list in the letter to Timothy consciously echoes Old Testament law. Therefore, it says:

> This addresses the current debate about homosexuality directly because it indicates that if we follow the lead of the New Testament we are not at liberty simply to disregard the stipulations of the old covenant with regard to same-sex activity: what was forbidden to God's people under the old covenant is still forbidden to God's people under the new covenant.[23]

The report quotes approvingly Peter Coleman in a 1980 study (*Christian Attitudes to Homosexuality*): 'Taken together, St Paul's writings repudiate homosexual behaviour as a vice of the Gentiles in Romans, as a bar to the kingdom in Corinthians and as an offence to be repudiated by the moral law in 1 Timothy.'[24] It does not explain why St Paul was the only New Testament author to mention the subject, or to return to it again and again.

Nor does it answer a point made succinctly by Christopher Rowland, Dean Ireland's Professor of Exegesis of Holy Scripture at Oxford University:

> Thanks to Paul, Christianity has never really been a religion that used the Bible as a code of law. In his Second Letter to the Corinthians, he writes: 'The letter kills, the Spirit gives life.' Throughout his writings he tries to get at what the Bible means, with the central criterion being conformity to Christ. ... We should not concentrate on the letter of the text but try to get at the underlying

point of his words. So, basing one's attitudes towards gay and lesbian people merely on two verses from Romans and Corinthians 1 runs the risk of ending up with a form of religion which is based on the letter of the text – something Paul emphatically opposes – rather than on what a loving God is doing in transforming lives in the present.

On the Damascus road, Saul's world was turned upside down. He encountered Christ in the outsiders, the heretics, the misfits and aliens, the very people he had been commissioned to round up. It was this experience that transformed his life. Such a turnaround was not the result of a minute attention to text and precedent.[25]

Back to the text of Timothy, Vasey, still doggedly on the track, contends that Paul was answering a query about the applicability of Old Testament laws in the light of their abuse by local teachers who were exploiting their flocks in their own interests.

These verses would be a slender basis on which to urge the church to a campaign for moral renewal based on Leviticus. Before Christians pursue this line of argument they need to examine the terrain into which it might lead them. Few modern Evangelicals advocate criminal prosecution for adultery, despite the death penalty required by Leviticus 20:10.[26]

In this, Vasey may have calculated without the US Fundamentalist Christian Reconstructionist movement. This argues for a restitution of Old Testament Biblical law as the basis for reconstructing society towards the Kingdom of God on earth. One of its theologians, David Chilton, says: 'The Christian goal for the world is the universal development of Biblical theocratic republics in which every area of life is redeemed and placed under the Lordship of Jesus Christ and the rule of God's law.'[27]

Another theologian of the movement, Rousas John Rushdoony, in 1973 published an 800-page explanation of the Ten Commandments and their application today as the foundation of the only true order: 'all law is a form of warfare'. In practice this means that capital punishment is central, not only to the crimes for which Americans still execute people but also for apostasy (abandonment of the faith), heresy, blasphemy, witchcraft, astrology, adultery, sodomy or homosexuality, incest, striking a parent, incorrigible juvenile delinquency and, in the case of women, unchastity before marriage. Some adherents suggest that women who have had abortions should be publicly executed, along with their doctors and advisers. The preferred means of execution is public stoning. In Rushdoony's stern words: 'God's government prevails and His alternatives are clear-cut: either men and nations obey His laws or God invokes the death penalty against them.'[28]

This unattractive plan for the Talibanization of American culture (Osama Bin Laden would surely approve) seems loopy, even rushdoony, in the context of the Biblical discussion we have been having in this chapter. None of the (largely) British authorities cited would remotely approve of Reconstructionism's ideas, at least publicly. John Stott, in his pamphlet, uses the threat of the death penalty, 'long since abrogated, of course', to claim that it shows how seriously homosexual practices were viewed in the Scriptures, without quite taking account of the fact that the Bible lays down the death penalty for quite a lot of offences that would be regarded as trivial today.[29]

The Reconstructionists are worthy of consideration, however, if only because of their influence over thinkers such as Marvin Olasky - influential for a time in the George W. Bush administration - and Howard Fieldstead Ahmanson Jnr, the Californian millionaire who is reported to have supported the insurgency movement in the US Episcopal Church in the build-up to its row over gays.[30] Mr Ahmanson's pastor in the Newport Beach church he attends was until recently the Rev. David Anderson, who is now the chairman of the American Anglican Council (AAC), the Washington-based conservative Episcopalian body most prominent in its opposition to the appointment of Gene Robinson.

Though stressing that he has moved on from Reconstructionism,[31] Mr Ahmanson has supported at least one Evangelical organization in Britain, and derives his wealth from the family's banking and real estate interests, which date right back to the Californian gold rush - his is indeed old money. His wife Roberta is a former journalist who is particularly interested in seeking to influence other Christian journalists and ensuring that the Bible message obtains prominence in the secular media. To that end the couple have attended conferences in Europe and the USA, which have also attracted a number of English Evangelicals eager to discuss ways of influencing the British media.[32]

A notable feature of the current strength of Evangelicalism within Anglicanism is how well Evangelicals have mobilized across national and continental boundaries, exchanging news and views via the Internet, as well as at conventions. English Evangelicals have made common cause and built close links with their American counterparts, both seeking a substantial realignment of their churches. It is the rapidity with which opinions have been shared, and the sophisticated manner in which strategies have been adopted to oppose the direction in which they perceive the church to be travelling, that have often left liberal Anglicans flat-footed. Evangelicals worldwide have generally been far ahead of their liberal opponents in the efficiency with which they have disseminated and discussed ways of how best to promote their vision of biblical truth. The liberals have lately tried to catch up. But they certainly have some way to go to match the accomplished and self-confident technophilia of their Evangelical brethren.

Conservative British Evangelicals use the Old Testament to argue that because Christ said he came to uphold the law and the prophets, he must have had homosexuality in mind, as we have seen in John Richardson's pamphlet. This gets round the inconvenience of Jesus never explicitly mentioning the subject, but it does cause difficulties elsewhere in interpreting which Old Testament laws are really no longer applicable and which Christ must have been anxious to maintain.

Academics like Gordon Wenham can get a little carried away with all this. Wenham, a professor at Gloucester University, whose chancellor is George Carey, in a speech to the Evangelical Congress in Blackpool in September 2003, conceded that homosexuality was condoned in Greece and Rome, opening the way to the revisionist interpretation that the Biblical authors were specifically critical of the practice because of its alien nature to the Chosen People. But instead, spectacles gleaming, Wenham veered off in another direction. Fortunately he found a modern relevance to Leviticus, littering his speech with exclamations in his excitement: 'Pre-biblical attitudes to homosexuality were remarkably modern! It is one example among many of how so-called modern attitudes are really ancient paganism raising its head again.'

Emerging triumphant from an ancient world apparently so like our own, he produced other examples of modern paganism: religious pluralism, abolition of Sunday as the universal rest day, abortion, cremation and easy divorce, adding: 'That is why the Bible is still relevant: it spoke to cultures, which in so many respects are similar to our own. We should not be intimidated by the charge of being old fashioned: it is the so-called liberals who are really taking us back to the dark ages!'[33]

Well, maybe the Romans did drop down to their local supermarket on a Sunday, not knowing what Sunday was for and maybe they were a bit hard on non-pluralist religions. But is the professor really saying that non-Christians (or non-Evangelicals) should not be allowed to worship, or that the elderly parishioner who opts for cremation is choosing a pagan ritual? And it seems he would prefer unhappy couples not to be able to divorce, in which case he is out of step with the Church of England, which now authorizes remarriage. Maybe the Church of England is pagan too.

This unhistorical, literalist nonsense does tend to afflict Biblical scholars of a certain sort after a time and serves only to undermine their academic case. Frankly it makes them appear dotty and it is only a short step from this to endorsing Biblical punishment.

For each of the Biblical references to homosexuality – all apparently hostile – scholars have come up with a range of interpretations and explanations. Some of the texts are ambiguous, or can seem so. They may refer to all homosexual practices, or only a few. Some appear more concerned with cultural practices or rituals or the dangers of idolatry rather than the nature of the act itself. None of them unambiguously or explicitly condemns the sort of relationship that Christian homosexuals claim to be their modern model: long-term, loving and monogamous. Indeed it is argued by some that the authors of the relevant texts may not have had any notion of such a practice, or of such a permanent orientation.

Even if it is contended that the Bible is unambiguously and in all circumstances opposed to homosexuality, that still does not explain why Jesus did not mention it, or why the references to it are so scattered and, in the New Testament, confined to the writings of St Paul. Nor does it explain why some similar injunctions against other practices are now ignored, or regarded as inapplicable: the defence of the eating of shellfish, as we have seen, entails exegesis and interpretation at least as convoluted as the Biblical literalists accuse the revisionists of employing. And if the Bible's lethal remedy for homosexuality is no longer appropriate (except to the American Reconstructionists), why do some Church of England divines have difficulty in describing the practice as a sin? Why not the death penalty, as prescribed?

There are interpretations according to choice in a burgeoning array of theological literature, but each interpreter seems to take his or her pick. And few of them are engaging the other side in an attempt to unpick the web.

It may be worth adding that the other great monotheistic religions, Judaism and Islam, drawing on the same traditions and the same stories – the Holy Qur'an contains the tale of Lot, though it appears to be more concerned with the level of heavy drinking in Sodom – reach the same conclusion: condemnation of homosexuality. In Islamic tradition (hadith), developed after the Prophet Mohammed's death, all sexual activity except between a married heterosexual couple is condemned – although a man may have more than one wife.

In Judaism, as in Christianity, there is a current split on the issue between Orthodox and Reform movements. Orthodox Jews follow Leviticus, the Reform and Liberal Jewish movements are much more tolerant of and welcoming towards homosexuals.

The Qur'anic references are scattered, just like the Old Testament – there appear to be just four – and seem to be concerned with poor hospitality. Nevertheless the text is uniformly negative, if not necessarily particularly explicit. It essentially states that homosexuality is wrong, but its practitioners should be forgiven:

> If two men among you commit indecency, punish them both. If they repent and mend their ways, let them be. God is forgiving and merciful. (4:13)

Islam's laws today, however, are complex and the punishments can be severe – much more so than the Qur'an lays down – according to the judge and the legal code he follows. The most severe, the Hanbali, is related to the Saudi Wahabi sect, the politically extreme, anti-Western movement which spawned the Taliban in Afghanistan and influenced Osama Bin Laden's Al Qaeda terrorist organization.

Technically the same standards of proof are required of homosexual activity as of adultery and other sexual crimes and misdemeanours – that the act be observed independently by four different male witnesses and be the subject of a confession – which may be why no one has ever been executed for homosexuality under Islamic law. But that legal detail has not stopped large numbers of gays and lesbians being executed in Iran since the overthrow of the Shah in 1979 and it may be wondered how openly a gay lifestyle would be tolerated in modern Pakistan, Indonesia or Saudi Arabia without the payment of bribes or the protection of influential friends.

Islamic injunctions against the practice have not prevented a considerable culture of homosexuality or homoeroticism within Islam and the Middle East at various times in the last 1,500 years among the Ottomans, the Janissaries, the Turkish soldiers who provided the sultan's guard, and the Taqiras, the Sufi brotherhoods. Indeed Sufi culture has a tradition of older men gazing at and exulting in the bodies of young men as integral to the contemplation of the glory of creation. Orthodox Islamic teaching celebrates male relationships in what was a segregated society and there are historic narratives of relationships between older and younger men.

There is now in the West even a Muslim society – Al-Fatiha – founded, perhaps inevitably, in San Francisco but with branches in Britain, which promotes the welfare of gays. But sympathizers need to be careful: two young imams who signed a statement of tolerance with Christian and Jewish religious representatives in the autumn of 2003 found themselves subjected to threats from co-religionists who accused them of being unrepresentative of Islam.

The Indic religions are more relaxed about homosexuality. Hindu laws sometimes prescribe a loss of caste but generally Hindu writers have traditionally been tolerant, assuming homosexuality to be not worth punishing. Lesbianism is more specifically condemned with one law stating that a woman who seduces a younger female should be paraded through the streets on a donkey and have two of her fingers cut off, while the younger woman should be fined or beaten. Sikh scriptures tend to be advisory and general so do not overtly criticize homosexuality, but the emphasis on family life and structure lead some Sikhs to conclude that the practice is wrong.

4

QUEER AS FOLK

'I hope you have not been leading a double life, pretending to be wicked and being really good all the time. That would be hypocrisy.' (Cecily in The Importance of Being Earnest *by Oscar Wilde)*

Richard Kirker, general secretary of the Lesbian and Gay Christian Movement, roars with laughter when told that his opponents see him as being at the head of a large liberal conspiracy, foisting the gay agenda on an otherwise peaceable and quiescent Church of England. Waving a hand round the LGCM's cramped second-floor, two-roomed headquarters above a community centre in the East End of London, he said: 'There's just me and one person who comes in three days a week and the rest are volunteers. We punch way above our weight financially. It's the strength of our argument that makes them think we are far more numerous than we actually are.'

Kirker, now in his early 50s, is at the heart of the LGCM and has been almost since its foundation in 1976. It is his waspish voice, his comments that pop up to air the pro-gay argument whenever there is a debate or a passing issue in the news.

It is a small irony that Kirker was raised in Nigeria, now the archdiocese of the gays' most outspoken enemy, Archbishop Peter Akinola, and first experienced discrimination not in relation to his own sexuality but the colour of his friends. As a young man he moved first to South Africa and then later, after a year's voluntary service in Pakistan, to England where he began training for the priesthood, first at Durham and then at the theological college in Salisbury:

> I had never been in the company of so many other homosexual men before. I should think 40 per cent of us were gay. The Church of England has given me more contact with homosexual people than I would otherwise have had. The principal was gay, four of the staff were gay. That was not the highest proportion – St Stephen's House in Oxford was 90 per cent. I had been intending to move to Ripon Hall in Oxford but I met my partner Michael at Durham and

he was moving to Salisbury, which was larger and had a gay-friendly reputation, so I went there too.

After three years at the college, Michael Harding was ordained a curate in St Alban's diocese by the bishop, Robert Runcie, who a year or two later would become Archbishop of Canterbury and who certainly knew that the new ordinand was gay. By contrast, Kirker was refused ordination by the Bishop of Winchester and was sent to the parish he had already been assigned in Southampton as a lay worker 'to see whether I could keep my hands off the choir boys'.

The two young men petitioned Runcie to see whether he would ordain Kirker and, although he initially refused so as not to undermine the decision of a fellow bishop, he did eventually ordain him a deacon. By this time Kirker had found a job in the diocese and the likelihood was that he would move on to ordination. Both he and his partner were becoming active in the fledgling Lesbian and Gay Christian Movement when Harding was killed in a motorcycle accident in February 1977 at the age of 25. Clearly he was the love of Kirker's life.

Any hope Kirker had that Runcie would ordain him was dashed as he became more active in the LGCM in the wake of his partner's death. On Runcie's part too there was perhaps some embarrassment at the openness of Kirker's grief for his dead partner – not enough stiff-upper-lipped discretion about it. The culminating incident, however, was at a meeting in July 1977 of Mary Whitehouse's Festival of Light organization at All Souls, Langham Place, John Stott's church, where an unseemly fracas took place. Kirker claims he was trying to ask a question and was seized round the throat by Stott as he attempted to take the microphone. The incident made the newspapers and Runcie told Kirker he would only ordain him if he gave an undertaking to end his involvement with the movement and never spoke on the issue of homosexuality again. Kirker refused and has remained a deacon ever since.

> Robert Runcie ordained a lot of gay people but the rest, unlike me, did not make an issue of it. He said to me: 'why can't you be like them? Although I am a card-carrying member of the Labour Party, I don't allow that to colour my judgement or opinions.' I was devastated. I had put so much energy into working the system. Runcie also told me that he thought I would have become unhappy with the C of E and that I would have ended up anyway wanting to leave. At the time I felt my vocation had been hijacked. I had never been happier than in my three years working in a parish. But now I think Runcie was probably right. I would have found it intolerable. With hindsight, I would not have found it a healthy place to be openly gay.

So many people are pushed into inappropriate relationships, or they are told they should give their relationships up. Far fewer questions are asked if they are only seen with the same person twice. It's iniquitous: an incitement to promiscuity. So many have said to me: 'I will tell my bishop when I have been ordained', but very few of them ever do. They are told they may be ordained but they will never get another job unless they keep quiet and they buckle under that inducement. People are given a much harder time these days; that's why so many good people have left the ministry.

Kirker's aged mother now lives in Winchester, in the diocese of another arch-opponent, Michael Scott-Joynt, one of the bishops who signed the open letter urging that Jeffrey John should not be appointed to the bishopric of Reading. She has long been reconciled to her son's orientation and is quietly proud of his campaigning zeal. Sadly, his late father never was and father and son were estranged for some time before his death.

✠ ✠ ✠ ✠ ✠

The Rev. Martin Reynolds said, 'I think I knew I was gay from the age of six, but I really knew it from the age of 11 when I went to the grammar school and my very best friend didn't. My first conscious memory of it being a problem was when the Sexual Offences Bill was passed in the Commons in 1967. I'd have been about 13 then and sexually active and I can remember my mother turning to me and saying: "These people aren't criminals any more, they're just mentally ill."'

Perhaps not so strange a reaction in a family in the South Wales valleys in the 1960s. Reynolds, a little more obviously gay than Kirker, has been a priest in the area now for a quarter of a century, living openly with his partner Chris, who is a hairdresser, for much of that time. The couple made headlines, albeit anonymously, in early 2003 when a Sunday newspaper reported that they were bringing up a teenaged boy they had first fostered and then adopted together.

This was about the time of Rowan Williams's consecration as Archbishop of Canterbury and, as a priest in his former diocese of Monmouth, Reynolds was well known to him. Indeed Williams could scarcely have avoided knowing him since Reynolds and his partner lived next door. On the night before the story appeared Reynolds wrote his resignation and popped it through the Archbishop's letterbox. 'Rowan knew he'd got fairies living at the bottom of his garden all right,' said Reynolds with a grin. It is obviously a practised remark.

With his dog collar and black leather jacket, sleeves rolled up to the elbows, the bespectacled Reynolds is a trendy vicar:

My first real boyfriend was at the age of about 13 or 14. He was my next-door neighbour. We were sexually active together and then he joined the army at 16, went to Northern Ireland and was killed a couple of years later. My father was a philanderer who left home when I was young and I was quite cynical about all that. I tried to be a heterosexual – people think homosexuals can't have sex with women – but I tried it and there was never a relationship there. It was just sex. I was never very comfortable about it. You know, I've never felt homosexuality was wrong: it always felt so right inside myself. There was something quite beautiful, magnificent, about our love for each other at the age of 18.

My father was a Catholic but we were not a church-going family. My faith experience came from an excellent teacher at school – I read a lot and it became very important to me. One day I had a vision – I don't talk about this much – and my life was completely transformed. I fell in love completely and absolutely with God. I couldn't give him enough – not the moon and the stars – that's how much I fell for him. I was sobbing with joy in my love for God. I had never heard of anyone having that sort of experience before. It was the beginning of a relationship. I have fallen in love since and I know what it means.

When I went to see my bishop about going to college, he could see I was Bible-read but almost completely unchurched. I had a deep understanding of the communion service, but not from any church doctrine. I found the communion service was like having intercourse with God. It was a very intimate, almost sexual experience. I felt I was part of the people. I still feel that, but less so. The Bishop of Llandaff sent me to theological college. I think he knew I was gay, I didn't have to tell him.

I was in college in Salisbury with Richard Kirker. I think he's mellowed now. Robert Runcie always used to say: 'He couldn't keep his mouth shut.' College was a wonderful experience for me. Everything was possible and nobody felt threatened. Everything was tested and tried and nothing was rejected.

After I graduated, I became a curate in Cardiff, 'the church with the highest of everything in Wales' – high unemployment, high poverty. There were 30,000 people in the parish and the church was central to the community: bingo, dances, 25 baptisms on a Sunday. I loved it. It was wonderful. I was there for seven years as a curate, I was deputy chaplain at Cardiff prison and I set up a home for young homeless people. It was about that time my boyfriend moved in – we've been together 23 years now. We used to go to gay clubs and everything and I'd go in a corner and talk with the people there about faith and religion, you know, counselling them – sometimes I'd still be wearing my white disco shoes when I took the early morning service and the old dears would nudge each other and say: 'Father Martin hasn't been home yet.' Oh, it was fantastic.

I was not promiscuous though. My partner was illiterate and wonderful. We're still together. He moved in with me in the curate's house. Everyone knew. One day my vicar walked in on us and he just said 'How very discreet' and walked out again. It was the most natural thing in the world. I never had any doubts that it might be wrong for me, for my faith or for my church. I've never been hidden about it with any member of the clergy. We have a very macho culture in Wales but also a strong male bonding society. My partner Chris and I go down the rugby club and we never have any trouble - well, only blokes trying to pick us up, see what it's like, see? I wouldn't do that: you've got to be faithful haven't you? I've also been propositioned by women, seeing if they could save me.

After Cardiff we moved to Pontyclun and Talygarn near Cowbridge for 13 years. There were three ministers, Baptist, Presbyterian and me and we did everything together. It was wonderful - no homophobia at all. Chris is a Roman Catholic and he attended his church up until Cardinal Ratzinger said homosexuality was evil. We felt that was too much. He hasn't been since.

About 11 years ago I was asked if I would take in a youngster, five years old, for respite care. His home life was difficult - when he came to us he was filthy and he only had one set of clothes. He had severe learning difficulties and very severe behavioural problems. They couldn't place him anywhere. We've had him, 100 days a year to start with, and then fostered him full time when he was 14. We had our doubts, yes; we thought he should have gone to an orthodox family but no one would touch him because of his difficulties. The social worker said the only other place they had for him, he would have been raped within five minutes and stealing cars within a day.

We felt we had a lot of love and a lot of luck. I had had 20 years of a brilliant ministry and we wanted to share that with a child who had nothing. Well it's transformed our lives. He was so damaged. We had to stay awake with him all night in case he damaged himself. The first hour he was in our house he broke 16 things. He'll unscrew all the light-fittings or throw everything out of the bedroom window if you're not careful. Everything takes so long with him around. You want to write a letter and it takes two hours because he's torn up all the paper or hidden all the pens. He certainly teaches you patience. Funnily enough, his greatest relationship now is with my mother who lives with us. They sit together and complain about Chris and me.

When the article appeared, even though we weren't named, we knew it would be difficult for Rowan and we also knew we could not give the child up so I surrendered my licence in the diocese of Monmouth. We'd been told by the journalist - who's been a lifelong friend - that the article would be about how gay parents could be good parents but it didn't come out like that. I posted my resignation through Rowan's door and he came rushing round to try and persuade me not to do it. I said that if they found out that we were living next door to him and our boy had played with his children it would make things difficult for him.

Later they issued a statement on Rowan's behalf saying he had felt obliged to accept my resignation. That hurt. He didn't have to say that. All he had to say was that the licence had been surrendered. I think they wanted that extra inch. I feel sad about that but I understand the politics - that's why I resigned in the first place. If the media knew we lived next door that would have caused him trouble, but the miracle was that no one told the national newspapers where we were. Every journalist in South Wales knew who I was and no one gave our identity up. The *Daily Mail* and other newspapers came sniffing round. But they didn't find out.

I still have my licence in Llandaff and I still supervise team ministries there. I have no intention of asking for my licence back in Monmouth. The new bishop, who's come from Reading, is an unmarried gentleman and he seems very nice. He says he's not gay and I guess he'd better be sure of that, because if he is and he were to be found out, there'd be hell to pay in the present environment. I wonder if he knows he's got fairies at the bottom of his garden here? Rowan certainly did.

That joke again.

Rowan has admitted ordaining one gay man but he has ordained lots. Let's not be stupid about this. So did Runcie and so did Carey. If Rowan did not know he was doing it, it was because he did not ask. He'd have been the only one who did not know. It's stupid to bring it down to one event when it's common in many dioceses. It's foolish to pretend it's only happened once. That's part of the duplicity of the whole thing.

✠   ✠   ✠   ✠   ✠

Vicky Gene Robinson is certainly the most famous homosexual priest in the world, the first openly gay bishop in the modern history of Christianity. He may even be - though it is far from certain - the most senior actively homosexual cleric in the world today.

His election as Diocesan Bishop of New Hampshire in the summer of 2003 was the event which precipitated the split in the Anglican Communion and the possibility of long-term schism. The Anglican primates warned that his consecration would tear the fabric of the church. Rowan Williams, the Archbishop of Canterbury, announced that he would not recognize the validity of his episcopacy or allow him to preach in the Church of England. One African archbishop announced that Satan was now stalking the US Episcopal Church, and Nigeria's Archbishop Akinola said he would find it impossible to sit down in the same room with such a person. Evangelicals who had been itching for the moment smugly announced that his consecration had split the church asunder, a self-fulfilling and self-willed prophecy if ever there was one.

Yet it was as well that most of his opponents who spoke so demeaningly had never met him. Robinson, a small, neat, sandy-haired man with rimless spectacles, is genial and just slightly camp though not offensively so. There is also a steely determination and strong ambition. He oozes charm and, if you did not know one thing about him, you would swear that he was an archetypal vicar. Or bishop. It has made it quite hard for his opponents to demonize him, though they have tried reasonably hard and, such is the vehemence of American society, at his consecration the risk to his safety from vengeful Christians was considered so severe that he was forced to wear a bullet-proof vest under his vestments.

Robinson was born in 1947, the son of Kentucky tobacco sharecroppers. He appeared to be paralysed and was not expected to live so his parents immediately christened him with the names they had prepared if their baby was a girl: Vicky Imogene, the latter after his mother. But the boy lived, the paralysis disappeared and he grew up attending a southern Nonconformist church. In time Imogene got shortened to Gene and the Vicky, although still there, has largely been revived only by his opponents.

Gene was a bright boy and in due course went off to college. He secured a place at Yale but eventually attended the University of the South at Sewanee, Tennessee, instead, graduating with a history degree in 1969. That means of course that to his conservative American opponents he was a member of that subversive 1960s generation, the anti-Nixon, anti-Vietnam War students, who they think have done so much to lay the USA low. It was one of the faults laid at Robinson's door by Diane Knippers at the October 2003 meeting of American Episcopal dissidents in Dallas. Ms Knippers, president of the Scaife-funded Institute on Religion and Democracy, told the conference: 'This is what happens when the church is led by the baby-boomers' generation. Ninety per cent of the bishops who voted for Gene Robinson were in seminaries in the 1970s.'[1] Fortunately George W. Bush, a Texan northerner with an expensive Ivy League education, who might have been yet another of that baby boomer generation, was too busy getting drunk at Yale at the time to notice.

Gene Robinson was indeed at a seminary in the 1970s in New York and then was in New Jersey as a curate, before moving to New Hampshire in 1975, where he co-owned and ran a girls' summer camp and horse farm and founded a spiritual retreat centre. He then managed a diocesan programme of spiritual growth and development called Living into Our Baptism and later became the diocesan youth ministries coordinator and then one of the originators of the national Episcopal Youth event. For the last 17 years before his election as a bishop, he was assistant to the previous diocesan, Douglas Theuner. He was canon to the ordinary for the diocese, coordinating diocesan staff, and he had also been for 20 years executive secretary of the Episcopal Province of New England, the last three years also spent on the board of trustees for the general theological seminary.

This in retrospect was an ideal curriculum vitae for a prospective bishop of New Hampshire, though, indeed, it was not his first try at an Episcopal post – he had been shortlisted for other dioceses twice before. But now he was well known and well liked among the clergy and parishioners of what is a small diocese in a small, conservative state: just 15,000 of New Hampshire's population of 1.13 million inhabitants count themselves as Episcopalians. It was a small number of church goers whose decision rocked the worldwide faith. But, lest anyone sneer at such a small parish, that number still exceeds, or is comparable with, numbers in the archdioceses of several of the Anglican Communion's primates, including those who have not hesitated to use their status to denounce the New England heretics.

Despite the smallness of the diocese, there were 150 candidates for the bishopric and it took 16 months, following the announcement of Bishop Theuner's retirement, to choose the new bishop, during which parishioners assessed each of them, heard their sermons and met them as they traversed the state, for all the world like the political primaries that New Hampshire also revels in each presidential election year. Whatever may be said about the state's democratic processes, they are certainly thorough. Nor was the field negligible: eventually the candidates were whittled down to a shortlist of five, one of whom subsequently withdrew on election as Bishop of Nebraska. Of the final four, two were women and thus almost as much of an anathema and as unacceptable to conservative co-religionists around the world as Gene Robinson.

In June 2003, less than two months before the looming triennial meeting of the US Episcopal Church's general convention in Minneapolis, Robinson, the favoured local son, was duly elected bishop. Had the process been accomplished a month earlier – three months before the convention – the appointment would not have had to go to the national body in open session at all. It would have been nodded through a national appointments committee instead. No diocesan bishop's appointment had been overturned since 1875. Because the choice, however, was so controversial, it may have been just as well that it required the convention's endorsement. It was probably even planned that way in recognition of the controversial nature of the appointment.

For what the Episcopalians of New Hampshire knew full well when they elected him was that Gene Robinson was gay and living with his male partner, Mark Andrew. That may have made him an apparently odd choice for the deeply conservative Republican Granite State, whose car licence plate motto is 'Live Free or Die'. It is a state which has strong libertarian instincts – does not levy a sales tax – and is indeed in the process of being invaded by civil libertarians who want to turn it into a government-free zone. In other words, as Richard Gerken, a retired corporate lawyer from Chicago and one of those disenchanted with Robinson's appointment, told me: 'I could never have imagined this happening in New Hampshire. I could have understood it if it had been in liberal Vermont, but not here.'

But the corollary was that the tiny band of local Episcopalians made their choice and did not like being told by outsiders that they should not have made it in the interests of the wider world. They liked Robinson and they were not going to be put off their man. Living Free meant making their own choices and not being too censorious about their bishop's lifestyle.

Robinson had been married for 15 years to Isabella ('Boo') whom he had met at college in Vermont in the early 1970s. The couple had had two daughters, Jamee and Ella, but Isabella had known from before their marriage that her husband believed himself to be gay. It was something he had known himself since seventh grade at school. During the marriage he had undergone therapy to tackle the problem. But eventually his wife met someone else – it was actually the reverse of his opponents' persistent smear that he had walked out of the marriage to live with his male partner, or their suggestion that he should have stayed with his wife, whatever the circumstances – and in 1985 the couple separated, before being divorced, so that his wife could remarry, the following year. After the court hearing, witnessed by their parish priest, the couple retired to their church for a ceremony at which they handed back their wedding rings, took communion, asked each other's forgiveness for the failure of their marriage and pledged themselves to bring up their daughters together. It was not until a couple of years later, on holiday in the Caribbean, that Robinson met Mr Andrew, who works in the state's department of health and human services. The couple had lived together for 13 years by the time of Robinson's election to the bishopric.

This then was the background of the man who split the Communion. Not exemplary perhaps – certainly a divorce would also count against him in many conservatives' eyes, though the Church of England at least now allows remarriage for the 'innocent' partner of a divorce – but scarcely a model of depravity either. During the confirmation process at the convention in August 2003, Isabella McDaniel sent a fulsome testimonial in support of her former husband and he was supported in person by his daughter Ella, now in her early 20s – his other daughter being otherwise engaged, giving birth to his first grandchild. This hardly sounds as if they felt that he had deserted his family.

The desertion smear leached into sermons delivered by men who should have known better and clearly did not bother to check their facts before publicly criticizing Robinson for his conduct. Sandy Millar of Alpha fame on the weekend of Robinson's consecration was telling his congregation 3,000 miles away at Holy Trinity, Brompton, in London, that Robinson had divorced his wife and left his children. In fact on the day that sermon was delivered, Robinson's wife and daughters, his aged parents and his partner were all present for his consecration as New Hampshire's ninth Episcopal Diocesan Bishop.

'I knew in school that I was different and that was very difficult in the South in the 1950s,' Robinson told me in the summer of 2003. 'Kids don't know the Bible but every single one of them can tell you that God feels they are an abomination. The culture has told them that in God's eyes they are despicable, even if they cannot actually find it saying that in the Bible. That is why I helped to found an organization in New Hampshire a decade ago called Outright to act as a support group for gay, lesbian and questioning teenagers.'[2]

Little did Robinson know at the time the trouble that would later cause him. He said:

> I did not come out for quite some time. It was a year and a half after the divorce before I met Mark and we dated for another 18 months before he moved to New Hampshire. I did not experience a great deal of negativity when he moved in but there were a few clergy who were troubled. They hung in there with me, however, and it was never made a big deal. More and more people got to know, but a lot simply had no idea that I was gay. Some didn't know until I was nominated for the Bishop of Newark in 1998.

> I promised myself and I promised God that I would be honest about it, to my family and to others. What makes families go crazy is secretiveness within the family, so no, I have never hidden it. The press here has been very respectful – perhaps more than it would have been in Britain. I have really not been pestered at all.

> It seems this issue is gaining momentum on all fronts and the church cannot bury its head to that. God is at work in the world and it is partly our duty to figure out where God is on this and to join Him there. Conservatives say this will destroy the Anglican Communion but I think the Communion is far

stronger than many folks believe. The church is not ours to win or lose. It's God's and God will not let it fall apart.

It seems to me that we can stay in communion, acknowledging we are all walking with God in our own way. I would welcome a meeting with Archbishop Akinola, so we could get together, share our love of God and find unity in our common belief in Jesus. I still want to be in communion with him, even if he does not want to share communion with me. You see, I have come to understand that this is not a sin. The Bible is not speaking about monogamous relationships between two people of the same sex. It just does not address that issue – the whole notion of sexual orientation is just a century old.

There is no reason why we should come apart over this. If someone chooses to leave or to declare themselves out of communion, that will be their doing, not mine. I want them in my church but if they decide not to be that is their responsibility, not mine. I am not going to take that on my shoulders. I care about it. I pray about it but I cannot take responsibility for every province in the Anglican Communion. There are still places where the ordination of women is prohibited and we did not come apart over that. Here it is impossible to remember when we excluded women, yet it was within our lifetime. Not many years hence, homosexuality will be accepted within the church too.

I am most eager to be a good bishop, not a gay bishop. I can do more for gay and lesbian people by doing my ministry well, by serving God and the people of New Hampshire well. That is why I was elected by the people of New Hampshire. No one here had a gay agenda – they had just known me for 28 years, experienced my ministry and believed I would be the best person to be their bishop. They are so excited and they would be outraged if it did not happen.

Gene Robinson would need all his steely determination to go forward to that destiny in the weeks ahead.

5

OLD AS THE HILLS

'This sin is now so frequent that no one blushes for it any more, and many indulge in it without perceiving its gravity.' (St Anselm, 1102)

It seems likely that homosexual practice is as old – or nearly as old – as humanity itself. Certainly the Romans and Greeks knew it, as generations of Christian schoolboys reading Plato, Horace and Catullus must dimly have perceived. How they must have puzzled about why something their religion told them was wicked should have been so indulged by the authors they were required to read.

Clearly the writers of the Old Testament did not think much of homosexuality, though what impelled them to consider it was also morally wrong, worthy of savage and extreme punishment, may be harder to judge. Those who take their guidance directly from the Bible on such matters believe that God just told them it is sinful. But why did He think homosexuality was so wicked? He does not speak directly on the subject but through a series of scattered messages mediated by men and framed by their culture, alongside other divine instructions that are now commonly ignored because they are rightly believed to have been culturally inspired. God-given punishments are also no longer exacted because of their ferocity. The last execution for homosexuality in Britain took place in 1835.

The motivating drive against same-sex practices for the Biblical writers seems to be the preservation of the race and its protection against outsiders, together with the maintenance of a distinctiveness of tribal practice and identity. Since males were dominant in the Middle Eastern tribal culture, as they have been universally ever since, there is clearly an element of distaste too for homosexuality, as if those who indulge in it are somehow demeaning themselves – maybe because one partner was likely to be taking a passive, un-masculine role.

This attitude was reinforced by the contemporary belief in the primary importance of the male seed, which was regarded by philosophers such as Aristotle as providing the sole means of reproduction. They thought it

blended with menstrual blood to produce the baby. Semen, it was believed, contained the foetus in embryo - the Greek physician Galen said
there was no difference between sowing the womb and sowing a field -
and so anything which aborted its progress to the female womb, such as
masturbation, contraception and homosexual relations, was akin to murder.[1] This idea of the waste of life has been a very persistent theme in
Christian thinking on the issue.

Such insights are evidently utilitarian rather than gynaecological or
even moral ones and so it may be best to quote Jeremy Bentham on the
subject at the outset: 'This crime, if crime it is to be called, produces no
misery in society'[2] - a line the prophet of utilitarianism composed in
1771, though it was sufficiently incendiary not to be published for another 160 years.

One very clear message starting with the Biblical references resounds
through history - that homosexuality is an alien sexual practice indulged
in by foreigners: Paul warns against the Gentiles' idolatry; in the nineteenth century to Englishmen it was known as the Italian vice, to the
French, l'amour allemand and to the Spanish something the Turks brought
up. A nineteenth-century New York paper called the Whip was apparently
glad to note that among the sodomites in the city in 1842, 'we find no
Americans as yet - they are all Englishmen or French'.[3]

This may explain the Biblical references in the context of temple
prostitution, an activity common in the Middle East, particularly Babylon
and Greece, at the time the authors were writing. Although knowledge of
what went on is cloudy, it appears to have been connected to fertility
rituals and was indulged in by both men and women and by both profes-
sionals and amateurs. Temples certainly benefited financially from what
occurred.

The Greek historian Herodotus, writing a thousand years after the
event about prostitution in the Hammurabi temples of Babylon around
the period 1750BC, had this to say: 'EVERY woman who is a native of the
country must once in her life go and sit in the temple and there give
herself to a strange man ... she is not allowed to go home until a man has
thrown a silver coin into her lap and taken her outside to lie with him.'[4]
How he knew, or how far Babylonian husbands really allowed this to
happen to their wives is unclear, but there seems no doubt that prostitution was practised around temples by qadishtu - sacred prostitutes - and
ishtaritu - servants of the goddess Ishtar. If women did it, probably men
did it too. Reason enough for the Old Testament authors to warn the
Chosen People against it.

There is ample evidence of Greek indulgence in homosexual practices: paintings on their vases show it, as do writings about their heroes. It was even associated with success in war (an interesting contrast to the US and British military's adamant rearguard refusal to countenance the admission of openly gay warriors to their ranks in the face of equal opportunities legislation in the 1990s). Plato wrote: 'A handful of lovers and loved ones fighting shoulder to shoulder, could rout a whole army. For a lover to be seen by his beloved forsaking the ranks or throwing away his weapons would be unbearable, He would a thousand times rather die than be so humiliated.'[5] Alexander the Great was gay and a whole succession of famous generals appear to have been murdered by their catamites.

None of this is to suggest that the practice was necessarily considered normal (though the depictions on the vases may mean it was sometimes regarded as comic) or even common, but it was also well acknowledged and maybe without heavy social stigma.

Religion changed all that. As the Roman Empire collapsed a new social order gradually emerged in Europe, with the church extending a moral discipline based on sin and the fear of retribution, if not in this life then in eternity thereafter, that civil society could not yet enforce. It was of course a morality based on the Bible and what the early Christian philosophers had to say about it. Gradually a set view emerged. The priority was the creation and maintenance of order.

This was not without a struggle. Some early texts, subsequently suppressed or discarded, seemed more equivocal than others. One was the so-called Secret Gospel of Mark, quoted by Clement of Alexandria in AD 180 during his attempt to crack down on a heretical Gnostic sect that worshipped Plato and Aristotle as well as Jesus:

> And going in immediately where the young man was [Jesus] stretched out his hand and raised him up, taking him by the hand. The young man looked on him and loved him and began to beseech him that he might be with him. They came out of the tomb and went into the young man's house, for he was rich. After six days Jesus laid a charge upon him and when evening came the young man comes to him, with a linen robe thrown over his naked body; and he stayed with him that night for Jesus was teaching him the mystery of the Kingdom of God.[6]

Even among references that remained in the Authorized Version, there were some slightly odd allusions. What are we to make of the relationship between David and Jonathan 'passing the love of women'? Or what about St John's Gospel which regularly mentions the author as 'the disciple Jesus loved' and has during the Last Supper story (13:23) John leaning on Jesus' bosom – an iconic image of the Evangelist that occasionally appeared in medieval statuary?

This is far short of suggesting a sexual relationship, but it has not stopped some from imagining one. The homosexual Tudor playwright Christopher Marlowe was accused of saying 'that St John the Evangelist was bedfellow to Christ and leaned alwaies on his bosom, that he used him as the sinners of Sodoma'.[7] That striking early example of dramatic licence, however, was echoed a few years later by no less a figure than King James I, who in 1617 defended himself before the Privy Council against charges of sodomy with his 'sweet child and wife' George Villiers, by shamelessly maintaining: 'Jesus Christ did the same and therefore I cannot be blamed. Christ had his son John and I have my George.'

The church in the Dark Ages and medieval period had a monopoly in the written word so that its views and those of its scholars – some of them clearly achingly personal – became unassailable and absolute. As the writer Reay Tannahill says: 'It is undoubtedly a tribute (if an ambiguous one) to such men as St Jerome and St Augustine that much of what the modern world still understands by "sin" stems not from the teachings of Jesus of Nazareth, or from the tablets handed down from Sinai, but from the sexual vicissitudes of a handful of men who lived in the twilight days of imperial Rome.'[8]

And sex was one of their obsessions, a distraction from loving and worshipping the Lord and a desire that could only partially be appeased by marriage if permanent celibacy could not be achieved. St Jerome suggested man should take a wife if he could not sleep alone through fear at night, and St Paul famously prescribed marriage only as better than burning with inflamed passions. Celibacy was the goal of Christian thinkers, sex 'an experiment of the serpent' and marriage 'a foul and polluted way of life'. Augustine, the man who prayed for chastity but not yet, believed intercourse was fundamentally disgusting and all women temptresses like Eve; Jerome thought sex unclean, Ambrose a defilement. Man was a sordid creature from the waist down and woman was just inherently evil all over.[9] To Tertullian women were the Devil's gateway, the cause of the Son of Man's death. To Aquinas they were just defective and misbegotten. So much for 2,000 years of Christian tradition sanctifying marriage and celebrating womanhood.

Adam and Eve were the culprits of course. When they ate of the apple 'and the eyes of them both were opened and they knew they were naked', the first thing they did was make themselves aprons to cover their pudenda (from the Latin pudere, to be ashamed). It was filth from the start. Sex was necessary for the maintenance of the species, but it was also shameful and so should be engaged in rarely and without passion, for one purpose only. By the eleventh century the papacy had taken this view far enough to prohibit marriage for the priesthood altogether, though not without a certain amount of grumbling from the clergy and, as we know, periodic individual lapses to this day.

There was even a debate about whether sex was an integral part of marriage, or was even necessary to it. Certainly such a shameful business was not possible outside matrimony, for that would be a mere surrender to lust. Even within marriage some recommended abstention on certain days of the week: Sundays in honour of the Resurrection, Mondays in commemoration of the departed, Thursdays in memory of Christ's arrest, Fridays to remember His death, Saturdays in celebration of the Virgin Mary. Plus of course the 40 days of Lent, Pentecost, Christmas and the weeks before taking communion. As recently as 1894 an American doctor was writing that any man who required intercourse except in pursuit of procreation was turning his wife into a private prostitute.

Abstinence must have been a useful means of contraception in the Middle Ages and is still the only valid form for Catholics. Sexual sins attracted a range of penances in medieval times, though homosexuality was not treated more severely than any others. You might receive seven days' penance for accidental seminal emission (20 days if manually assisted), there would be 30 days for a monk caught masturbating in church, 50 days for a bishop.[10] Contraception, including oral and anal sex, was almost as culpable as murder and received penances, including fasting and abstinence, of up to 15 years' duration. Abortion attracted lesser penalties if only because the woman knew she would go to Hell three times over: as a suicide (if she died as a result of the operation), an adulteress to her heavenly bridegroom, Christ, and as the murderer of her child. Although this was the view in the Middle Ages, anyone who has seen the recent film *The Magdalene Sisters*, about how young Irish women regarded as immoral were treated by Catholic nuns as recently as the 1960s, will know that it was an idea whose potency lasted until very recently indeed.

Homosexuality was, said Pope Gregory III, 'a vice so abominable in the sight of God that the cities in which its practitioners dwelt were appointed for destruction by fire and brimstone'. The Sodom story had evidently by then acquired its modern reading. Nevertheless the penalty he imposed for homosexual acts – one year's penance – was only a third of that imposed on priests caught going hunting.[11]

The declining Roman Empire was slow to introduce legislation against homosexuality even after its emperors had converted to Christianity, possibly because it would have opened many members of its armies to prosecution. It was not until the third century that it did so and even then the punishments were not harshly enforced. By the fourth century, however, a succession of natural disasters had led emperors in the eastern capital of Constantinople to look for blame in the sinfulness of their subjects. After plague killed a third of the city's inhabitants in AD541, the emperor Justinian averred that God had been provoked to anger by the city's sins, 'especially ... the defilement of males which some men sacrilegiously and impiously dare to attempt, perpetrating vile acts with other men'.[12] Sodom was conveniently invoked as it too had been destroyed by a natural catastrophe blamed on its inhabitants.

Homosexuals thus became a threat both to the secular realm and to Christian morality. They were denied baptism and instruction in the faith until they changed their behaviour. Aware that this might not be enough to curb the proclivities of their celibate inhabitants, monastic houses began to invoke rules designed to eradicate any thought of sinfulness: monks (and, much later, nuns) were forbidden to sleep two to a bed and dormitory lamps were left burning all night. At the Council of Toledo in 693, Spain was described as being rife with sodomy and as a consequence: 'if any one of those males who commit this vile practice against nature with other males is a bishop, a priest or a deacon, he shall be degraded from the dignity of his order and shall remain in perpetual exile, struck down by damnation.' The king added the extra punishment of castration for good measure.

The medieval church created a wide and complex range of punishments for the range of unnatural acts that it gathered together under the single description of sodomy, recognizing degrees of culpability according to what the activity was and the amount of positive participation as well as the age and occupation of the offenders. And there were different penalties in different areas: in sixth-century Wales homosexuals were given three years' penance, in eighth-century Burgundy, ten years'. The punishment for oral sex ranged from seven years to life. The seventh-century Frankish Cummean Penitential laid down sliding scales: for mutual masturbation by men aged 20 or over, 20 to 40 days' penance, 100 days' for a second offence, separation and penance for a year if habitual; for fellatio or oral intercourse, four years' rising to seven years' for repeat offenders; for anal intercourse seven years' for a first offence.

These punishments were no more severe than those for contraception, but prosecution began to change and grow harsher in the eleventh century at about the time of the introduction of the celibacy rule for priests. Crimes were referred to bishops for punishment rather than being dealt with locally by priests. This was perhaps a mark of improved communications and a recognition that the imposition of years-long penalties could not be effectively implemented at a very local level (or maybe not even at an Episcopal one).

In the thirteenth century St Thomas Aquinas exerted his enormous moral authority to insist that homosexuality was unnatural in the sight of God and accordingly disordered. Like Augustine (and some Evangelicals even today) he maintained that the Creator had designed the genitalia specifically and only for procreative purposes, so that any other sexual use of them was wrong, unnatural and heretical. This is the source of the Christian churches' specific teaching on homosexuality as a moral disorder. Thus, conveniently, the church's suspicion of sexual activity as a central source of sinfulness conjoined with the secular hostility of outsiders and a concern for the continued propagation of the family and racial line. The church promoted a vision of what was natural and what was not and imposed a succession of harsh penalties for those seen to undermine it. As the secular state apparatus grew more effective the criminal law took over from religious penance. In England it was from 1533, the time of the dissolution of the monasteries, that the 'detestable and abomynable vice' of sodomy became a civil matter.

That reinforced rather than diminished religious condemnation. Even in 1976 when the Roman Catholic Church issued its *Declaration on Certain Questions Concerning Sexual Ethics*, it was still announcing that there was no justification for homosexual acts that opposed the moral sense of Christians, the teaching of the Bible and 'objective moral order'. In 2003 it denounced homosexuality as evil. Tannahill quotes a homosexual Jesuit priest as hoping that 'once the Church is aware of the destructive impact of its policies on hundreds of thousands of lives it will have to change its policies.' After 700 years it would probably be best not to hold one's breath.

Yet in recent years historians studying court records have concluded that the incidence of homosexual prosecution was not especially high through the late Middle Ages, that enforcement was not particularly consistent or invariably harsh except at times of moral panic and that magistrates and the communities from which offenders sprang were often relatively tolerant. It has always been a condition that has neither been eradicated nor discouraged by the severity of the potential penalties.

The incidence of homosexuality in cities across the world appears scarcely to have varied over time either. This further suggests that homosexuality affects only a small but relatively constant minority of the population and that it is therefore unlikely to be susceptible to fashion, personal choice or lifestyle decisions. All major cities had generally rather well-known gathering points – Holborn and later the statue of Achilles in Hyde Park in London, Central Park in New York, the wild boar statue in the Tuileries Gardens in Paris, the Victoria Theatre in Sydney. The authorities knew this too and periodically clamped down.

Statistics are difficult to interpret because records are incomplete and the rationale behind prosecutions may not be clear, but a recent study by William Naphy estimates that in Paris 80 sodomites were executed between 1565 and 1640, notwithstanding that King Henri III, who kept a succession of mignons – male royal favourites – was on the throne for part of that time. In Geneva, a smaller city but with fuller records over a slightly longer period (1555–1678), 30 were executed.[13] Thereafter, prosecutions died down but when in 1787 a particularly notorious sodomite called Jacob Ponçon was caught soliciting local soldiers for sex, the magistrate was surprised to find that his activities had been well known for some time. His doctor, Louis Jurine, told the court that he had been treating Ponçon for seven years for various complaints associated with anal problems and had advised him to change his habits, for medical rather than moral reasons, but he had never reported him to the authorities.

This would seem to have been common too – if people were discreet, they were quite likely not to be bothered too much, unless there was a complaint (sometimes by a spurned lover). Told of a gay community living in Chartres in 1805, Napoleon decided against prosecution: 'Nature has seen to it that [these offences] are not frequent. The scandal of legal proceedings would only tend to multiply them.'[14]

Prosecutions for sodomy across Europe appear to have remained remarkably static over time, rising just slightly in line with the increase in the general population and forming a small proportion of overall criminal convictions. Robb has pointed out that although 46 people were executed in England for sodomy between 1810 and 1835 – a further 32 were condemned but reprieved – that represented fewer than 3 per cent of all executions during that period, well below murder (21 per cent) and property crimes.[15]

During all this period too, there appears to have been a presumption against prosecution of the rich and powerful unless their crimes were particularly egregious. Kings were above the law even though Henri III had his catamites and in England James I and earlier Edward II, and maybe Richard II and William Rufus, had their close favourites.

Ralph, a medieval archbishop of Tours, installed his boyfriend John as Bishop of Orleans – though perhaps the separation involved meant that their ardour was already cooling – with the blessing of the pope and the king of France. Archbishop John Whitgift, the man who crowned James I, took as his close companion Dr Andrew Perne, the ex-Master of Peterhouse, Cambridge. His successor Archbishop William Laud, who fell foul of the Puritans for other reasons and lost his head on Tower Green in 1645, wisely kept his homosexual thoughts for his diary.[16]

The unfortunate Percy Jocelyn, bishop of the Irish diocese of Clogher, caught with his breeches round his ankles in the company of a young guardsman at the White Hart Inn in Westminster in 1822, was an exception. After his prosecution 'the mitred reprobate' went off to live in Paris and then later ended his days quietly in Glasgow and Edinburgh where his neighbours knew of his identity but never divulged it.[17]

In the United States, which broadly followed the English law of 1533 on the matter though without the death penalty, prominent people could also be protected until recent times. President Franklin D. Roosevelt defended his placeman Sumner Welles, the Under Secretary of State, for three years during the Second World War, following allegations about his behaviour towards a coloured porter on a train coming back from Alabama, despite pressure from J. Edgar Hoover of the FBI and others. Welles was of the same social background, had been a page at Roosevelt's wedding and was close to his wife Eleanor. 'Well, he's not doing it on government time, is he?' the president said.[18]

There is some evidence for the celebration of close friendships, occasionally even sanctioned and blessed by the church. This is controversial since it is not always clear whether the partnerships were sexual ones or merely platonic. Sometimes the power and influence of the couple may have rendered objections otiose or simply imprudent. Certainly the late Yale historian John Boswell uncovered startling evidence of church ceremonial as in the case of Basil I, the seventh-century ruler of the Byzantine Empire, who appears to have been married twice to men, one of them a monk named Nicholas who was 'ceremonially united with him and kept him as his housemate and companion'.[19] John Stott is dismissive of Boswell's evidence – and one can see why he would have to be – saying that the scholarly assessment by fellow historians has 'ranged from the sharply critical to the dismissive to the devastating', though as that judgement comes from something called the Human Relationships Foundation of Auckland, New Zealand, he clearly had to go quite a long way to find it.[20]

What then to make also of the British gay historian Alan Bray's analysis of English funerary monuments,[21] such as that from the seventeenth century in the chapel of Christ's College, Cambridge, marking the joint burial of John Finch and Thomas Baines, or the fourteenth-century brass in Merton College chapel, Oxford, linking John Bloxham and John

Whytton and depicting them lying side by side like a husband and wife? Bray also found the tomb of two English knights in Istanbul, which depicts them exchanging a ritual kiss. He found a monument to two eighteenth-century gentlemen in Launceston, Cornwall, which describes them as *conjunctissimi*, a word normally referring to married couples. The Cambridge monument bears the Latin inscription: 'And as in life they were one at heart and in kinship and friendship, so after death they were even then not divided, most faithful pair of friends.' Nor were they alone, so to speak: other similar monuments are dotted about.

Bray, who died in 2001, is rightly cautious of claiming these to be necessarily homosexual partnerships. But he does point out that the church in generations past was happy publicly to affirm and bless same-sex friendships, citing a fourteenth-century Dalmatian rite, *ordo ad fratres faciendum*, as a service 'for making brothers'. This would appear to be much the same as the sort of blessing service that got the Canadian diocese of New Westminster into trouble in the summer of 2003. And it must be doubtful whether those Evangelicals who claim their opposition to such things is sanctioned by 2,000 years of Christian tradition would permit two men to be buried together these days, still less commemorated with a depiction of them kissing as the church allowed in the past.

When we come to the nineteenth century too, we find passionate, though not necessarily sexual, friendships at the heart of the religious schism of the 1840s. This split high-church Anglicans and Evangelicals and led some to follow John Henry Newman into the Roman Catholic Church. How ironic that 160 years later the next great split in Anglicanism should also have been precipitated in Oxford, the home of lost causes.

If we feel the rhetoric in the current Anglican dispute a trifle overheated, we should try the Oxford Movement row, which occurred just as the first academic challenges to the literal truthfulness of the Bible were being mounted and Charles Darwin was agonizing over the publication of *The Origin of Species*. The Tractarian Henry Liddon's declaration that Jesus believed Moses to be the author of the first five books of the Bible and anyone questioning this or the assertion that Jonah lived in the belly of the whale was effectively calling Christ a liar and so was not fit to be a Christian, does have some eerie echoes in the debate at the turn of the twenty-first century.[22] The religious disagreements and the intensity of those Oxford dons involved in it now seems quite strange and alien to us, but did not to the Victorians. Newman, incidentally, when he died many years later, old, famous and a cardinal, was buried without a whiff of sexual scandal in the same grave as his best friend at the Oratory cemetery outside Birmingham.

In attitudes towards homosexuality there has always been a certain Christian presumption – just as among the writers of the Bible – that it was a chosen lifestyle, a perversion perpetrated by men who were essentially heterosexual and so could be coerced by prosecution or converted by persuasion into 'normal' sexual practices. This is a belief which persists, most recently in New Hampshire, where one of Gene Robinson's Episcopalian critics, Bill Hamilton of St James's Church, Laconia, insisted to the local press in November 2003: 'What Robinson did wrong was that he chose to become a homosexual.'[23]

Some Christian conservatives, particularly in the USA, believe that homosexuality can therefore be 'cured', although the evidence for this is pretty slight. Most psychiatrists recognize such an approach as seriously simplistic. The Evangelical Courage Trust, which after 20 years ministering to homosexuals in England decided that 'healing' was not an effective approach, lost its grant from the Evangelical Alliance in 2001 as a result of reaching that conclusion.

The view that homosexuality is somehow chosen has been challenged for more than 200 years now, though it was only gradually that a few began to argue that they could not help the way they were made. In 1726 in London a convicted sodomite told the magistrate: 'I think it no crime in making what use I please with my own body,' and a Dutch preacher of the same period insisted that his interest in men was 'proper to his nature'. The Marquis de Sade, admittedly not an unbiased witness in the field of sexual liberation, argued: 'Is it not clear that this is a class of men different from the other, but also created by nature?'[24]

In London following the Restoration in 1660, toleration of sexual misdemeanours seems to have grown for a while, with 'mollies', 'margeries' and 'poufs' – male prostitutes – patrolling the streets of London and invading the stage. It is no accident that the foppish characters in the comedies of Congreve and others have a somewhat camp air. That changed under the influence of Puritan protests which resulted in 1726 in a raid on the most notorious mollie house, run by Margaret 'Mother' Clap in Holborn, who found herself in the pillory as a result. This was a common fate for mollies, who found themselves pelted with dung and sometimes blinded as a result.[25]

Worse outcomes did occasionally await them, including execution if their crime was particularly notorious. Capital punishment for sodomy remained on the statute book in England until 1861 (in Scotland it was not finally abolished until 1889). By then the punishment was considered to have outlived its usefulness. But it was still a crime and in 1885 parliament enacted one of the most regressive measures and one that came when other European countries including Belgium, Italy, Portugal and Spain were repealing their homosexual legislation instead of tightening it up.

This was the Criminal Law Amendment Act which was designed for 'the protection of women and girls, the suppression of brothels and other purposes' but which at a late stage was amended to include male prostitution as well. The relevant clause, introduced by the MP Henry Labouchere stated that: 'any male person who, in public or *private*, commits or is party to the commission of, or procures or attempts to procure the commission of any male person' was liable to two years' imprisonment with hard labour. What had started out as a liberating measure for women became a blackmailers' charter for men. It emphasized that they were liable for offences committed in private – these had always been illegal, though not always pursued – and, because the sentence was less severe than capital punishment, it meant that they were more likely to be prosecuted. Clearly the law was only partially motivated by Christian morality – it was more immediately driven by social concern.[26]

Some have argued that there was no significant rise in prosecutions after the passage of the 1885 Act. But it was undoubtedly of assistance during subsequent periodic fits of public moral outrage and during the first half of the twentieth century prosecutions steadily rose. The last years of the nineteenth century were also a period of mounting concern about public decadence and immorality leading to some of the most celebrated – or notorious – cases of the era. As has often been the case, public prurience and ridicule – Gilbert and Sullivan's *Patience* with its 'greenery-yallery, Grosvenor Gallery,/Foot-in-the-grave young men' had its premiere in April 1881 – mingled with outrage and disgust.

The Cleveland Street scandal of 1890, in which a male brothel staffed by off-duty telegraph boys was raided, aroused gossip about the high-born clientele (including, it was said, Prince Eddy, Queen Victoria's grandson and second in line to the throne) – one reason why the police may have been rather slow to act in the case.

Then, most famously of all, in 1895 came the Oscar Wilde case, the humiliation and conviction of one of the best-known literary figures in the country after his ill-advised attempt to sue his boyfriend's choleric father, the Marquess of Queensbury. Though often portrayed as an act of vengeance by a repressive state, the authorities in fact were rather dilatory in pursuing Wilde, in the hope that he would follow the example of Lord Arthur Somerset, the prime culprit in the Cleveland Street case, and flee to France. He had brought the criminal prosecution on himself. But homosexuality's most prominent martyr, while the subject of some vicious moralizing and social ostracism, was by no means universally condemned even at the time.

Although the *Daily Telegraph* cheerfully proclaimed: 'Open the windows! Let in the fresh air', after his conviction, *Reynold's News* refused 'to gloat over the ruin of the unhappy man' and pointed out that he had corrupted none of the knowing young men who had testified against him.[27] An Anglican clergyman paid half his bail. As the radical editor W.T. Stead noted: 'Should everyone found guilty of Oscar Wilde's crime be imprisoned, there would be a very surprising emigration from Eton, Harrow, Rugby and Winchester to the jails of Pentonville and Holloway. Until then, boys are free to pick up tendencies and habits in public schools for which they may be sentenced to hard labour later on.'[28]

Thereafter, through the twentieth century, in Britain there were occasional moral seizures: an otherwise justly obscure Conservative MP during the First World War produced a list of alleged homosexuals in politics and the arts whom he alleged were treacherously subverting the war effort.

In 1916 the personal diaries of Sir Roger Casement, detailing his homosexual encounters, were ruthlessly and successfully deployed to prevent public sympathy in both Britain and America following his conviction for treason over Irish independence. Attempts, particularly in Ireland, to prove that the diaries were forgeries have continued to this day, as if to admit that Casement's homosexuality would necessarily devalue the man and somehow diminish his patriotism in the eyes of his Catholic compatriots.

Between the wars and after 1945, police prosecutions continued to increase. It was a relatively easy way of helping the prosecution statistics and harassing a generally subservient section of the population and if an element of provocation and entrapment was involved, the police were not particularly fastidious about it. Where public figures were involved there was the added stigma of newspaper publicity when the court case was heard and many an obscure man must have had his career and local reputation ruined too. There were periodic enforced resignations of MPs caught in the bushes of public parks – the former Welsh Secretary Ron Davies could still find his political career ruined in the year 2000 when he was beaten and robbed while cruising on Clapham Common, though he faced ridicule rather than prosecution. In the 1950s Lord Montagu of Beaulieu endured much worse when he was sent to prison on the trumped-up evidence of some boy scouts, sedulously prompted by the police.

By then, however, the moral and social climate was slowly changing. In the early 1960s capital punishment was abolished and official censorship was collapsing in the wake of the failure of the *Lady Chatterley* prosecution. Harold Wilson's Labour government decided that the time was right to support the repeal of the 1885 legislation – though it shielded behind a private member's bill in order to do so. Homosexual law reform was by no means accepted by all and the cabinet was divided. But the Sexual Offences Bill passed the Commons in one overnight sitting, Labour having a large majority and receiving support from the Liberals and some Tories, early in the morning of 4 July 1967. The reform legalized private sexual relations between consenting adults aged over 21. Roy Jenkins, the Home Secretary and a supporter of the legislation, noted in his memoirs: 'I remember recuperating at a pre-luncheon American Embassy Independence Day party followed by an afternoon at Wimbledon.'[29]

That did not mean, however, that all the attitudes of those in authority were changing. Prosecutions for indecency actually rose in the years following the passage of the act and only slowly began to fall thereafter. Traditionalists claimed both that it was the perversion of an unnatural minority and yet that they could also somehow subvert vulnerable members of the 'natural' majority into sharing their filthy ways and so undermine society as a whole. To underline the point, their use of language became more extravagantly extreme and condemnatory as if their vehemence alone could turn would-be homosexuals from their private pursuits.

In the United States too, where state laws persisted, the era of peace and love did not usher in a period of greater tolerance. Despite a poll in *Time* magazine in 1977 in which 70 per cent of those questioned subscribed to the statement that there should be no laws regulating sexual practice and 57 per cent said they did not regard homosexuality as morally wrong, the resurgence of the conservative religious and political right in the 1980s showed the distinct limits of toleration. In 1988 the same magazine was publishing a letter from a Virginian stating that it was a matter of urgency for America to return to 'the God-fearing moral standard of yesterday. We need people with the guts to stand up against the evils of Communism, homosexuality, abortion and gun-control.' In 1986 the Supreme Court would revive the states' right to outlaw sodomy. Chief Justice Warren Burger said: 'To hold that the act of homosexual sodomy is somehow protected as a fundamental right would be to cast aside millennia of moral teaching.'[30]

Perhaps remarkably, the Church of England had supported the change in the law, though not necessarily from any real sense of social liberalism. Some of its bishops had even campaigned for repeal. In the House of Lords, the Archbishop of Canterbury himself, the venerable and much-loved Michael Ramsey, spoke in favour of decriminalization, though he referred to homosexual behaviour as 'utterly abominable'. But his remarks paled by comparison to those of the ageing war hero Lord Montgomery who believed 'the act of homosexuality in any form [was] the most abominable bestiality that any human being [could] take part in, which reduces him almost to the status of an animal.'

Dr Robert Stopford, the Bishop of London, while insisting he did not condone homosexuality or regard its practices as any less sinful, told his colleagues during the second reading debate that the church was concerned mainly for the reformation and recovery of people who had become victims: 'if this bill becomes law we hope that more people will come forward for that help, guidance and reformation which we believe it is our duty to provide for them.'

This was therefore by no means a change in the church's attitude to homosexual practice, merely to a law perceived to be unjust or unworkable. Dr Ronald Williams, the Bishop of Leicester, told their lordships that while he accepted the new tolerance, if it arose from a sense that moral values no longer mattered that would be regrettable: 'It would be a bad day for Britain if things came to the point where the law was reduced to a status no longer related in any vital way to the law of nature or the law of God.' The Bill passed through the Lords by 111 votes to 48.

The *Church Times* maintained a dignified reticence during the whole proceedings as if the subject was beneath mention, perhaps just too dirty to be considered. Its pages show scarcely any references to the bill's passage and none at all of the Commons debate, but eventually, a fortnight later, it ventured a leader:

> The passing of the bill into law will confirm the fears of those who have seen in it a major threat to public morality and a new step down the slippery slope to civilization's corruption and decay. The strongest argument in favour ... has always been that it will remove the temptation to a particularly sordid form of blackmail and that private conduct is a matter for the choice of individuals, who should feel free to follow their inclinations without the interference of the state. ... The enactment of the bill should be an occasion for Christian campaigners in favour to make crystal clear in public that they at least still recognise homosexual conduct as an offence against the moral law.[31]

When he was asked why the homosexual reform legislation had passed through the Lords when a bill to protect badgers had not, Lord Annan, the bill's sponsor, was succinct: 'Because there are more buggers than badgers in the Lords,' he said.

6

THE DAY BEFORE
YESTERDAY

'This mysterious and unfortunate condition.' (Dr Derrick Sherwin Bailey, Secretary of the Church of England's Moral Welfare Council, in Homosexuality and the Western Christian Tradition *(1955))*

The Church of England found itself bowled along by the social changes of the 1960s, which produced unwelcome social developments, including a decline in deference and respect for the old conventions, sexual liberation and the rise of feminism, that it found exceptionally difficult to deal with or even comprehend. There was also an accelerating decline in church attendances. Whereas in the 1950s nearly half the population had attended church on a Sunday, by the turn of the century the figure was down to about 7 per cent, many of those committed not to the established church but to Charismatic and Pentecostal, often black, denominations that had barely existed a generation earlier.

It was a climate in which for the first time the church was not entirely assured about its survival, when its fundamental tenets were sometimes being attacked from inside and its status and personnel ridiculed from without, when projected statistics appeared to show that at some point in the foreseeable future no one would be attending services at all, in any church. Its message grew more uncertain and muffled, its rituals and prayers chopped and changed and its beliefs were first challenged and then attacked either for being too changeable or not changeable enough.

No wonder the trumpet gave forth an uncertain sound. Michael Ramsey, the Archbishop of Canterbury, was asked in the 1960s whether he thought the church would survive into the next century. His answer: 'Well, you know, that is not certain, not certain, not certain at all. Not certain. It might easily, easily, it might easily, quite easily, just fall away after 20 years or so. Just fall away,'[1] was regarded as shocking. While his prediction has not come to pass, the question could still be posed today (and might well receive a similar answer from a senior churchman).

Within the church the greatest uncertainty was about sex in a climate where traditional Christian attitudes and censure could for the first time no longer be assumed to be automatically and actively shared by the population at large. With single parenthood losing its stigma, divorce common, premarital and juvenile sex assumed normal and homosexuality eventually open and accepted, there was a huge dilemma. Should the church move slowly towards a new acceptance of different moral norms or stand out against them and preach a message that fewer and fewer people could be bothered to listen to? It has indeed gradually shifted its position on many of these issues: the baptism of illegitimate children, the marriage with no questions asked of couples who are already living together, the remarriage of divorcees in church. Only with homosexuality is its response paralysed.

In 1963 John Robinson, the Bishop of Woolwich, published that rare thing, an ecclesiastical bestseller, *Honest to God*, which posited for the first time that God might not be a bearded benign old man up above the bright blue sky and, incidentally, that divorce and sexual relationships outside marriage might be acceptable. And, while in the years that followed, the Vatican maintained its traditional and historic line that homosexuality was intrinsically disordered, other faiths were beginning to consider slightly more positive attitudes towards those attracted to the same sex. The Quakers were first with a pamphlet in 1963 arguing that every sexual act should be judged by its inner worth, concluding that, 'homosexual affection can be as selfless as heterosexual affection and therefore we cannot see that it is in some way morally worse.' The Methodists too edged towards a more tolerant view.

For the Church of England though, acutely conscious of its established status and its uneasy alliance of a wide range of theological opinions, there was no straightforward response to homosexuality. When a month after the passage of the Sexual Offences Act, in August 1967, the vicar of Great St Mary's, Cambridge, pondered whether Jesus had not married because he was gay – a pretty otiose not to say frivolous form of speculation – a torrent of criticism descended on his head. Canon Hugh Montefiore merely mused in a conference speech in Oxford that 'the homosexual explanation is one we cannot ignore'. But the remark was taken sufficiently seriously for the Archbishop of Canterbury himself to issue an immediate rebuke. Ramsey said: 'There is no evidence whatever to support [the] reported ideas. Christians believe that Christ's dealings with men and women were those of a perfect man.'

The *Church Times*'s correspondence column bubbled for some weeks with the outrage (seemingly more than it had with the earlier homosexual reform legislation) with only the Rev. John Hester, of Dean Street, Soho, standing up for Montefiore:

> If the canon's suggestion is wicked and even its consideration is an outrage, what are the implications for those who know themselves to be homosexual? Is it possible that our Lord really meant: 'Be ye perfect like me – but not if you are a homosexual of course, you haven't a chance of success then, poor thing.' Surely it is this proposition which is itself the outrage.[2]

This argument too has had echoes throughout the succeeding debate. The controversy ultimately did the turbulent canon no harm. Montefiore went on to become Bishop of Birmingham.

Throughout the 1970s the gay issue rumbled on as a kind of background noise. Gay activists became more aggressive and open, aided and abetted by high-profile events such as the Festival of Light (founded by Lord Longford who, as a member of the Wilson government, had supported homosexual law reform) and the *Gay News* prosecution. In 1976 the Lesbian and Gay Christian Movement was founded and, while its approach was largely non-confrontational, its very existence was an affront to those who believed there were no homosexuals in the church, or that, if there were, they should keep quiet about it.

As the then Bishop of Chester told his diocesan newsletter 'no goodwill can come out of activities which sought to parade publicly that which should be essentially private.'[3] In 1975 the anonymous author of the introduction to *Crockford's Clerical Directory* asserted: 'Christians should never be so charitable to deviants as to cease to oppose the flaunting of homosexual behaviour.' The preface added that it was not a fit subject for discussion since to do so might turn people away from matrimony for, 'the category of the marriageable includes large numbers with some homosexual inclination and experience.' Why Christian heterosexuals might wish to incur such wrath and disapproval by experimenting with homosexuality, or whether it was desirable for homosexuals to engage in a married relationship with a woman against their true inclinations was not explained. These are still questions which hang in the air in Anglican discussions.

More luridly a lieutenant colonel from Oxfordshire who had served as a pathologist claimed that many murderers and suicides portrayed an element of sexual aberration. A priest had to enter family life at times of birth, death and bereavement and 'one does not want to wonder, even for a second, whether he is making advances to one's teenage son.'[4] It might not be a fear so openly voiced today, but it still exists in the muttered asides of some churchmen.

There were other, incidental, changes that affected the debate within the Church of England and its relations with the country at large, of which one was the creation of the General Synod, effectively the church's parliament, with lay as well as clerical and Episcopal members, called together twice and sometimes three times a year to debate issues of interest to the community and hence with the ability to kick up a genteel fuss when it wished to do so. This is not an institution that most other religious organizations outside Nonconformism tend to have – they are almost entirely unused to consulting their members about anything. Certainly the pope, to coin a phrase, would sooner take advice from his camerlengo than from his one billion-strong congregation. Anglicanism is quite democratic even on matters of faith and ritual and accordingly takes decisions rather slowly. Even then they often have to go to parliament for secular approval.

There was also a moral tide among politicians which fostered a greater political interest in the activities of the church, particularly insofar as it was perceived to be too liberal. And there was a question of relations with other churches: the liberal Methodists were casually rebuffed in the 1960s, but the Catholic Church was wooed in a palsied ecumenical game which produced warm words of mutual appreciation but very little movement – apart from avoiding giving offence to the Vatican – over very many years. Every time the Church of England envisaged a radical step, there were plenty to warn that the pope in Rome might not like it and that therefore it should not be done for fear of harming the relationship.

By the 1980s the struggle within the Church of England centred on just such an issue: the ordination of women, a long battle which threatened to divide the Communion (though, in the end, only a small if noisy minority of 430 instead of the predicted 3,000 clergy actually left) and which was ultimately seen as a triumph for liberalism. Among the collateral developments of the debate were the formation of factions and alliances among the theologically conservative wings of the church and the tactical making of common cause at times between Evangelicals and Anglo-Catholics. There was an accumulating sense among traditionalists that the church was moving away from them and had to be steered back.

Both groups were divided on women's ordination, however, especially the Evangelicals. But there was a realization among them that a united front must be developed to see off future challenges. Conservative Evangelicals realized that they were likely to lose the women's ordination debate. Too many people in the church knew women and some were even married to them. Although the Bible was clear enough on the subject of women in leadership, it was a debate that could be stalled but not won. There were other issues on which they could unite the flock and have a chance of winning. Inter-faith services was one such issue but that too was ambiguous: for every Evangelical who thought they represented a dilution of God's message, there were others who believed they were a worthy exercise. By the mid-1980s some conservative Evangelicals were beginning to recognize that homosexuality was the next issue that would present itself. It was most assuredly a sin, the constituency did not like it, the church was weak on the subject and it had all the makings of a unifying issue. They must be prepared.

The decision to ordain women priests took many years, from the early 1970s to November 1992, but the long struggle not only produced a higher degree of organized factionalism but also a number of other innovations that came to play their part in the gay debate. Firstly, the church eventually found a way round St Paul's injunction that women should keep silent in church and hence reinterpreted the Bible for modern times. Secondly, it restructured authority within the church to allow parishes that could not tolerate the idea of women's ordination – or those bishops who had ordained women or touched them – to come under the authority of provincial Episcopal visitors (PEVs), more often known as flying bishops, who would minister specifically to them. This effectively undermined traditional diocesan Episcopal oversight and set a precedent that would effectively allow parishes to choose their own bishops. If they could do it for this reason, why not for some other in the future?

It was a separate irony, not missed by many, that the Anglo-Catholic wing of the church which broadly, but not entirely, opposed women's ordination on the grounds that females were not qualified to lead a congregation, was also the part with the highest proportion of gays. Nor was it lost on those supporting women's ordination that the Anglo-Catholics had made common cause with the conservative Evangelicals, who opposed women's ordination on the grounds that it was unbiblical and who under other circumstances would have been most censorious of the Anglo-Catholic gays' behaviour. The debate created strange bedfellows. Indeed the ultimate effects of the women's ordination debate were to create highly politicized factions, to focus church attentions inwards and ultimately to weaken the Anglo-Catholic wing of the church. This all had repercussions for the gay debate.

In the words of the religious commentator Andrew Brown:

One of the prejudices shared by almost all supporters of women's ordination was that their Anglo-Catholic opponents were fundamentally just gays who were jealous of potential priests who might look better in skirts than they did. On the other hand, it was reasonably common to encounter men who believed that any unmarried woman who wanted to be a priest was probably a lesbian. As so often in the Church of England, there was some truth on both sides of this argument.[5]

The coming of women priests was a shock to the Anglo-Catholic constituency. They really had not realized that their views would not prevail, that they were in a minority and that life and society had moved on. For Evangelicals too it was a time of coming to terms with the rest of the Church of England, as well as with society at large, and of realizing that their vision of the church and the Bible was not shared by everyone else.

The decision in November 1992 did not ultimately provoke the widely anticipated split – almost as if everyone was too exhausted by the long campaign – although those who could not agree with it were rewarded with lavish pay-offs for the cost of their conscience, ultimately costing the Church of England £26 million it could not afford. For the church authorities the lesson seemed to be that division could be managed, with good will.

Unlike the Anglo-Catholics who were welcomed into the Roman Catholic Church with unseemly haste, the Evangelicals did not have a more congenial place to go. Nevertheless this was a dry run for the row over gays a decade later.

By now the US Episcopal Church had already voted to ordain women in 1976 and had ordained its first woman bishop, Barbara Harris, who was also both black and divorced, in 1988 – placing it far ahead, even in an impaired Communion, of the rest of the church. Some bishops initially refused to wear their ecclesiastical robes in Bishop Harris's presence as a stern mark of disapproval, or to hold meetings with her. This, however, all seemed to have been forgotten in 2003 when Gene Robinson was consecrated and a new split was announced, or perhaps the same split all over again, by amnesiac prelates.

The Church of England was in an anxious state by 1987, still at war over women's ordination – it had just taken the decision that they could be ordained deacons – and under attack from Margaret Thatcher's government, which appeared to see eye to eye with the Church of England over very little and was not afraid to say so. The prime minister, who had not volunteered in the Second World War herself, took umbrage at the behaviour of Robert Runcie, an Archbishop of Canterbury who had won the Military Cross, who insisted on praying for Argentinian dead after the Falklands War in 1982. His idea of Christian forgiveness was not hers.

Then when the church produced a report discussing the plight of the inner cities, another ministerial bruiser and his allies in the press could think of no better counter-argument to its findings than to denounce it as a Marxist document. Its bishops were told in no uncertain terms that they should shut up about social issues, which were no concern of theirs, and stick to God, so long as He busied Himself only with non-contentious and preferably conservative matters of moral discipline. This was not the sort of relationship with the government of the day that the church was used to or expecting. It was rattled by media ridicule too.

And it was denounced as excessively liberal in the case of the appointment of David Jenkins, the loquacious Bishop of Durham who swapped the college seminar room for the bishop's palace and thought he could continue to indulge publicly in the sort of theological speculation that had previously mildly amused his students only in private. That there was a lightning strike on York Minster shortly after his consecration was just too good to be true for the media. Nevertheless, if he was a figure of fun to the newspapers, his views, particularly his seemingly insulting dismissal of the Resurrection story, were taken extremely seriously by many in the church. They were hurt, distressed and annoyed by his insouciance and seeming imperviousness to the feelings of those whose faith depended on the sort of beliefs he appeared to ridicule. Evangelicals thought he should never have been appointed. They could not comprehend how someone with Jenkins's views could be an ordained minister of the church, let alone rise so far. If there was a single spark which lit the conservative resistance to the direction in which the church was travelling it was caused by the appointment of the Bishop of Durham. The fire at York Minster was coincidental, but was not taken as such by some.

Gavin Reid, the Evangelical former Bishop of Maidstone, who served on the Synod with Jenkins, says that his appointment was seen as symbolic of the liberal tide in the church:

> Jenkins was cavalier with other people's views and he knew what he was saying because he had been brought up as an Evangelical. He'd even been wheeled out to attack Bishop Robinson's book in his younger days. I think he was a bit of a fool. Loveable, but a bit of a fool. He said a lot of things that Evangelicals might have been able to agree with and he believed it was important to speculate and to push Biblical interpretation, but it was how he said it that did the damage.

In 1986 the House of Clergy even went into private session during one
Synod and passed a confidential motion asking that the likes of David
Jenkins should never be appointed ever again. By then, however, the
damage to the Evangelicals' confidence and trust had been done. They felt
they had worked hard for the church and that their views had been either
ignored or, in the case of Jenkins, thrown scoffingly back in their faces.

Into this febrile climate stepped a clergyman with a mission, not to say
an obsession: the Rev. Tony Higton emerged from the parish of Hawk-
well, out in the wilds of Essex, with a motion that struck at the heart of
the moral panic gathering ground in the nation about the emerging
worldwide AIDS epidemic. Higton's target was all forms of sexual immorality, including divorce and other heterosexual sins, but it was the attack
on homosexuality that grabbed the attention.

Higton, now working for an organization called the Church's Ministry
among Jewish People and acting rector of Christ Church, Jerusalem, says:

> I was very concerned about the deterioration in standards in the church,
> about doctrinal belief and belief in morality. There was a trend rather than
> specific events. I knew that while homosexuality would dominate attention I
> was equally concerned about heterosexual immorality. My motivation was not
> to attack the homosexual community but their beliefs. What precipitated it
> was, yes, the Bishop of Durham. I thought you couldn't have bishops denying
> half the Gospel. I felt very strongly that enough was enough, but I never
> wanted to pillory anyone. I didn't have particular people in mind. I was not
> political in that way.

This was a pot that could not be kept from boiling. Evangelicals like
Higton were shocked as they engaged with the rest of the church that it
could harbour so many gay clergy and apparently not mind about it.
Evangelical clergy did not attend theological colleges swamped with gays
and a camp culture as Anglo-Catholics did. Vicars outside London and
the metropolitan areas often did not realize that homosexual colleagues
even existed, or rarely came across them – 'there was a little bit of it happening round Southend, not far from my parish,' says Higton now. It was
a sort of half-hidden secret that had been kept from them. This was a side
of the church they rarely saw and if they occasionally came across exotic
creatures at Synod, flamboyant in flowing capes and strangely shaped hats,
they were told that this was just an alternative, that these vicars were 'not
the marrying sort'. When the truth slowly dawned on them they were
shocked that such things were tolerated in defiance of the Bible under
their very noses. It reeked to high heaven.

Higton, an Evangelical to the roots of his abundant hair, produced
with help from similarly inclined conservatives such as David Holloway,

the turbulent vicar of Jesmond – who was political – a motion for Synod calling for the reaffirmation of Biblical standards of morality, condemning fornication, adultery and homosexual acts in all circumstances and demanding of Christian leaders that they should be 'exemplary' in all spheres of morality. The motion was a shot across the bows of the bishops for what the Evangelicals suspected was coming – an attempt to soften the church's opposition to homosexual practice in the likely recommendations of a forthcoming report.

It caught the bench of bishops flat-footed. They had not expected it and it was precisely the sort of debate they did not wish to hold in public because it tore at the roots of their discreet policy not to inquire too deeply about the activities of those they chose to ordain. Runcie, who had himself knowingly ordained gay clergy, admitted as much a decade later during his retirement: 'There have been in my ministry occasions when I have acted in a "don't-want-to-know way and why-should-I-inquire" way. I never liked the prospect of inquiring into what happened in a man's bedroom unless he's prepared to tell me.'[6] He insisted, however, that he had not ordained anyone he knew to be actively engaged in a homosexual relationship, a caveat that members of the LGCM still regard with incredulity.

Higton had earlier that year founded an organization called Action for Biblical Witness to Our Nation (ABWON) and in the run-up to the debate published a report with Holloway called *Sexuality and the Church*, which demanded that any candidate for ordination who was prepared to justify homosexual practice should not be allowed to proceed to holy orders. Higton also wrote to all 44 diocesan bishops demanding their support for his crusade about sexual morality in the church: 20 replied and 24 did not. The Archbishop of Canterbury's response was magisterial in its disdain: 'The Archbishop is himself deeply concerned about the moral issues to which you draw attention. However, he cannot respond to every request he receives for a statement of his views on moral questions. It is his practice to make such statements when he judges the moment to be opportune and in an appropriate context.'

At a previous Synod meeting earlier in the year, Higton had asked the Archbishop why the church's statements on ministering to those with a homosexually transmitted disease (i.e. AIDS) had omitted references to the need for repentance. Runcie loftily replied that the bedside of sufferers was not the place for pastors to be working out their own feelings and that they had to be sensitive to the needs of sufferers.

But the motion with its simple argument received wide support among lay members of the Synod and could not be avoided, ignored or patronized out of existence. It placed the bishops in a particularly cleft stick: opposing the motion would expose them to the charge of supporting immorality in defiance of the commonsense view of the worshippers in the pews.

Evangelicals' suspicions that they were being sold down the river on the homosexual issue had been roused for some time, ever since the Church of England's first modern attempt to tackle the subject theologically had been published in 1979. A working party led by the Bishop of Gloucester, John Yates, had produced a report entitled *Homosexual Relationships*, which suggested that 'there are circumstances in which individuals may justifiably choose to enter into a homosexual relationship.' This was a considerably more liberal approach than the church would subsequently adopt. The *Church Times*, some years later, noted that disapproval was no longer an adequate response:

> The Church of England has homosexuals among its priests, among its ordinands, among its worshippers. These are people who have the same need of sexual expression in its many forms, for companionship, for acceptance as heterosexuals. It becomes increasingly difficult to deny them those things and argue the denial is merciful, or truthful, or practical. ... The Church ... cannot long defer the time when it will have to consider withdrawing disapproval of homosexuals. That would mean most notably that homosexuality ceased to be an obstacle to ordination.[7]

In some dioceses of course it had already ceased to be an obstacle. By the mid-1980s though, the scourge of AIDS and the public fear of a 'gay plague' had caused a renewed secular public panic, which conservative Evangelicals could exploit. They may not have encouraged it, but the publicity attendant on the debate led to a spate of arson attacks on London churches whose clergy were suspected of being homosexuals. The atmosphere was feverish.

It is questionable whether the Church of England was itself running in advance of public opinion at this time on the question of homosexuality, which was still an object of scorn when it was not the subject of ribald ridicule. National newspapers had still not learned the commercial value of the pink pound, and respected public figures who were gay kept their identities firmly closeted. Only slowly would more tolerant attitudes prevail among some though by no means all of the middle classes – and some of the last to change were those who regularly attended church.

AIDS was not the only cause of concern in the pews. There was a sense that gays were flaunting their sexuality. There were suspicions of a homosexual mafia wielding undue influence in an effete church, of gay bishops and gay clergy running rampant and securing preferment through the institution.

Not only had subversive liberals introduced a dull, modern-language liturgy (the 1980 Alternative Service Prayer Book) in defiance and betrayal of all the church's loftier, hallowed, poetic traditions, but homosexuals were running the place. It was the fear of what might come out that scared the bishops most. Higton himself attacked the appointment of Bishop Yates to chair the church's Board for Social Responsibility, saying it was a matter for deep distress. The Bishop had not been forgiven for the 1979 report.

In the event the debate, on 11 November 1987, was successfully finessed, and its publicity relatively limited because of events in Northern Ireland, where three days before the IRA had perpetrated one of the worst atrocities of its long campaign, at Enniskillen, killing and maiming many peaceful people attending a Remembrance Day service.

In Synod, Higton denied that he wanted a witch hunt, but demanded Godly discipline which supported the Scriptural teaching that homosexual practice was an abomination and a perversion. He read from letters he had received about 'rampant' practices at theological colleges, of clerics frequenting gay bars and clubs, of an unnamed rector displaying explicit posters and pamphlets in his church and of priests being moved and reappointed to new parishes following convictions for indecency.

> Today the nation and the world are going to make a decision, not about morality but about the credibility of ... the Church of England. Whatever decision we take will send out a message either that the church is courageously true to its Biblical and traditional foundations or that it is not. ... We must help homosexuals to see the error of their ways and unashamedly proclaim Biblical beliefs and morals. Let us stand up and be counted.[8]

Later in the debate David Holloway, in McCarthyite fashion, claimed that there was a homosexual mafia in the church, even in high places: 'Too many of us have first-hand knowledge that confirms part of what is being alleged. The church of Jesus Christ is being scandalised in the eyes of the watching world.' He wanted appropriate discipline against such priests. But he did not name names. Holloway argued that the homosexual issue was more likely to split the Anglican Communion than the ordination of women. He said some African bishops had already talked of boycotting the following year's Lambeth Conference of bishops because of the Church of England's tolerance of homosexual practice among its clergy.

All but unnoticed, a single Synod member, Barnaby Miln, a Hereford JP, told the Synod that he was gay. He believed, he had told the *Daily Mail* earlier, that if the motion was passed the Church of England would shut down.[9] Later he was to move in with Derek Pattinson, secretary-general of the Synod, the Church of England's most senior (and stately) civil servant and a man who, when he retired in 1990, would himself receive a knight-hood from the Queen and a fast-track to ordination.

The bishops themselves rallied around a much more moderate (though still pointed) amendment proposed by the conservative Evangelical Bishop of Chester, Michael Baughen, affirming traditional teaching on chastity and fidelity and asserting that fornication and adultery were sins against the ideal of a total commitment within a permanent married relationship.

This was at the nub of the bishops' case and what ultimately doomed Higton's jihad: by spreading the attack wide to heterosexual sin as well as the homosexual variety, he had effectively undermined his case and cast it beyond the pale. Everyone could agree that homosexual activity was sinful but one had to be a bit more careful about the 'normal' kind which might not be unknown to the people in the pews. As Baughen once said on another occasion, the church had to evangelize where people were, 'in their golf clubs' – though whether there are more golfers than gays in most parish churches remains a matter of conjecture.

Having agreed therefore that everyone in a general way was a sinner, the amendment continued: 'homosexual genital acts also fall short of this ideal and are likewise to be met by a call to repentance and the exercise of compassion. ... All Christians are called to be exemplary in all spheres of morality ... and holiness of life is particularly required of all Christian leaders.'

Runcie himself told the Synod that the more grateful they were for a blessing like marriage, the less they should use it as a stick with which to beat the less fortunate:

> While there are both homosexual and heterosexual people whose conduct is undisciplined, self-centred and out of control, questions arise over our response to homosexuals who are seeking to behave responsibly towards other people, who are not sleeping around, not molesting children, not breaking up other people's marriages and friendships. ... I want to insist that to be homosexual by nature is to be a full human being. We need to listen to what such homosexuals say about their situation.

> Only when we allow people to be more open and honest about themselves can we respond with serious pastoral care and effective discipline. Clergy behaviour is best left to their Father-in-God within the present terms of the law. In this earthly tabernacle of Christ's church there are many mansions – and they are all made of glass.

With some relief the Synod voted by 403 to eight for the amended motion, with 13 abstentions. All the bishops, including those who were and would continue to be ordaining gay clergy, supported the motion. The outcome left the question of disciplining gay clergy just where it had been before. Such unsavoury measures were left to their diocesan bishops, some of whom were more tolerant than others but all of whom were inclined to let sleeping dogs lie. David Jenkins, the Bishop of Durham, correctly but tactlessly went so far as to say that in his experience, practising homosexuals made good clergy so long as they avoided scandal and promiscuity. For good measure, he added that some of his colleagues thought the same. The issue had been temporarily scotched but it would not go away.

Higton told me:

> Some bishop said after the debate that it had set back the gay cause for ten years. I think he was being prophetic. I always felt that the tide would turn again, just as it has. Recent events have not surprised me. My views have not changed. I have never been antagonistic towards gay people. I don't have any negative reaction to them. My issue is simply with the morality of the behaviour. There is a lot of hate in this issue. I am more concerned about reconciliation in my job now.

The Thatcher government, busily reforming the education system, decided to take up the homosexual issue in populist terms by introducing into the 1988 Local Government Act the notorious clause 28 which prohibited local authorities from 'promoting' homosexuality or gay 'pretended family relationships'. In the face of pretty slender evidence and the private reservations of some ministers (I was the education correspondent of the *Daily Mail*, one of the clause's most enthusiastic promoters, at the time) the clause effectively prevented councils from spending money on projects, including advice services, which could be alleged to make gay lifestyles somehow more attractive. The clause was symbolic of the electoral advantage the Conservative government perceived to be gained from attacking homosexuals, whose votes it clearly felt it did not require.

Although there was no doubt that some Labour city authorities were behaving provocatively in the 1980s and engaging in gesture politics of a sometimes infantile and extravagant kind, there was very little evidence that they were aggressively proselytizing for gays (should such a thing be possible). The evidence really came down to the elusive presence of a single schoolbook, imported from Denmark, called *Jenny Lives with Eric and Martin*, which showed in sober prose and pictures aimed at counteracting prejudice how a young girl lived normally with her father and his male partner. The most shocking image showed a chaste photograph of

the two men sitting up in bed with the little girl, though there was naturally no suggestion that the two shaggy-haired and moustachioed
archetypal 1970s characters were sexually attracted to her. I kept the book,
which I never saw in any school or public library, in my bottom drawer at
the *Mail*, just in case it ever needed to be taken out for the titillation of
our readers.

The clause was never invoked but its very threat prevented libraries
stocking gay newspapers, or websites, and even forced the Glyndebourne
Touring Opera to abandon a staging of *Death in Venice*. It was finally
repealed by the Labour government in 2003, not without some difficulty
and opposition by former Conservative ministers who had gone on to
their just rewards in the House of Lords. Repeal was by then described as
a 'triumph for twenty-first-century tolerance over nineteenth-century
prejudice'.

Back in the 1980s, within a month of the Higton debate, there was
further confirmation of the Church of England's ineffectuality in the
ghastly debacle of the *Crockford's* preface, which appeared to confirm all
the worst prejudices about a church turning in on itself, losing its Christian purpose, fighting bitterly and hounding a righteous cleric to his
death. This at least was one version, though it only bore a glancing resemblance to the truth.

Crockford's, the annual directory of the ordained clergy of the church,
was accustomed to carry an anonymously contributed preface from a
senior churchman outlining the events of the year in a sometimes vaguely
waspish manner. In 1987 the preface was somewhat more pointed than
usual, attacking Archbishop Runcie for a lack of principle, 'taking the line
of least resistance on each issue' and suggesting that preferment went to
his friends and those who thought like him rather than to Evangelicals or
Anglo-Catholics. To some sections of the press this was a jolly passing
fancy since it confirmed their prejudices about the Archbishop and it was
useful to be able to report similar, but presumably authoritative, criticisms
in a semi-official source. The hunt immediately began for the author,
largely on the basis of offering him money to write more boldly and
publicly what he had already said under the cloak of anonymity.

The hunt was almost at once narrowed down to Gareth Bennett, the
chaplain and history tutor of New College, Oxford, a conservative of the
old school, who was known to be disgruntled after being passed over for
promotion to a bishopric and who – it was less widely known – was a
specialist in the anonymous church pamphleteers of the early eighteenth
century. If he thought he could emulate his hero, Francis Atterbury, the
Bishop of Rochester, who had penned Tory diatribes during the reigns of

William of Orange and Queen Anne, however, he reckoned without the interest of the modern media.

In this I must record a small interest, since Bennett had been one of my tutors a decade earlier. I remembered a diminutive man, simpering camply behind rimless spectacles, who seemingly derived mirthless pleasure from lacerating hapless adolescents with sarcasm, chuckling dryly at the discomfort of 18 year-olds. I should imagine he was latently homosexual, but he was certainly misogynistic – when the debate over whether the college should admit women undergraduates was raging, I remember him hissing prissily at a sherry party: 'Of course, we could never have them here. Whatever would we do about the *sanitary* arrangements?' A few years later the college indeed went co-educational, but Gary (an extraordinarily demotic misnomer for such a frigid man) had not left. He was becoming increasingly bitter that he would never get the promotion he coveted and for which, with his chilly personality and conspiratorial nature, he was entirely unsuited.

When the *Crockford's* story broke it was Bennett's misfortune that not one but two New College history graduates were working at the *Daily Mail*. It was the paper most anxious to identify him and offer him money to work out his frustrations in a page six opinion column about why, oh why, the Church of England was going down the tubes. I was one of those journalists; Leaf Kalfayan, the deputy news editor, was the other. We both recognized the unmistakable style immediately.

Bennett denied his authorship. He was apparently worried that Robert Runcie really would prevent any further advancement if his authorship became known – not realizing that the Archbishop already knew perfectly well who had written the preface and was quite relaxed about it. When a day or two later Bennett returned from a weekend in Cambridge to his lonely bachelor home in a drab Oxford suburb to find his aged pet cat had died in his absence, he repaired to his garage and gassed himself using a hose from the car exhaust.

The recriminations were enormous: the church blamed the press (particularly the *Mail*) for its scurrilous pursuit of the hapless, insufficiently worldly, cleric, the press blamed the bishops who had previously attacked the author for hiding behind his anonymity. Internally there was also a vicious campaign to saddle Runcie with the whole affair or at least to discredit him over it, which saw an unlikely and temporary alliance between Holloway and some of the gay Anglo-Catholics for giving insufficient moral leadership on the one side and for failing in his duty of care on the other. Runcie himself believed, and said bitterly in retirement, that he had been 'stabbed in the back' over the incident, especially by the gays.

Bennett never realized that his momentary celebrity (and commercial value) was already waning as newspapers were turning to the next day's sensation before he ever turned on the car ignition. But the chief effect of the terrible story was to show a callous church rounding on one of its own and forcing a decent, and vulnerable, man to suicide. A great deal of guilt went around.

One unresolved question was whether Bennett's mental turbulence had been partly caused by his own campness. Certainly over succeeding years the homosexual issue gave rise to a number of high-profile casualties among bishops and senior clergy as a succession of outings occurred in the tabloid press, bearing out all the worst allegations of the conservative Evangelicals in the most prurient and salivating fashion.

Among them were the Bishops of Gloucester and Jesmond. The Bishop of Durham who succeeded Jenkins barely escaped the revelation that he had been prosecuted 25 years before for an incident in a public toilet. The flamboyant Father Brian Brindley, vicar of Holy Trinity Church, in Reading of all places, a leading member of the General Synod and a man who could not have announced his campness more clearly if he had strung a message above his vicarage in fairy lights, fell foul of a *News of the World* man with a tape recorder and was forced to resign his living. Brindley, who had spelled out his fantasies about young boys in some detail and who had once declared, 'a woman can no more be a priest than a goat can be a Christian', repaired to Brighton, converted to Catholicism and 12 years later ended his days in spectacular fashion by collapsing during his 70th birthday celebration dinner at the Athenaeum, shortly after the hors d'oeuvre course.

The Rev. David Holloway lost no time in circulating photocopies of the *News of the World*'s Brindley story ('Evil Fantasies of Kinky Canon') to every member of the General Synod in self-righteous justification, accompanied by an unctuous letter. This was somewhat ironic, since Brindley and he had collaborated in the wake of the Bennett affair against Runcie. The campaign reflected little credit on him: Holloway lost his seat on the Synod at the next election, but went on to co-found the pressure group Reform.

The *Independent*'s Andrew Brown and then the *News of the World* also eventually caught up with Sir Derek Pattinson, the former secretary-general of the General Synod ('Sin at the Synod'). This happened some time after his young Irish chauffeur had died in an accident at King's Cross while on an expedition to buy cocaine for Pattinson's friend Barnaby Miln, the man who had declared himself homosexual during the Higton debate.

Miln himself subsequently went to prison for fraud and Pattinson retired into obscurity. They resurfaced in the autumn of 2003 by which time Sir Derek was in a nursing home and Mr Miln was exposed as running a ring of homosexual prostitutes from his partner's flat, furnished with drugs, bondage equipment and a large set of canes for corporal punishment. The flat, close by Westminster Abbey, had been sold to Pattinson on advantageous terms by the diocese of London. It was far from clear whether he was aware of what was happening at his property since he had allowed Mr Miln the run of his home in his absence. Miln happily boasted to an undercover reporter about promiscuous gay sex and offered his services for a modest £60.

The late 1980s was a difficult and unsavoury period for the church's hierarchy, hardly helped by the tactics of the militant gay campaigning organization called OutRage!, led by the political activist Peter Tatchell, which periodically, when it felt the need for publicity, threatened to 'out' gay clergymen in high places, including ten bishops all at once in 1994. This was the mirror-image of Holloway's tactics and had an unpleasant, bullying air about it, kicking at inoffensive men who somehow impertinently chose to keep their sexuality private in defiance of Mr Tatchell's clear wishes. The tactic left the LGCM distinctly uncomfortable, though some members would later claim that the campaign pushed the church's debate forward in the 1990s.

OutRage!'s actions certainly alienated many within and beyond the church and gave an unattractive impression of gay militancy which won it little support outside its narrow constituency. In the words of Jeffrey Heskins, a vicar by no means ill-disposed to gays:

> Outing gay individuals is part of the liberationist ethos because it purports to challenge the boundaries of public and private. ... Ironically the deployment of such extreme tactics seems to do little to empower or liberate the oppressed individual. Instead [it] just compounds a stereotype of gays and lesbians, one that depicts them either as immature anarchists or as unstable predators and bullies who select soft targets like the Church to vent their anger on.[10]

The chief object of OutRage!'s campaign was David Hope, then Bishop of London, later Archbishop of York, a witty, genial man, an unmarried priest in the Anglo-Catholic tradition, much more concerned about the church's traditional spirituality than its bureaucracy. At an earlier stage of his career, sent to sort out the gay antics at St Stephen's House, the high-church ordination training college at Oxford, Dr Hope had earned the aggrieved nickname 'Ena the Terrible' – some versions said it was 'Ena the Cruel' – after Ena Sharples, the elderly female battleaxe of the television soap opera *Coronation Street*, from the disgruntled students. It was a nick-name which stuck, resurrected in every subsequent profile ever written about the high-flying bachelor bishop. Here too.

After receiving a particularly nasty letter from Tatchell warning that the group had enough information about him to out him as gay, in early 1995 the Bishop issued a statement acknowledging his sexuality was 'a grey area' but insisting that he had chosen to lead a single celibate life: 'This is a positive way of life for me. I am happy and content with and within myself.'[11] It is difficult to imagine any previous bishop ever being required to make so demeaning a statement.

The assault on Hope's sexuality came at a time when the primates of the Communion were meeting in London. Such was their fellow feeling for their beleaguered colleague that they were persuaded to issue a liberal and supportive statement on his behalf. This was in stark contrast to their reaction to Gene Robinson, whom they had never met, a few years later. Even this humane gesture, however, perturbed the moderator of the Church of Pakistan, who was petrified that his name would be associated with such a statement, even though he privately supported it, for fear of how it would be interpreted back home.

By then the church had a new Archbishop. George Carey succeeded the urbane Runcie in 1991, reputedly as Margaret Thatcher's revenge on a Church of England that had made little secret of its distaste for her social policies. It is said that she ignored the favoured candidate, John Habgood of York, as too much part of the establishment and dismissed other poten-tial archbishops such as David Sheppard, the Bishop of Liverpool, despite his impeccable establishment and cricketing credentials (he had once been the England cricket captain) as far too liberal. She had had enough of smooth men and chose instead, out of the blue, the obscure Bishop of Bath and Wells.

Carey, who had only been a bishop for four years, was an Evangelical – thus maintaining the relatively recent tradition of selecting Anglo-Catholics and Evangelicals in turn – but, more importantly from the government's point of view, this was not an archbishop likely to cause trouble. Indeed not: such trouble as George Carey created was because of his inability to provide inspiring and decisive spiritual leadership either within the church or to the nation at large.

This may have been because of a lack of intellectual self-confidence: Carey, gap-toothed and bespectacled, smiling as though he was somehow vaguely missing the joke, was the first archbishop for many generations, perhaps since the Middle Ages, who had not been university educated or raised among the landed gentry or middle classes. Instead he had admirably worked his way up from a childhood on a council housing estate in Dagenham, Essex, leaving his secondary modern school aged 15 to become an office boy with the London Electricity Board. His was an interestingly meritocratic appointment but he was perhaps rather too similar in his inexperience to his contemporary, John Major, the prime minister, who had also risen from nothing and also had insecurities as a result.

Carey was at least a man, as some said admiringly, who knew what it was like to go round Tesco's supermarket shopping, but he was limited in his vision. Like a good Evangelical should, he wanted to convert the nation to Christ and was perhaps rather surprised when it did not respond to his call. The result of the decade of evangelization, inaugurated before his arrival but enthusiastically adopted by the new incumbent at Lambeth Palace, was that there were fewer people attending church at the end of the 1990s than at the beginning. This was a particular disappointment because the new archbishop was also the first Evangelical to rise from the post-war revival of Evangelicalism, the previous Evangelical archbishop, Donald Coggan, having been a desiccated and uninspirational academic raised in dour pre-war traditions. The new man represented Evangelicalism's big chance. It was scarcely Carey's fault that his spiritual ambitions were thrown awry by the discovery in 1992, a year after his arrival, that the Church Commissioners, guardians of the Church of England's budget, had contrived to lose at least £500 million in ill-conceived property speculation. That threw many hopes off track.

In the circumstances Carey's concentration on managerialism was not surprising. It kept the show on the road but it was not inspiring. Equally his overriding concern to keep the increasingly diverse and fissiparous Communion together at all costs by attempting to finesse divisions, was worthy but not often courageous. It did not bring him many thanks in the Church of England. Across the rest of the world the dignity of his office brought him wider respect.

Carey's position on the gay issue wavered occasionally. He too was battered by Tatchell, not on the grounds of gayness, since the Archbishop was happily married, but because he had not accepted OutRage!'s naming agenda. On Easter Sunday in 1998 the Australian campaigner even popped up in the pulpit beside him at Canterbury Cathedral where, until the police arrived, the pair briefly formed an unlikely double act, one in vestments the other clinging to a banner, locked together rather like Judy and Mr Punch.

There is always a nagging feeling, however, that Tatchell is more interested in self-publicity and confrontation than the promotion of reasoned
debate.

Generally the Archbishop could talk as well as anyone about listening
to homosexuals, but when in 1992 the SPCK planned to publish a collection of prayers for gays and lesbians that it had commissioned from the
lesbian theologian Elizabeth Stuart, he ensured that the publisher withdrew by threatening to resign as its patron if the book went ahead.

Carey's position wobbled though. In a speech at the Virginia Theological Seminary in February 1997 he announced: 'I do not find any
justification from the Bible or from the entire Christian tradition for
sexual activity outside marriage,'[12] but in November 2003, less than a year
after his retirement, he was happy to muse on BBC television's *Breakfast
with Frost* programme about the possibility of civic ceremonies for gay
couples, saying that there was not necessarily anything sinister about
them: 'there may well be a case for looking sympathetically at civil partnerships as long as this is not the thin end of the wedge to try and get gay
marriages in.'[13] He seemed entirely uncomprehending of the moral ambiguity, not to say double standards, of such a position for one such as he.
This equivocation was one reason why some Evangelicals came eventually
to despair of his leadership and to regard him with disappointment and
even in some quarters contempt.

Shortly before Carey's appointment, in the late 1980s, to show it
meant business, the Church of England chose to crack down rather more
publicly than before on the Lesbian and Gay Christian Movement, evict-
ing it from St Botolph's, the church in Aldgate in the City of London
whose rector Malcolm Johnson had provided the movement with office
space in the church's tower room. He had not troubled to seek diocesan
approval for this and, in the wake of the Higton debate, was suddenly told
he would have to acquire it. The Bishop of London and the Archdeacon,
George Cassidy, apparently oblivious to the number of gay clergy in the
capital, chose to make an example of the church and, egged on by Mr
Higton and sections of the press, decided that it was inappropriate that
the LGCM should be housed in an ecclesiastical property.

Chief among the charges against it was the sale of advice booklets and
academic studies of homosexuality to members and inquirers. Some of
these were fruitier than others and the sale of *The Joy of Gay Sex* on church
premises, even though it was 'not the kind of book to put into the hands
of one's grandmother' in Sean Gill's words,[14] made allegations about
peddling pornography easy to sustain. The parish was forced to give in but
the diocese found itself having to pay all the legal costs.

The diocese's actions incurred considerable criticism for its apparent vindictiveness. Seventy London clergy complained to the Bishop:

> Most of us have no link with LGCM and may not support all its aims, but we believe that the resort to law in this way was an inappropriate response to a pastoral problem. Members of LGCM are our brothers and sisters in Christ and the rest of the Church should listen to them with respect and love, especially at this time of increasing hostility to gay people. But again the church has been seen as intolerant and rejecting, driving gay people out both physically and symbolically.[15]

Their complaint was joined by one Rowan Williams, Lady Margaret Professor of Divinity at Oxford University, who wrote in the *Church Times*: 'The deliberate will to humiliate which seems to be evident in the way this case has proceeded is very scandalous for the Church.'[16]

By now, however, the Church of England was making yet a new effort to reach an agreed position on homosexuality. Another working party had been set up in 1987 under the chairmanship of the Rev. June Osborne, a deacon in Tower Hamlets in the East End of London, to advise the bishops on the issue. This was the report that the tacticians behind the Higton debate had hoped, successfully as it turned out, to preempt. The committee proceeded with some secrecy, as if unnerved to be tackling such a sensitive topic at such a delicate time, and when it completed its work in 1988, its report was not published. This scarcely mattered – except insofar as it precluded another debate in Synod – for the findings were eventually leaked to the media.

They were resolutely even-handed, except in suggesting that the church needed to be more welcoming to gay people:

> The church needs to be very careful lest it opt for those insights which match its own tradition and abandon the possibility that it may have to learn from insights less amenable to such an easy marriage with Christian views. We need to keep clearly in mind that if what we stand for makes no connection with the real dilemmas and questions experienced by homosexual people we are in danger of failing in the basic pastoral task. ... Bishops, as the chief pastors of the church, have a particular responsibility to set a tone of welcome and acceptance in these matters.[17]

The report suggested that the church could not judge all homosexual genital acts as morally identical or equally blameworthy: 'Homosexual promiscuity and lustful self-indulgence is one thing; homosexual activity in a young person's exploration on the way to maturity is another; deliberately chosen physical expression in a mature and long-standing relationship yet a third.'

It added, presciently:

> No serious work on moral growth can be achieved in an atmosphere marked
> by a judgemental and fearful spirit. When people think they have nothing to
> learn and that their duty is to make others conform to their views it is very
> difficult for growth to happen. ... Those who wish to stress the inclusive char-
> acter of the Gospel and therefore of the Church can appear to be suggesting
> that anything goes in the Church. ... On the other hand there are those who
> seem to be saying in effect we would rather not have fellowship in Christ with
> homosexual people. Life in the Church would be more comfortable without
> them. That is how homosexual people hear much of what the Church appears
> to say to them.

In retrospect this may have been a more fruitful and less convoluted way
forward than what emerged the following year, which was a compromise
that both sides could apparently live with, but which exposed the church
to accusations of double standards and hypocrisy.

This was the slender, 48-page custard-yellow and red-covered pamphlet
called *Issues in Human Sexuality*, which was produced by the House of
Bishops in December 1991. The title itself was a misnomer since it was
almost entirely concerned with homosexuality. It remains the church's
policy even though the then Archbishop of Canterbury, George Carey,
stated in the preface that 'we do not pretend [this] to be the last word on
the subject.' The report went on to add that those who disagreed with it
were free to argue for change – remarks that Evangelicals like David
Banting and William Taylor tend to overlook when insisting that *Issues* is
the definitive word and that those like Jeffrey John who disagree with it
must instead give it their full-hearted endorsement.

The report bizarrely introduced the desiccated and faintly repellent
term 'homophile' in preference to 'homosexual' because it was thought to
be 'as yet free of some of the negative overtones' and because it could,
apparently, help avoid clumsy circumlocutions in referring to same-sex
love.

The report recognized that committed same-sex partnerships could be a
blessing for those involved in them and for society at large and that homosexuals were 'as valuable to and valued by God as heterosexual people'.
But it added even so that they fell short of the heterosexual ideal. It commended them to a life of abstinence: 'a path of great faithfulness, travelled
often under the weight of a very heavy cross' but suggested that in some
circumstances 'a loving and faithful homophile partnership in intention
lifelong, where mutual self-giving includes the physical expression of their
attachment' could be accepted.

But clergy could not have this possibility. They could not 'claim the liberty to enter into sexually active homophile relationships'. It explained:

> Because of the distinctive nature of their calling, status and consecration, to allow such a claim on their part would be seen as placing that way of life in all respects on a par with heterosexual marriage as a reflection of God's purposes in creation. The Church cannot accept such a parity and remain faithful to the insights which God has given it through Scripture, tradition and reasoned reflection on experience.[18]

However, while the report indicated that sexually active homosexual ordinands might not be accepted, it rejected the witchfinder-general approach to those who were already ordained, saying that it was grossly unfair to assume that two people of the same sex living together were in an erotic relationship: 'Although we must take steps to avoid public scandal and to protect the Church's teaching, we shall continue, as we have done hitherto, to treat all clergy who give no occasion for scandal with trust and respect and we expect all our fellow Christians to do the same.' In other words, don't ask, don't tell.

Issues in Human Sexuality from its title onwards was therefore an uneasy attempt to square the divergent views that existed on the bench of bishops, trying to force an incoherent pastoral and theological position into a rounded policy. The inconsistency was rapidly identified: how could a loving and faithful partnership be deemed acceptable for lay people, but not for clergy, unless they were discreet about it, and certainly not for potential ordinands? Twelve years later when the question of gay bishops arose, senior churchmen found themselves in a similar position, being unable for the most part to say whether, if it was unacceptable for Jeffrey John to be a bishop, it was acceptable for him to be in holy orders at all. Most seemed to suggest that he could remain a clergyman, but not be a candidate for a senior post because that involved leadership and setting a good example.

Most bishops themselves were aware of the inconsistency. The pamphlet's main author, John Austin Baker, the Bishop of Salisbury, himself disowned it once he was safely retired. Giving a public lecture in London in April 1997, he said: 'The bishops saw same-sex erotic relationships as incompatible with the clerical vocation. ... I find myself obliged now to dissent from that judgement. If the Church is willing to accept the ministry of homosexuals, then to impose on them a condition which most clergy are not prepared to undertake would seem to be unjust.'

He added that it was unjust for married heterosexual clergy to deny their gay colleagues 'the potential spiritual blessing of a sexual relationship when they themselves enjoy that blessing' and dismissed the argument that congregations would not have confidence in gay clergy by saying that their views 'tell us nothing about the essential moral status of such relationships'.[19]

These sentiments startled George Carey, who described them as 'a significant departure from the church's current mind', adding that there was no question of any sudden change in the church's official position. Richard Kirker of the LGCM said the speech showed the need to consign *Issues* to the dustbin of history, and Reform, not for the first or last time, warned that the whole Anglican Communion was in danger of collapse.

7

THE DIGNITY
OF DIFFERENCE

'There is only one Jesus Christ and all the rest is a dispute over trifles.' (Queen Elizabeth I)

Throughout its history the Church of England has always been riven by the contradictions inherent in its foundation. It was formed in the 'crucible of unsolvedness' and retains its traditional disparities - between its Catholic and Protestant roots, between Episcopal and Synodical government, between Biblical and sacramental approaches to belief and worship. These inherent tensions help define what it has been and what it is today and have created an ongoing struggle between its Evangelical and Catholic wings. This is a contention for the character of the church, with both traditions attempting to seize and claim its authority. What we are seeing now is perhaps a consequence of fundamental beliefs vehemently held and thus not amenable to compromise or flexibility - or sometimes moderation of language.

Certainly the Evangelical tradition has been more fissiparous than most, and the debate within its ranks and between its factions over the interpretation of the Bible and other matters has bubbled periodically to the surface at least since German theologians in the 1860s first posited that not all its passages were necessarily factually accurate. This convulsion, along with the contemporaneous publication of Darwin's *The Origin of Species*, caused serious questioning of what the Bible said, how it should be interpreted and whether Protestant Christians could live with what resulted. This and the developments that sprang from it remain at the root of the current contention about Biblical authority.

Of course not all Evangelicals are members of the Church of England: they belong to a range of denominations across the Protestant tradition, including Methodists, Baptists and Pentecostalists. Some indeed believe that their links with other denominations are closer than those with other

Anglicans. There are Anglican Evangelicals who see themselves as primarily members of the Church of England, and Evangelical Anglicans who consider themselves Evangelicals who happen to be members of the Church of England. Since the eighteenth century, Evangelicalism has always been a tradition within a tradition, sometimes more or less consciously a church within a church. Increasingly, with its success in recent years inside a church in numerical decline, it has become more prickly and assertive of its position, certain that it is in the right, puzzled that others within the church do not always see things in the same way, but convinced that its views, beliefs and traditions should prevail, both because they are right and because they bear the democratic mandate of the weight of numbers.

It has never been an entirely cohesive force even within the Church of England, divided not only on Biblical interpretation but also on forms of liturgy and prayer and church hierarchy and organization. When in 1878 Edward Batty of St John's, Fulham, told the Islington Clerical Meeting that they should 'admit that certain historical parts of the Bible were allegorical or open to different interpretations and show that they were fully alive to the importance of the claims of just, honest, reverential and scholarly criticism', he was greeted with cries of 'No, no'.[1] There was great suspicion and fear of a loss of control of the text: 'theological interpretation like every other branch of knowledge is a progressive science', said the vicar of Islington in 1905.

Thereafter, Evangelicals had to cope with a succession of blows to belief and worship. The First World War caused crises of confidence, even to the level of deciding how the dead should be regarded: should they be prayed for even when they were destined for heaven anyway and was that indeed where they were heading after death in battle? Would they automatically enter into salvation even if they were impenitent, merely because the British cause was just?

New-fangled, sometimes foreign, ideas could undermine the teaching of the Bible, as James Mountain, Baptist Minister of St John's Free Church, Tunbridge Wells, declared in the 1920s: 'Shall the floods of German criticism overwhelm the ripened fields of ... Truth, even as the hordes of German Huns overran the stricken fields of Belgium?' The solution was to organize to defeat error, perversity and untruth, often by splitting from the source of the pollution – in Mountain's case by founding a separate Bible Baptist Union for his disgusted flock in Tunbridge Wells.

These and other problems, which seem arcane to us, periodically wracked the Evangelical community. Should believers shun places of entertainment or sporting activities, or were these harmless ways of recruiting potential believers and spreading the Good News? Should they encourage adherents to listen to the wireless, which occasionally played uplifting music for the benefit of the housebound? Did the cinema have any worth or was it 'one of the Devil's chief agencies for keeping [Christians] away from the cross'? Should they engage in civic society at all, or shun it as a distraction from God's purpose? Even church bazaars could be suspect and any form of gambling such as a raffle or whist drive was absolutely out of the question, second only to drink as a cause of wickedness. This made it increasingly hard to engage a wider constituency. Some on the farther fringes of Evangelicalism, groups such as the weird and malign Jehovah's Witnesses and the isolationist Exclusive Brethren, still feel this way.

In the USA, where the gospel of Social Darwinism - the survival of the fittest translated into factory working conditions - was more fiercely espoused and politicized, evolution was the cause of strife. The uncertainties of modern life - economic dislocation, agricultural depression - helped encourage a movement to return to old Biblical certainties, 'the Fundamentals'. This occurred especially in the Southern states, which had never fully recovered their prosperity since the American Civil War 60 years before.[2]

Just as British Evangelicalism had spawned several of the great social reformers of the nineteenth century - men like William Wilberforce, eager to free slaves in order to convert them to Christianity, Lord Shaftesbury and Dr Barnardo - so the US Fundamentalist movement was by no means necessarily a conservative one to start with. Its greatest early champion, William Jennings Bryan, had been the most radical politician ever to run for the White House - he had been the Democratic candidate for the presidency three times and had more genuine social reforms to his credit - factory conditions, working hours, minimum wages, graduated taxation - than any other single American politician before or since. But Bryan died in the wake of his humiliation at the Scopes Monkey Trial in Tennessee in 1925 and Fundamentalism moved steadily towards reaction thereafter.

It was not until after the Second World War that Evangelicalism really began to emerge from its shell, both in Britain and the USA. The dropping of some of the exclusionist, negative, disapproving rhetoric and the arrival of sharp young proselytizers such as Billy Graham helped to start the conversion of a new young generation seeking uplifting spiritual answers in a confusing and demoralized world that had recently confronted evil on an unparalleled scale. More than 80,000 people attended the first week of Graham's first revivalist meeting in north London in 1954 and ten months later 64 per cent of previous non-church goers who had come forward at his meetings were still attending church.[3]

These people were not, as their successors a couple of generations on would be in the 1990s, largely ignorant of Christianity. They had been taught the basics at school and Sunday school and probably dragged to church each week by their mothers. The decline of religious education, the disinclination of women to lead their families to church each week and the rise of other Sunday possibilities such as shopping and leisure pursuits generally combined to create a largely Biblically ignorant though spiritually inquisitive population.

A new menace to post-war religion also loomed in the shape of Soviet Communism. The world faced a conflict of ideologies – maybe even imminent destruction through Man's own power of invention – and a choice was necessary for all thinking people. Salvation, for oneself, for the world, was an urgent consideration. Some historians have noticed that Evangelicalism seems to flourish in times of social upheaval and uncertainty as people strive for something secure to grasp.

From being a movement that seemed to disapprove of all forms of pleasure, however innocent, Evangelicalism broke out in several joyful directions after the Second World War. It became more informal, more welcoming and more friendly, in keeping with a less deferential, more permissive and questioning age. It was the time of the Charismatic revival, an offshoot of the pre-war Oxford Group. This exuberance did not mean a tolerance of sin, least of all sexual sin, which tended to be the most personal and prevalent of all, but it did mean a degree of self-expression and witnessing to the way God had changed one's life. It also meant less formal services, fewer traditional hymns and prayers – indeed hymns of a mindless vacuousness to match the new Alternative Service Book – more guitars and, ultimately, overhead projectors obscuring the chancel, less ritual and fewer occasions where vestments were deemed necessary, more folksinging and irreverence and, sometimes, less evident thoughtfulness.

When current Evangelicals in the course of the gay debate criticize '1960s culture' and the exaltation of personal feelings and experience as part of the gays' self-absorption and indiscipline, they tend to forget that modern Evangelicalism has roots in precisely the same sort of culture. Just as American Anglicans attacked their liberal bishops in 2003 for being part of that irresponsible, baby-boomer generation, so the leaders of the Evangelical movement in the new millennium were often those whose conversion had come at precisely the same period and probably for very similar reasons.

Some of this charismatic stuff was uncomfortable, even Satanic, to more traditional Evangelicals but the two strands of the movement intertwined and from 1967 those who formed part of the Anglican Church had a new sense of purpose. In that year Evangelicals gathered at Keele University to discuss among other things whether their future lay within the Church of England or outside it with others as a separate interdenominational group. John Stott, who chaired the meeting and who resisted any separatism, helped to swing opinion towards full participation. He noted with satisfaction that all the conference speakers were conservatives. David Atkinson, the Bishop of Thetford, wrote in the September 2003 issue of *Church Times*: 'Keele turned Evangelical Anglicans churchwards: we understood that we belonged within the Church of England and had a part to play in its life. It also turned us outwards: there was a recognition that Evangelical Anglicans had some hard work to do in the world of work, mission, ethics and education.'[4]

Since then some Evangelicals have regarded the church as 'a convenient boat to fish from', providing buildings, facilities, a structure and an established position in society from which to seek souls for salvation. They would be lost without it, or confined to a few scattered buildings, holding annual meetings in obscure country village halls. This is what has happened to some splinter groups.

The church into whose waters the Evangelical movement sailed was a strange and even alien one, from Anglo-Catholics with their strange superstitions and suspicious ritualism to low-church men who were practically Presbyterians. It was a tweedy church and, within the same communion, sometimes within the same city, there were effete young men who clustered together in clergy houses and believed in using incense. Whatever it was, it was broad and to some it did not seem serious.

Nor was it at all welcoming to the enthusiasts erupting in its midst. 'Evangelicals were pretty nearly persecuted in the 1950s and '60s,' said Gavin Reid, later Bishop of Maidstone, who was himself ordained in 1960:

> If you were an Evangelical in those days you did not get senior appointments or plum livings. There was only one Evangelical bishop on the bench and if the diocesan clergy were taken off for a conference, you could be sure there would be no concessions to your worship and the Eucharist would be catholic. It was not a good career move to be an Evangelical. We found ourselves sent to difficult parishes and having to turn them round and make them work, and that of course eventually made us better.
>
> By the 1980s, having gone to work in the church following Keele and got stuck in, we were surprised to find it had not made much difference. That is

what made us more assertive and in the late 1980s there was a new generation entering Synod. That's when there was support for the Higton motion. It was something Evangelicals could vote for.

The Evangelicals were on an upward tide against the prevailing wooliness of the Church of England. Evangelicals filled the need for certainty. The number of ordinands claiming to be in the Evangelical tradition rose, became vicars, some even bishops, and spread the word with confidence and often aplomb. By contrast the liberal message appeared uncertain and wan: a belief- and certainty-free zone. By the 1990s, with an Archbishop of Canterbury who was one of them, they felt ready to take over and were only puzzled that the outside world did not seem to share their confidence.

Evangelicalism has some determined strengths: the emphasis on personal responsibility, the joy and vigour of worship and often an accessibility and friendliness that builds a warm and caring church community, although it can also lead to a banality and a tooth-furring mundanity in services, a loss of spiritual depth and a perfunctoriness in the celebration of traditional offices. In the words of Monica Furlong in her book C of E: The State It's In:

> To spend much time around Evangelicals is to feel oneself caught up into a mood of cheerfulness, vigour, enterprise, hope – it is a bit like going out with a likeable puppy which not only jumps all over you and licks your face but travels five times the distance you are travelling out of sheer joie de vivre and exuberance.

> The Evangelical church offers a simple and simplified teaching which anyone can grasp. A close study of the Bible, a strong emphasis on the crucifixion as being related to an individual's sins, an emphasis in being in some special relationship with Jesus that is reached by a conversion experience, the importance of witnessing to one's belief and so converting others, a strict moral sense – all of these, together with a warm social climate are of the essence.[5]

There is room for debate about just how effective the Evangelical movement has been in recent years. It likes to assert that its churches are among the most vibrant and active within the Church of England – and there is a lot of truth to this, at least in the urban suburbs where the middle classes have flocked to some large parishes in their search for spirituality and the meaning of life and have helped to make them wealthy. But it is also true that church numbers continue on a downward trend with little sign of the mass conversions that Evangelicals have always craved.

Three main strands are now evident in modern Evangelicalism: the Charismatics, the 'open' Evangelicals and the conservatives. They are not always in agreement with each other and are sometimes mutually scathing or even antagonistic. An article by the Rev. Graham Kings, an Evangelical, one of the organizers of the new, moderate Fulcrum group and vicar of St Mary's, Islington, in the *Church Times* in September 2003 set out some characteristics.[6] The Charismatics – sometimes characterized as the 'happy-clappies' for their joyful, even ecstatic forms of worship, their waving arms and occasional attempts to talk in tongues – have a conservative view of Scripture but also believe in the importance of receiving God's Word today through prophecies. They are committed to the dynamic authority and trustworthiness (though not necessarily the inerrancy) of the Bible and the exercise of spiritual gifts in church, such as prophesy and healing. They are open to ecumenism, women's ordination, the use of the media, the importance of the church as a community and the exploration of creative and alternative forms of worship.

Open Evangelicals believe in the intrinsic authority of the Bible, 'which is to be interpreted in context and with insights from the world-wide church', and work for renewal within the structures of the Anglican Communion. They are open to ecumenism and to learning from other traditions, have an active interest in the outside world and its issues and believe in the importance of the sacraments and liturgy.

The third and perhaps best organized and most vociferous group in recent years, certainly on the gay issue, are the conservative Evangelicals. Although they may be open to some limited Biblical interpretation, they essentially believe in the inerrancy and infallibility of the texts and in punishment and repentance as the means of atonement for sin. They are not therefore happy with what they see as the subversion of Biblical doctrines, such as the ordination of women – placing women in a position of 'headship' in either the church, the home or the family. Church structures are less important than proclamation of the Word: thus they may use non-liturgical worship, work across denominational boundaries and 'plant' non-parochial churches where they perceive a need, even if there are already parish structures (of a different sort of Anglicanism) existing in place.

Planting churches may be fine where there is no similar local worship available – indeed an official report welcomed the idea in January 2004[7] – but these can be potentially disruptive and difficult impulses for other churchmen and women where there are other active churches even within the Evangelical tradition. Thus Tom Wright, the newly installed Bishop of Durham and a theologian who appeared as a guest speaker at the Blackpool Evangelical Conference in September 2003, was extremely irked to find a conservative church under a Holloway-ite cleric attempting to establish itself right under his nose in the middle of the city of Durham, without his permission or approval.

This form of church planting is a divisive issue, championed by Peter Jensen, the Archbishop of Sydney, Australia, whose pursuit of proselytizing for his own brand of chippy, aggressive churchmanship spreads well beyond his own diocesan heartland. Bishops are not the only ones annoyed to find the Archbishop (who has appointed his own, like-minded brother – a man who compared homosexuality to bestiality during a talk to Cambridge undergraduates in early 2004 – as dean of his diocese) invading their patch, claiming their forms of mission are flabby and inadequate, decrying the work of others and calling on the faithful to set up their own churches instead. Jensen has little truck with ecumenism, because he simply knows he is right. But he is also viewed with nervousness because of the disruptiveness such methods can cause and because his idea of diocesan authority – the bedrock of Anglican tradition – is a strictly conditional one. If you don't like your bishop then ignore him or find yourself another from outside. Preferably someone just like Peter Jensen.

This has implications not only for parish structure and Episcopal authority but for diocesan funds as well. If you don't like your diocese, why not be like William Taylor at St Helen's Bishopsgate in the City of London and refuse to support it by withholding your contributions? Dr Jensen started a week-long speaking tour of England in January 2003 by giving a day of lectures from Mr Taylor's pulpit. This is a diminution of collegiality, potentially an undermining of the diocese but also, more crucially, of less-well-off parishes, less able to hold their heads above water, with less affluent parishioners or greater social needs.

Conservative Evangelicals don't like to see this as a form of blackmail – and some of them don't like the tactic at all – but it is an inevitable consequence of the congregationalism that the Jensenites and those of like mind espouse. After all, you cannot support those who preach error and, if there is a need, you can always plant a church in the area to shine as a proselytizing beacon of truth in a sea of struggling and contemptible iniquity.

From such ideas and such mindsets and in the absence of clear leadership of the Evangelical movement as a whole – Stott was ageing by this time – there emerged the pressure group Reform in February 1993. Reform claims its purpose is to 'win the nation for Christ' and says: 'The Church of England seems to have lost confidence in the truth and power of the gospel and we believe that responsibility in changing this must belong to the local church.' The group's founding statement in its original leaflet says: '[We are] Christians first, Evangelicals second and Anglicans third. ... We are committed to the reform of ourselves, our congregations and the world by the gospel. ... Reform is urgently needed [because] the gospel is not shaping and changing our church and our society: our society seems to be shaping and changing us.' It has a pretty profound distrust of bishops as well evidently as the Church of England and wants to complete the Reformation which petered out in the seventeenth century.

Formed by the likes of Wally Benn (who seems to have survived his subsequent promotion within the Church of England to the suffragan bishopric of Lewes without too much of a personal crisis of conscience) and David Holloway, Reform was set up initially to resist the ordination of women. Since then it has moved on to homosexuality. Multi-faith worship was a concern to the conservative Evangelicals in the 1980s, until they found that Muslims shared their reservations.

Monica Furlong, in her book, refers to Reform as having 'a brutal, blackmailing approach ... holding the church to ransom'.[8] It can certainly appear self-righteous and rancorous, permanently angry and intolerant, as if it regards other church people as inferior backsliders or even not fully Christian. Opponents enjoy the group's annoyance at being called the C of E's Taliban tendency but it also periodically claims to be the largest pressure group within Evangelicalism. It has certainly made a lot of noise in a short time.

In an interesting recent study, Canon Martyn Percy, a liberal theologian and director of the Lincoln Theological Institute at Manchester University, argues that Reform identifies its particular stance as 'orthodox' and implies that the rest of the denomination has lapsed in belief, confidence and responsibility. The enemy in the new Reformation is not the papacy but modernity and liberalism.[9] During the course of 2003 in the gay bishops' controversy, there was indeed much bandying about of the word 'orthodoxy', as if this was all the justification necessary, and much laying claim to its possession. In this religious view, everything – self, church and world – must submit to the pre-determined will of God that has been so clearly and unambiguously revealed. Moral decay is all around and the only hope of salvation is Bible teaching.

Percy notes 'a particular kind of elite conservative Evangelicalism' in Reform, which has drawn some of its leaders from a relatively exclusive, public school and Oxbridge group. A surprising number of them seem to be former army officers: William Taylor at Bishopsgate, Paul Carter, now in New Westminster diocese, Canada, another. No wonder their philosophy seems full of battlefield analogies. They were trained in the muscular and masculine Christianity of student summer camps run by groups such as the Inter-Varsity Fellowship and the Universities and Colleges Christian Fellowship. It is a world in which women are allowed in as helpers – doing the dishes, that sort of thing – but not as full participants, certainly not as leaders. These camps encouraged a back-to-basics Biblical teaching, not a touchy-feely Alpha-like proselytizing, of which conservative Evangelicals are usually deeply sceptical, when not outright hostile.

Percy argues:

> Reform leaders are not simply arguing for a particular kind of moral coherence as the basis for ecclesial communion: they are also advocating a specious form of Protestantism that will exclude the excesses of Charismatic Renewal and the aesthetics of Anglo-Catholicism. In other words, Reform is promoting a kind of clear, morally certain and pedagogically cerebral Christianity. ... There is little scope for ambiguity or difference, for the Bible is held to be clear on all matters of importance. It is a case of Trust and Obey – there is no other way. ... It is important to understand the association as a movement of *resistance* ... the themes of correction, confrontation, reformation and reassertion are prominent.

In the light of this and the subversive message that the church and its bishops are letting down the flock, it is perhaps understandable that Reform is not universally popular even among other Evangelicals. But it makes them nervous too. Its focused targeting of specific issues and its tactics – decentralization and reform of church structures – are disquieting.

Only one vicar has so far gone the whole hog and exiled himself from the Church of England and he, of course, is a Reformista. Charles Raven, the vicar of St John the Baptist, Kidderminster, decided in 2000 to declare himself out of communion with Peter Selby, the Bishop of Worcester, because of the Bishop's liberal views on homosexuality. He not only invited two retired Ugandan bishops to conduct a confirmation service in defiance of his own diocesan's instructions, but also refused to have any dealings with anyone who had been licensed by Bishop Selby, including the cleric who had been appointed team rector instead. The poor man, Harold Goddard, found himself barred from the church. Raven was the author of a booklet called *Conflict and Growth*, which indicates that the latter can only grow out of the former. In this he may have miscalculated, as the Bishop eventually refused to renew his licence. Raven took his ideological purity out of the church and down the road to a local hall, where some of the remnants of his flock followed him.

In the circumstances of such belief, there is no scope for any compromise whatsoever, certainly not on the gay issue, because gays are just sinful. If a group lays claim to 'orthodoxy' and defines the term as it wishes, it may be attempting to annexe and define the whole church in its own likeness - a church it doesn't really like and whose traditions it does not respect very much - but it is also very hard to argue with. Freedom and tolerance of others are not options for Reform because such qualities are seen as amounting to a rebellion against and a rejection of God's sovereignty. It is a Manichaean struggle. There can be no tolerance for its self-defined enemies and no place, ultimately, for them in the church, Reform wants to reform.

The Church Society's autumn 2003 magazine provided an interesting insight into conservative Evangelicals' entryist thinking in an article by a retired army officer called Edward Armistead, member of the General Synod from the diocese of Bath and Wells and chairman of the Oak Hill training college council. It could almost be taken from a 1980s Militant Tendency instruction sheet. Called 'Surviving as an Evangelical in a non-Evangelical rural church', Mr Armistead's article outlines subversive tactics for circumventing opposition from what he terms 'the old guard' in a parish - i.e. those who might oppose what a zealous Evangelical might want to do. He clearly regards such people as not being really Christians at all.

Thus the area you move to may have a 'beautiful' church but

> it is often impractical for effective gospel work: access by foot or car is restricted and car parking limited; there is no loo or kitchen and no meeting room for mid-week groups and children's work on Sunday. The priority for the parochial church council is so often the preservation of the building and its contents, including the organ. ... Any suggestion that the church could be reordered to make it more user friendly by, for example, replacing the pews with more comfortable chairs or the installation of a sound system - let alone the provision of pew Bibles! - is met with derision and opposition.

> The rural church is likely to be dominated by the 'old guard' who are suspicious of innovation ... and who are determined to preserve the church and all that takes place in it in accordance with what makes them feel comfortable. ... The result is ... that Christians go elsewhere ... rural congregations shrink ... and archdeacons impose ministers who will conduct services in accordance with the wishes of the 'old guard' but who have no experience of, or training for, teaching the Bible.

The answer, Mr Armistead says, is to decide whether the old guard is worth engaging with - 'Do they actually understand the issues or even care about them sufficiently to make intelligent dialogue worthwhile?' - and then to organize small Bible study groups, sometimes with like-minded folk from neighbouring parishes, to nurture Evangelical Christians 'and to help others, including the "old guard", see the need to repent and believe in the Lord Jesus'. Eventually even they can become 'targets' for God's good news of salvation. A conservative Evangelical vicar in Staffordshire was taken before a church court in February 2004 precisely for altering his listed church – ripping out pews, installing carpet over Victorian floor tiles – without permission.

The rise of this form of Evangelicalism coincided with the church's disarray over homosexuality and the rise of a gay lobby of sorts within it and in society as a whole. The foundation of the Gay Christian Movement in 1976 – the 'L' for Lesbian came rather later – followed the first stirrings of the gay liberation movement in Britain and particularly the USA. Gradually there was a new assertiveness and a willingness to stand up and be counted, although the movement within the church has generally been a rather responsible and supplicant one. It has been steered by Kirker and others away from direct confrontation on the whole – it has never advocated promiscuity or the removal of the age of consent – while making its voice heard for acceptance with increasing vociferousness. It is this that has been most resented – as Gerald Ellison, the Bishop of London, told the Rev. Malcolm Johnson, vicar of St Botolph's, on the day he allowed the movement to hold its inaugural meeting in his local church school: 'Why don't you keep quiet? I don't tell everyone what Mrs Ellison and I do in bed.'[10]

Discretion would certainly have been the better part of valour as far as the bishops of the Church of England were concerned. The church would really prefer the gays to remain in the closet and it is an unanswered question whether Jeffrey John and Gene Robinson would have been promoted to the episcopate with a clear conscience had they kept quiet about their sexuality. After all, it has done so often enough in the past. The LGCM estimates that there are at least seven homosexuals on the current bench of bishops, though some of those, maybe all, are likely to be celibate. It is the increasing refusal of gays in the church and in society generally to keep quiet that leads their opponents in the Anglican Communion to claim that they are in thrall to a powerful lobby seeking to subvert the church's teaching.

In fact, as those opponents know, the practices they rail against, such as same-sex blessings, have been relatively common within both the Church of England and the US Episcopal Church for years. By the late 1990s the LGCM was receiving about 500 inquiries a year about blessing services and had a confidential register of 40 clergy willing to carry them out.[11] In 1976 the vicar of Thaxted, Essex, conducted a blessing service for two lesbian couples – an event that only came to be known about because the press reported it – and in 1978 St Luke's in Charlton followed suit.[12] Compare and contrast the altogether more heated reaction 20 years later when the Canadian diocese of New Westminster introduced something very similar.

The point was that gays were seeking not just acceptance by the church but recognition and participation within it, even on its terms rather than theirs. One of the first discussions within the Gay Christian Movement was about liturgy, as Mr Johnson of St Botolph's said: 'If clergy can bless battleships and budgerigars we can bless two men and two women who are in love and wish to make solemn vows to each other.'[13] In this desire for acceptance, the gay men who founded the movement found it hard to make common cause with women, but also with the wider gay movement which, with some reason, saw the church as a hostile and oppressive force.

The gay movement also developed its own theology, first in the 1980s seeking to develop a reinterpretation of the Biblical texts on homosexuality and also to increase acceptance for the notion that the condition was not a matter of choice or perversion but of natural orientation and so should not be regarded as sinful. This cautious approach was gradually replaced by a rather more assertive and less apologetic philosophy – queer theology – in the late 1980s and 1990s. This sought to change churches themselves by becoming more demanding that they should accept what the American gay theologian Robert E. Goss christened 'translesbigays' and abandon what he called the Biblical 'texts of terror'.

Such language gives some of the flavour of this new offshoot, though many of the writings of the queer theologians are clotted, convoluted, opaque and laden with jargon. Thus, Goss:

> Queer theologies proceed from critical analysis of the social context that forms our sexual/gender experience in the web of interlocking oppressions and from our innovative and transgressive practices. Queer theology is an organic or community-based project that includes queer sexual contextuality and our particular social experiences of homo/bi/transphobic oppression and other forms of oppression and our self-affirmations of sexual/gendered differences will impact upon the future developments of liberation theologies.[14]

This is clearly still a priesthood talking to itself in a language only it can appreciate. We are a long way from C.S. Lewis – or perhaps from any engagement with a wider community. Between militant conservative Evangelicalism and queer theology there can be little meeting of minds.

Yet the secular gay movement as a whole has been making accelerating progress in social acceptance during the last decade. The media now finds it much harder to demonize gays as it did during the church debates of the late 1980s. This was a startling revelation to some Evangelicals during the Jeffrey John and Gene Robinson sagas in 2003, for they had calculated on at least some sympathetic editorializing in the conservative press, but found scarcely any.

Newspapers in Britain which a decade before had railed against kinky canons and pulpit poufs now shrugged their metaphorical shoulders in indifference. Indeed life had changed: coming out was no longer such a furtive thing to do. The most popular television soap opera, *EastEnders*, watched by a huge audience every week, introduced a gay character played by Michael Cashman, who was himself gay, in the late 1980s.

The omens at first were not good: 'The tabloids were screaming. They outed my partner, we had bricks through the window and there were questions in parliament about whether it was appropriate to have a gay man in a family show when AIDS was sweeping the country,' Cashman told the *Guardian*.[15] But gradually assumptions changed: 'This was a flagship BBC show, the most popular series in the country, and Colin and Barry [the characters' names] were there day in, day out. The relationship wasn't sensationalized and the public devoured it.' After three years in the show, Cashman left and later went on to become a Labour MEP. Another gay actor, Sir Ian McKellen, was not only knighted, but is now one of the most popular public figures in the country.

By the late 1990s Britain had its first openly gay cabinet minister in Chris Smith. There were also openly gay MPs – one of whom, Ben Bradshaw, saw off a particularly homophobic, ostentatiously religious Conservative opponent in the 1997 election in Exeter to win a previously safe Tory seat. Even the Conservative Party eventually saw the advantage of having gays in its ranks. One Tory MP, Alan Duncan, eventually came out as gay to a deafening wave of indifference, though insinuations about the past of one of the party's leadership contenders, Michael Portillo, contributed to his defeat in the 2001 leadership contest. The Prince of Wales's chief adviser was openly gay, living with his partner who happened to run the Press Complaints Commission before going off to be chief media officer of, yes, the Conservative Party.

In the USA the daughter of Dick Cheney, the Republican Vice-President, came out as a lesbian, and Dick Gephardt, the leading Democrat and sometime presidential hopeful, included his daughter and her female partner on the family Christmas card. In November 2003 one of the least controversial parts of the Queen's speech to parliament, outlining the government's legislative plans, was the proposal to authorize same-sex civil partnerships. In Massachusetts the supreme court ruled that gay couples should have the same rights as heterosexual ones, and in February 2004 the mayor of San Francisco authorized same-sex civil weddings. Soon the practice spread across the USA. President George Bush, facing re-election and an opponent from · 'liberal' Massachusetts, immediately spotted a 'wedge' issue to divide the Democrat opposition, and announced plans for an amendment to the US constitution – only the 17th in its 217-year history – to define marriage as being solely between persons of the opposite sex. John Kerry, the Democrat contender, agreed with that definition. Both men, however, also supported an improvement in the rights of non-married couples. Even as a partisan political issue, same-sex partnerships were by no means straightforward.

These developments do not, of course, eradicate anti-homosexual prejudice, but together, cumulatively, they build a general acceptance of gays as a fact of life.

In an interesting study based on analysis of the British Social Attitudes and British Household Panel surveys of the 1980s and 1990s, Alastair Crockett of Essex University and David Voas of Manchester University trace a clear change in public attitudes.[16] They show that in a country where half the population has no memory of the practice of homosexuality being a criminal offence, attitudes have evolved dramatically. In 1983, in the first survey of its kind, just over half of the adults questioned believed that sexual relations between same-sex adults were always wrong and only 20 per cent said they were not at all wrong, or rarely wrong. By 2000 more than a third said they were not wrong at all and only slightly more than that believed they were always wrong. Overall, those who thought same-sex relations were always or mostly wrong – 46 per cent – only just outnumbered those – 41 per cent – who thought them rarely or not at all wrong.

Although Crockett and Voas say that the figures should disabuse the liberal temptation to suppose that homosexuality is now condemned only by a small minority, the change in the balance of views has been extremely rapid. What is even more marked is the change in attitudes differentiated by age and gender. The proportion of people in 2000 saying that homosexuality is wrong is about a quarter in all age groups up to the age of 55 and then the proportion increases sharply after that age. For comparison, in 1983, 38 per cent of those under the age of 35 considered homosexuality was always wrong. Women too find homosexuality easier to accept than men, though this is a trend that may be changing.

Among religious groups, however, the researchers found that differences in attitudes were more marked than in the general population as a
whole: liberal Christians, especially among the young, being more than
usually accepting of homosexuality than the population as a whole and
conservative Christians, including the young, being more than usually
disapproving. The study says:

> Young Anglicans are less likely to hold anti-gay attitudes than non-Anglicans
> at age 18, but there is a positive interaction between Anglicanism and age,
> such that for each additional year of age the odds of an Anglican having anti-
> gay attitudes increases than by more than would be expected for others ...
> while the odds of an 18-year-old Anglican having anti-gay attitudes are half
> those for non-Anglicans, the odds are equal just beyond the age of 50 and by
> 65 they are a third higher for Anglicans. Society as a whole is split over
> whether homosexuality is wrong and Christians are even more divided than
> others.

But at the same time, the Anglican Church seemed to be talking fren-
ziedly and obsessively to itself. The opponents of homosexuality in its
ranks grew more implacable than ever, taking the secular world's be-
musement as proof that they were right.

In 1996 the LGCM obtained acceptance of sorts with the holding –
not without fierce and unprincipled opposition from some Evangelicals –
of a celebratory service to mark its first 20 years, in the cathedral at
Southwark. Reform thought the cathedral should have 'banished and
driven away' the gays and wondered whether the cathedral would have
made itself available to neo-Nazi groups – an interesting illustration of
how it saw the gay movement and how it thought it could best demonize
it in the eyes of the public. The gays seemed to be winning the argument.
And then came the 1998 Lambeth Conference.

8

DOING THE
LAMBETH WALK

'The thing I love most about this rainbow Communion is the way it has always lived with disagreement without breaking apart.' (George Carey, Archbishop of Canterbury, at the Lambeth Conference, 1998)

By the time George Carey summoned the Lambeth Conference of all the bishops of the Anglican Communion to meet in July 1998, attitudes on both sides of the homosexuality debate were hardening. It would be a most divisive and rancorous conference and, however much Dr Carey might wish it otherwise – at one point he said that if the meeting came to be remembered only for its debate on sexuality it would have failed – it became a pitched battle over homosexuality between conservatives and liberals, between the developing world and North America, with Church of England bishops caught uncomfortably somewhere in the middle. The issue had not even been on the agenda of the previous conference ten years earlier; now it was to be almost all consuming. For many outside the church the abiding image was of an African bishop screaming that Leviticus called for the death penalty against homosexuals and attempting unsuccessfully to exorcize the gayness from the LGCM's Richard Kirker. It was an unfortunate sight for a supposedly loving Christian church to convey.

Almost 750 bishops attended the Conference from 37 separate provinces and 164 countries, many more than ever before, because suffragans as well as diocesan bishops were invited for the first time. Despite its name, the Conference had been moved in the 1970s from Lambeth Palace to the university campus at Canterbury, so that all the delegates could be accommodated in a large tent-like structure erected within a sports hall. The conferences, held every ten years, had been inaugurated in 1867, initially in response to complaints of heresy from Canadian bishops against the missionary Bishop John Colenso of Natal in southern Africa, a

man who at the time was attempting to convert the Zulus and who had
recently contributed to a book in which he had suggested that the Bible
stories could be interpreted and that some might even have been myths.
One hundred and thirty years on there would still be an issue of Biblical
interpretation, but this time the Canadian bishops would be largely on the
side of liberalism and the Africans (though not the South Africans) on the
side of tradition. The issue of how Anglicans could define and enforce
uniformity of belief in culturally and racially different societies had grown
even more pressing in the intervening century. One other legacy of the
first conference also remained: that the meeting and its resolutions should
be advisory on the Communion's autonomous provinces, not mandatory.
This was not something that the traditionalists by this stage wanted, nor
one, once they won their way, that they wished to observe.

A considerable head of steam had already built up by the time the
bishops met. The American Episcopal Church was increasingly out of line
with the rest, both on the ordination of women priests and latterly women
bishops – an issue that had divided the Conference ten years earlier in
1988 – and over the open ordination of gays. In 1998 there would even be
11 women bishops present at the Lambeth Conference, eight from the
USA, two from Canada and one from New Zealand, at a time when half
the Communion still did not allow the ordination of women to the most
basic offices of holy orders. The men who a decade earlier had said they
would not recognize their orders or sit down with them, now found them
sitting in the same cathedral and the same hall.

Now America was going further still and ordaining openly gay men (as
well as closeted ones). There were many gay priests: a swathe of dioceses
across the northern states and their cities – Illinois, Wisconsin, Indiana,
Michigan, Chicago, Milwaukee – were known as the 'biretta belt'. 'Father's friends' were relatively common in many areas, their behaviour and
lifestyle tolerated or at least overlooked. Everyone knew it but they were
too polite to comment. Now there were lesbian women priests as well.
The US church's decision-making convention was divided on the issue of
homosexuality. But it had not only already voted down a motion insisting
that clergy should 'abstain from genital sexual relations outside of Holy
Matrimony' but had also decided to leave it to local dioceses whether they
ordained gay and lesbian candidates or not. Otis Charles, the former
Bishop of Utah and recently retired Dean of the Episcopal Divinity
School in Massachusetts, had even come out publicly in 1991 to an-
nounce that he was gay: 'the choice for me is not whether or not I am a
gay man, but whether or not I am honest about who I am with myself and
others. It is a choice to take down the wall of silence I have built around

an important and vital part of my life, to end the separation and isolation I have imposed on myself all these years.'[1]

At the same 1991 convention in Phoenix, Arizona, the church announced that it had surveyed 18,000 members in more than three-quarters of its dioceses and found that almost 100 per cent believed one could be a faithful Christian and yet be divorced, or divorced and remarried; three-quarters believed that one could be faithful while living unmarried with someone of the opposite sex, and 70 per cent believed that being active as a homosexual or lesbian was not contrary to being a faithful Christian.

In 1992 some traditionalists attempted to arraign Walter Righter, the former Bishop of Iowa, on charges of heresy, on the grounds that he had ordained a known homosexual to the diaconate. After a year of wrangling the church court ruled that there was 'no core doctrine prohibiting the ordination of a non-celibate homosexual person living in a faithful and committed sexual partnership with a person of the same sex'. The bishops who had brought the charges called the decision 'stunning': 'In a single pronouncement it has swept away two millennia of Christian teaching regarding God's purposes in creation, the nature and meaning of marriage and family.' It was an argument that would be heard again, as was the call from developing world bishops for ECUSA to be expelled from the worldwide Communion.

What the Americans did not have was a genuinely Evangelical movement in the English sense. Conservative Evangelicals in the USA have many other denominations to choose to belong to, rather than the Episcopal Church. It remained a socially progressive, doctrinally traditional church, united by a common prayer book. Conservative Episcopalians who would make common cause with the English Evangelicals in years to come in truth had little in common with them liturgically and ritualistically. It was remarkable that the oppositionists on both sides of the Atlantic ever saw eye to eye at all.

By the 1997 convention in Philadelphia, the city of brotherly love, the Episcopalians had gone even further, coming within one vote in their house of deputies of asking for the preparation of a rite for blessing same-sex unions and issuing an apology to gays for 'years of rejection and mal-treatment by the church'. They also elected a liberal presiding bishop, Frank Tracy Griswold III, scion of a long-established and wealthy Philadelphia family and a bishop who had certainly ordained gay men during his time in charge of the diocese of Chicago.

Such developments spurred traditionalists elsewhere towards a more explicit statement of belief. In November 1995 a group of English Evan-

gelicals – largely academics – had produced the St Andrew's Day statement, 'an examination of the theological principles affecting the
homosexuality debate', which both affirmed Biblical traditions and attempted to apply them: 'there is no place for the church to confer
legitimacy upon alternatives. ... Pastoral care, however, needs a certain
flexibility.' It insisted that 'those who understand themselves as homosexuals' – implying they had some choice in the matter – like anyone else
were liable to 'false understandings based on personal or family histories,
emotional dispositions, social settings and solidarities. ... Our sexual
affections can no more define who we are than can our class, race or
nationality.' Worthy as its intentions were, the statement could not help
talking *at* rather than *to* homosexuals. Indeed it patronized them. Its
message of the need to reaffirm the good news of salvation in Christ,
forgiveness of sins and transformation of life, was scarcely novel and its
insistence that there were only two vocations, marriage and singleness, did
not tell anyone anything they did not already know.[2]

In February 1997 80 of the bishops of the developing world, assisted
by Evangelical conservatives, met in Kuala Lumpur, the Malaysian capital,
and drafted an altogether more uncompromising statement. It affirmed
that the future of Christianity now lay with them in the developing world,
and then complained that their experience of life was overshadowed by
ethnic hatred, political instability and neo-colonialism, social injustice and
marginalization, plus international debt, pollution and environmental
damage, religious strife, unbridled materialism and pervasive corruption.
They wanted the IMF and the World Bank to remit debt but then
launched into an all-out assault on sexual immorality or 'brokenness',
almost as if it was the cause of all their problems: 'The Holy Scriptures are
clear in teaching that all sexual promiscuity is sin. We are convinced that
this includes homosexual practices between men or women as well as
heterosexual practices outside marriage.' It was a startling emphasis and
one that could only be explained by an attempt to head off any Western-
world moves towards toleration at the following year's conference.

This was the opening of a second front. Archbishop Maurice Sinclair,
the English Evangelical primate of the so-called 'Southern Cone', the
geographically enormous Anglican province that stretches from Peru to
Tierra del Fuego in South America, asserted that the US Church's failure
to prosecute Righter showed 'an apparent lack of awareness of implications for the Communion as a whole in the failure of the majority to
identify and affirm church discipline in this area of sexual ethics'.

His solution to this was a reduction in the independence of individual
provinces – something he was keen to see so long as those provinces acted

in accordance with Evangelicals who thought like him: 'Is it really Christian to be autonomous? Isn't Christ's way mutual subjection even in church government? ... Some light-handed but wise-headed supervision of a collegial nature would do us all good. Authority in the Anglican Communion would continue to be distributed authority but it would gain the necessary coherence.'[3]

Both Sinclair and his successor, another Evangelical, Greg Venables, were so successful in their evangelizing mission to the Southern Cone that they ministered to a total congregation of 22,000 souls thinly spread across the vast wastes of the Andes and the Pampas - rather less than many English deaneries - so it was no wonder that they had so much time on their hands to lecture the rest of the Anglican Communion and be taken seriously as world leaders. Venables spent much of his time in England during 2003, emerging from obscurity in Buenos Aires to lecture rather larger and more successful provinces than his own on their failings.

Another primate, though of a communion approximately one hundred times larger than Sinclair's, Desmond Tutu of Southern Africa, spoke out on the opposite side of the argument. The southern Africa province, partly no doubt because it struggled for so many years against apartheid - a political system ostentatiously taking its rationale from the Bible - and partly because it had been proselytized by the more liberal missionaries of the Society for the Propagation of the Gospel rather than the Evangelical Church Mission Society which had ventured into Equatorial Africa has been notably more socially liberal than its fellows further north. It has also not in recent years experienced competition from the rise of militant Islam.

Tutu, like his successor, Winston Njongonkulu Ndungane, was notably liberal on the issue. He also held considerable moral authority and influence throughout the African church as a man who had led the struggle against apartheid. Cape Town was even to appoint the openly gay Rowan Smith as dean of its cathedral. Smith, a Cape Coloured, was to remark that it was just as well he was not a woman as well.

Tutu declared:

It is a matter of ordinary justice. We struggled against apartheid in South Africa because we were blamed and made to suffer for something we could do nothing about. It is the same with homosexuality. The orientation is a given, not a matter of choice. It would be crazy for someone to choose to be gay, given the homophobia that is present. .... Our Anglican Church says that orientation is okay, but gay sex activity is wrong. That is crazy. We say the expression of love in a monogamous, heterosexual relationship is more than just the physical but includes touching, embracing, kissing, maybe the genital act.

In September 1997 conservatives in the US Episcopal Church, to-gether with English Evangelicals particularly from the Oxford Centre for Mission Studies – whose leaders would claim for themselves an increasing role in coordinating international opposition on the gay issue in the years ahead – met 50 bishops largely from Africa to coordinate tactics. The meeting was held in Dallas, home of one of the most conservative of the US bishops and was largely paid for by the diocese.

The statement issued at the end of the meeting declared that there was a socio-political campaign to promote homosexuality within the church: 'It is not acceptable for a pro-gay agenda to be smuggled into the church's programme or foisted upon our people and we will not permit it.' It called for the primates of the Anglican Communion to provide 'a place of appeal for those Anglican bodies who are oppressed, marginalized or denied faithful Episcopal oversight by their own bishops'. This was precisely what the same people would call for, from the same place, six years later follow-ing the consecration of Gene Robinson in 2003.

The liberals did not respond well to these increasingly belligerent assertions. The most outspoken among them was Jack Spong, the Bishop of Newark, New Jersey, a man out on a limb theologically even among his colleagues and one who was seemingly as little able as David Jenkins to know when or how to keep quiet. He produced *Twelve Theses* of sufficient radicalism to cause the English Evangelicals of Reform to demand the cancellation of his invitation to Lambeth as well as that of other bishops of whom they disapproved. Spong's document claimed, among other things, that Christ's death to atone for the sins of the world was a barbar-ian idea, that the bodily resurrection never happened and that the concept of Original Sin was nonsense. It was a deliberate provocation. In the *Church Times*, Rowan Williams, still Bishop of Monmouth, described the document as empty and sterile: 'I cannot in any way see [this] as represent-ing a defensible or even an interesting Christian future.'[4]

Spong followed up this triumph by sending a paper on homosexuality to all the African bishops, accusing Archbishop Carey of showing no moral credibility and being ill-informed on the subject, and the Southern Cone Archbishop, Sinclair, of using the Bible as a weapon of oppression. He demanded that the issue be 'openly and authentically' discussed at the Lambeth Conference.

As a method of persuasion, Spong's approach had its shortcomings. Carey accused him of a hectoring and intemperate tone and, in a letter to the world's bishops, warned of a 'very negative and destructive conflict' at Lambeth if the issue was pressed in such terms: 'Do come in peace, do come to learn, do come to share – and leave behind the campaigning tactics which are inappropriate and unproductive, whoever employs them.' Not one to quit while he was behind, Spong responded by accusing his opponents of ecclesiastical blackmail, adding to Carey: 'By your silence in the face of these affronts' – he meant the Kuala Lumpur and Dallas statements – 'you reveal quite clearly where your own convictions lie. That makes it quite difficult to have confidence in your willingness to handle this debate in an even-handed way.'

Many American bishops themselves were furious with Spong, not just because many of them were hostile to his views and knew their congregations were too, but because they felt he was undermining anything that they themselves might want to say at the conference. He was successfully stirring up anti-Americanism and arousing old anti-colonial resentments.

The Evangelicals had cultivated the African bishops, stroked their egos and shared their pain and they would do so assiduously throughout the Conference. The strategy was highly effective in coordinating policy. The American Anglican Council, made up of conservative Episcopalians, set up headquarters in a Franciscan study centre on another part of the campus – 'the Catholics were only too happy to rent it to us,' said one who was involved – and offered open house. It was all most un-Anglican and organized like an American political campaign. Developing-world bishops, some with very little money or experience of life outside their own countries, who were ignored or patronized by the first-world bishops, found their every need assiduously met by a team of helpful young American, British and Australian graduates. 'We gave them food, we ran errands, if they wanted a cup of tea or coffee they just had to raise their hand, we provided them with mobile phones and free telephone links home and we cast their speeches into good English,' one of the team told me.

There were lunchtime meetings and strategy talks, discussions on the tactics to be adopted and the resolutions to be supported. At one point crib cards were drawn up offering counter arguments for Evangelical bishops to refer to during debates. The message to the developing-world bishops was that the Americans were not going to force their agenda on anyone. They didn't need to. 'Our philosophy was, if we stacked up the rocks next to the pit, the Africans would be more than happy to throw them,' said the team member.

Assisting – and later claiming credit – was the Oxford Centre for Mission Studies. The OCMS is a group based in a converted north Oxford church, whose raison d'être is to liaise with and foster educational opportunities for developing-world Evangelicals, and it was to take an increasingly partisan and shrill stance on the homosexual issue over the coming years. It was also happy to see the ex-Christian Reconstructionist, the American multi-millionaire Howard Ahmanson – and other wealthy Americans – give support to its projects and to place one of Ahmanson's employees on its management team. The centre would have a more important role in rallying Anglican Communion opinion during the Jeffrey John affair five years later, but for the moment they were regarded as useful helpers rather than prime movers: 'they were directable', I was told.

The operation cost an estimated £40,000, made up, I was told, from donations by individual churches in the USA. There were mixed motives on all sides, apart from opposition to homosexual practice and promoting the conservative Evangelical agenda: the Americans were concerned with their own internal divisions and wanting to do down Spong and his fellow liberals and the English to restore the centrality of the Church of England to the life of the Anglican Communion. 'George Carey had done a lot of travelling and loved to play the big white father around the world but he had a tin ear for the church. His trips promoted him and his persona but the Church of England was left behind him in the dust,' one Oxford Evangelical told me. The Africans themselves wanted, as the Kuala Lumpur statement had said, to demonstrate their importance within the Communion.

Significantly, the Franciscan Centre operation was hardly noticed, except by those to whom it mattered. George Carey never paid a visit, though Rowan Williams, the Bishop of Monmouth, came several times for lunch.

As if to underline the widening division still more, Spong went further just before the conference in an interview for the Evangelical *Church of England Newspaper*, with Andrew Carey, the Archbishop's son, in which he cast doubt on the Africans' intellectual ability. He said they had moved into a 'very superstitious kind of Christianity', had not faced the intellectual revolution of the West that had influenced the likes of Copernicus and Einstein and were therefore not reading from the same radar screen. New understandings of homosexuals had not percolated down to them. 'If they feel patronized that's too bad. I am not going to cease to be a twentieth-century person for fear of offending somebody in the Third World.'

The interview appeared under the mischievously misleading headline 'Africans one step up from witchcraft' – something he had not said – and unsurprisingly caused a storm of protest, not least because the American

Evangelicals assiduously poked copies of the article under the door of every developing-world bishop they could find.

Spong finally offered a grudging apology for 'unintentionally alienating' the Africans, but did not retract what he had said. 'He looks down on Africans. He thinks I am a naïve person who has not been educated enough to know Scripture. I do not accept his apology,' announced Archbishop Emmanuel Kolini of Rwanda, a small country which had recently experienced inter-tribal genocide.

In such an atmosphere the bishops gathered in Canterbury fractious and mutually suspicious, conspiratorial and affronted, little inclined on the homosexuality issue at least to reach accord in a friendly spirit of tolerance, freedom and generosity of spirit. Archbishop Carey at least entered the proceedings in a frame of mind that was probably not conducive to charitable feelings towards gays. Peter Tatchell had chosen the opportunity of the agenda planning meeting at Lambeth Palace before the Conference to make one of his sudden invasions. Carey was entertaining his colleagues in the Palace garden when Tatchell and some friends clambered over the wall, rushed the group and started screaming alarmingly in the Archbishop's face. The demonstrators were eventually dragged off – Tatchell himself by a gay member of the Anglican Communion staff – but it was a disconcerting moment. Jim Rosenthal of the Anglican Communion office said: 'The incident had a devastating effect. Carey was traumatized.' The demonstration was therefore entirely counterproductive for what was to happen next.

The tradition for the Lambeth Conference is for a series of sections to be set up reviewing broad areas of church policy, then to split up into sub-sections to discuss particular issues arising out of them before returning to plenary sessions of all the bishops to vote on the resolutions drawn up from their reports. The sub-section on human sexuality was evidently going to be the most contentious.

It was clear that there was a vast gap in comprehension on the homosexual issue. Bishop Robert Haines of Washington told his diocese in a report: 'I was in a group with a bishop from a diocese in the South Pacific consisting of small island villages. There is no term in his language for homosexuality and he had never discussed the subject, taboo in his culture. When I asked what happens to individuals who feel or act out same-sex attractions, he replied: "The village elders take care of them".'[5]

At the Lambeth Conference in 1988, the African bishops had successfully argued for the recognition of cultural diversity with regard to polygamy in their countries. Polygamous marriages were shaped by social and political culture and context. It was a significant move, showing that culture and social context do make a difference in determining the church's pastoral attitudes whatever the Bible says.[6] But it was a toleration the developing-world bishops and their Evangelical allies were not prepared to extend to gays in the West a decade later.

Over the first two weeks of the Conference a committee of bishops, largely chosen from among those with the strongest opposing views on the subject, attempted in an angry atmosphere to cobble together an agreed statement. In an attempt to reach an accord they moved out of a lecture theatre to somewhere a little more congenial, less set up for confrontation. The Evangelicals offered them a room in the Franciscan Centre which they gladly and innocently accepted.

The idea of an international commission to review the matter – as had happened over women's ordination under Archbishop Robin Eames of Ireland a decade earlier – was mooted. Indeed that was probably the preferred option of those in charge. Bishop Richard Holloway believes he was promised as much by Archbishop Carey. It would have been a traditional way of kicking the issue into the long grass before coming up with an unexceptional but inclusive message. That at least was what the liberals expected to happen.

Spong welcomed the idea. But the Evangelicals were having none of it. Wally Benn, the Suffragan Bishop of Lewes and member of Reform, told the Church Times: 'If it looks to be headed in the liberal direction, the balloon will go up. But if its brief is to uphold the Biblical position, then that will be fine. What we don't want is a commission which Spong is happy with.'[7]

Bishop Duncan Buchanan of Johannesburg, chairing the committee on human sexuality, told the newspaper: 'It is not necessarily the worst issue facing the Church. It is a second-tier issue and not one on which we need to be split down the middle. We can hold together in Christ and that is the key.'

It probably did not help that Bishop Buchanan was white and known to be relatively liberal on homosexuality. Observers recall that he frequently seemed close to tears as the acrimony continued. Suspicions were aroused when he at one stage mislaid the resolution the section had agreed on and, attempting to rewrite it from memory, succeeded in leaving out certain reservations. Fortunately the Evangelicals had a copy of the original and quickly supplied it.

The Franciscan Centre operation was in full gear. Over their free box lunches, the bishops would gather to hear the views of white Evangelical bishops, led by Bishop Harry Goodhew of Sydney, and to place their orders with the keen young stewards who could not do enough to help them. An American journalist, Katie Sherrod, working for *Ruach*, a magazine published by the Episcopal women's caucus, wrote:

> The conservatives' on-campus headquarters at the Franciscan Centre was a high-tech model of a US political campaign office. With admirable efficiency and obvious effectiveness, they hosted meetings, tutored bishops in procedures and rhetoric and generally made sure they 'owned' the agenda at Lambeth. ... It was the conservatives' canny marriage of US-style political organization with the scriptural fundamentalism of many of the African and Asian bishops that enabled the conservatives to so dominate. ... The conference deliberations revealed an ideological colonization of Anglicanism driven by the politics of the Episcopal Church USA.[8]

There were rumours of cash passing from the American conservative bishops to the Africans, newly minted dollar bills still in their bundles, produced from suitcases to secure votes. The Rev. Ran Chase, a member of the Rhode Island diocesan staff, told his Bishop, Geralyn Wolf, one of the 11 women bishops:

> I was in line at one of the campus banks and an African bishop turned to me with 500 dollars in crisp new bills in his hands. He said: 'What do I do with this? Can I use it?' and I said: 'No you can't use it unless you go in the banks and exchange it for pounds.' I said: 'Where did you get dollars?' He said: 'Oh, I didn't get it. That nice bishop from Texas gave it to me.'[9]

This story, which has now become an Anglican urban myth, a tale of conservative bishops handing out wads of cash from suitcases, was nearly but not quite true. What happened according to one who was involved was that he was approached over lunch at the Franciscan Centre by Bishop Macleord Baker Ochola of Kitgum diocese in Uganda, who had no money at all. He had already tried tapping Archbishop Carey and Bishop Griswold with no success and now was getting desperate. He had a large family at home and needed to buy them presents. The stewards rallied round and one, Todd Wetzel, of the conservative group Episcopalians United, emptied his pockets to provide £200. They decided they could not give the money directly to the Bishop so asked Bishop Jim Stanton of Texas to hand it over as a present from the diocese of Dallas. The Bishop then trotted off to a bank, where he bumped into Mr Chase in the queue. What he was actually intending was to change the pounds into Canadian dollars so that he could attend a Mennonite World Council meeting in Canada. He hadn't divulged this detail to the Evangelicals.

When the story got out, the Americans decided not to challenge it because it made the American Anglican Council seem richer and more powerful than it actually was. That anyway is their story.

Rhode Island's Bishop Wolf was, and is, one of those bishops on the liberal side of the argument and did not need any convincing of what was going on. She told her diocesan newspaper: 'Under my door every single night was information from [the conservative American Anglican Council]. Some of it was just obnoxious ... [it was] indicative of an evil spirit in the church. There's a lot of evil at work here.'

She claimed that some African bishops were motivated by fear: 'Some were told by their governments that should they take any kind of conciliatory line on homosexuality, they would risk being imprisoned on their return. ... One of my group was petrified even to talk about it. We underestimate the tensions that some of our fellow Christians live under.'

Actually there is no doubt that a great many developing-world bishops did not need much persuasion to condemn homosexuality. But they certainly benefited from a number of perks, including free flights – a disproportionate number of African clerics turned up in Dallas in October 2003 for the AAC's conference there, which was supposedly for Americans aggrieved at the Robinson decision.

What was also going on behind the scenes was a power-play for the leadership of the African Communion, in the wake of Tutu's retirement. Any hopes his successor Ndungane had of succeeding to the saintly mantle were dashed because of his support for the liberal line on homosexuality. Nigeria seized the leadership and has not relinquished it since.

Eventually the committee charged with reporting on human sexuality produced a unanimous report, though they agreed they were 'not of one mind' about homosexuality. It stated that the bishops recognized that there were 'persons who experience themselves as having a homosexual orientation', many of whom were members of the church, that they were loved by God and, if baptized and believing, full members of the body of Christ. They should not be victimized, all discrimination against them on the basis of orientation should end and homophobia should be opposed. A clear majority of the bishops were not prepared to bless same-sex unions or ordain active homosexuals.

The conservative bishops went into secret conclave at the Franciscan Centre, its letter of invitation, signed by 27 bishops from the USA, Africa, England and Australia, saying there needed to be a 'consolidation' of the orthodox position and a review of the resolutions on which they would be voting in the coming days. A letter signed by eight primates called the conference 'a turning point in our history' and added: 'A crucial question is how we relate to the modern globalisating culture which, although originating in the West, in one way or another powerfully impinges on us all. ... We must ask whether we are in danger of allowing this culture with its philosophical assumptions, economic system, sexual alternatives and hidden idols to determine what we become.' It called for a commitment to Biblical renewal, the suspension of the ordination of practising homosexuals and an end to the blessing of same-sex relationships.

Meanwhile some African bishops were calling for bishops who supported equal rights for homosexuals to repent or leave the Communion. There could be no tolerance: Bishop Emmanuel Gbonigi of Nigeria was quoted as saying: 'I won't listen to them because it would be a sheer waste of time. It's not because I'm a bigot but, as far as I am concerned, it is against the word of God. Nothing can make us [African bishops] budge because we view what God says as firm.'

It was Bishop Emmanuel Chukwuma of Nigeria who best encapsulated the atmosphere, however, when, on the day that the report was to go before the full conference, he encountered Richard Kirker of the LGCM. Chukwuma announced that Leviticus ordained the death penalty for homosexuals. 'Would you be prepared to stone us to death?' asked Kirker, who was handing out leaflets, whereupon the Bishop attempted to lay his hands on the top of his head. 'In the name of Jesus, I deliver him out of homosexuality,' he declared as Kirker ducked out of the way, 'I pray for God to forgive you, for God to deliver you out of your sinful act, out of your carnality.'[10]

Kirker civilly replied: 'May God bless you, sir, and deliver you from your prejudice against homosexuality.'

'You have no inheritance in the kingdom of God. You are going to hell. You have made yourself homosexual because of your carnality,' the Bishop riposted, sweat streaming down his face and his voice rising. As his wife nearby murmured 'Alleluia', Bishop Chukwuma shouted: 'We have overcome carnality just as the light will overcome darkness. ... God did not create you as a homosexual. That is our stand. That is why your church is dying in Europe – because it is condoning immorality. You are killing the church. This is the voice of God talking. Yes I am violent against sin.'

When another South African bishop intervened, saying Archbishop Tutu supported homosexual inclusiveness, Bishop Chukwuma replied: 'Desmond Tutu is spiritually dead,' and stalked off. The brief encounter was gleefully replayed on that evening's television news bulletins. Indeed the image spread around the world. The Conference press office received incredulous calls from abroad asking whether the incident could really have happened. Chukwuma's moment in the spotlight did Anglicanism enormous damage.

Inside the big tent, the resolution that finally went to that day's debate, hammered out through two and a half weeks' 'pain and anger' in Bishop Buchanan's words, affirmed the traditional understanding of marriage, said celibacy was right for those 'not called' to married life and called on 'all our people' to minister pastorally and sensitively to others, regardless of sexual orientation. The resolution condemned homophobia along with violence in marriage and 'any trivialization and commercialization of sex'.

But the two-and-a-half-hour debate was hijacked, with a succession of amendments put forward by African bishops, who had not been in the section or listened to the debates there, hardening condemnation of homosexuality as a sin. It was highly unusual for outside cabals to intervene in this way and the liberals thought it should not have been allowed. But in the emotional atmosphere, attempts by some bishops to move away from what one called 'this trivial business' were swept aside. The Conference was reminded that Ugandan Christians had been martyred in the nineteenth century for refusing to have homosexual relations with their king: 'they would laugh at us now and say, "We died for the Gospel, now where are you going?",' said Bishop Michael Lugor, a Sudanese bishop. He said that the church should say to homosexuals: 'Why do you come out and tell us what you do? Go to God and confess your sins. A man who sleeps with his wife doesn't come out and blow a trumpet about it.'[11]

Some American and English bishops attempted to warn against hardening the resolution: Catherine Roskam, Suffragan Bishop of New York, claimed it would be Evangelical suicide. But, in a measure of the way things were going, the Conference voted to incorporate the assertion that homosexuality was incompatible with Scripture. The amendment was allowed, even though it was submitted out of time, for fear that the African bishops would walk out if it was not included. The amendment had been personally brokered by Archbishop Carey.

Further amendments changed 'homophobia' to 'an irrational fear of homosexuals' and 'chastity' to 'abstinence' – the latter put forward by Bishop John Sentamu, Ugandan-born Bishop of Stepney, who feared that chastity might eventually come to include committed same-sex relationships.

The motion was gradually firmed up: in the words of the Canadian Bishop Barry Jenks of British Columbia: 'a document whose face ... was a face of love and compassion is gradually, bit by bit, step by step, turning into a judgement and condemnation.'

Finally, before the final vote, George Carey came out and spoke in support of the amended motion. He had sat on a dais during the debate, applauding hardline speakers and he now abandoned his neutral chairmanship entirely to endorse the motion. 'I believe that [it] is simply saying what we have all held, what Anglican belief and morality stands for. ... What disagreement ought to do is to lead us closer together. We are aware that we have to go on listening. The dialogue continues.'

As amended, Resolution 1:10 upheld faithfulness in marriage between a man and a woman in lifelong union and believed that abstinence was right for those not called to marriage, recognized that 'there are among us' persons who experienced themselves as having a homosexual orientation, committed the church to listening to their experience and assured them that they were loved by God. It added: 'While rejecting homosexual practice as incompatible with Scripture [it] calls on all our people to minister pastorally and sensitively to all irrespective of sexual orientation and to condemn irrational fear of homosexuals.' It added that it could neither advise the legitimizing or blessing of same-sex unions nor the ordaining of those involved in same-gender unions. It also requested the primates to establish a means of monitoring work carried out on the subject of human sexuality.

In some confusion, a vote was taken and the amended motion was passed by 526 in favour, with 70 opposed and 45 abstaining. The African bishops strode out shouting 'Victory!' and slapping each other on the back. Archbishop Eames of Ireland who had chaired the debate announced, 'we have displayed how we can disagree and still love each other'. Peter Selby, Bishop of Worcester, in contrast likened the poisonous atmosphere generated by the debate to a Nuremberg Rally.

Shamefacedly some liberal American bishops also voted for the amendment. One of them, Bishop Calvin Onderdonk Schofield Jnr, whose own son was known to be gay, said that the Communion had spoken on the issue and he wanted to affirm that. Rowan Williams abstained.

Outside there was no doubt who had won. Bishop Kenneth Fernando of Sri Lanka said: 'It does look as though the liberals lost out.' Bishop Richard Holloway, primus of the Scottish Episcopal Church, decried Carey's 'pathetic' leadership: 'He thought that the vote had been taken, so he tried to add a nice fluffy epilogue. It would have been better if he had stayed silent.' When asked what he thought about the Archbishop's leadership, Holloway snapped back: 'What leadership?' He said he was 'gutted, shafted, depressed'.

Bishop William Swing of California later told the Church Times: 'I thought the bishops who worked on the human sexuality resolution at Lambeth came up with a broad, deep, inviting statement that could have been a marvellous document for the whole of Anglicanism. But some folks just couldn't stand to leave it at that: they wanted winners and losers in the Anglican Communion before we went home.'[12]

Five years on, Holloway, now retired, remained bitter. He told me:

> I hated that conference. It was the worst experience of my life. Quite a few bishops felt physically threatened in the atmosphere that was generated in that debate. George Carey could have stamped on it but he didn't. He seemed oblivious to what was going on, grinning away on the platform while the most awful things were said.

> I thought there would be a commission, the sort of benign displacement that usually occurs in Anglicanism. It is a good mechanism because it buys you time to receive new ideas and gives a mechanism to reconcile people who can't agree. I tended to think it would work. But there was a deep, visceral view on homosexuality in untutored people. I think that sort of prejudice is there in all of us, like xenophobia and racism, some sort of evolutionary gene. We listened to the African bishops and their attitude to sexuality is all about male ownership, male rights to have sex.

Carey met the Conference chaplains after the vote. They threatened to leave the Conference and denounce its outcome. Several explained emotionally to the Archbishop that they themselves were gay. The Archbishop pleaded with them for understanding of his difficult position and begged them not to polarize the situation further.

Shortly after, 146 bishops, evidently including a number who had voted for the resolution, signed a statement of apology to lesbian and gay Christians, regretting that it had not been possible 'to hear adequately your voices and we apologize for any sense of rejection that has occurred because of this reality. ... It is our deep concern that you do not feel abandoned by your church.' Among the signatories were 42 English diocesan and suffragan bishops.

The liberals were sore, outplayed and out-voted in ways they had loftily never imagined, guilty of taking the developing world for granted and casually insulting and patronizing them. They came across as rancorous and spiteful. It was game, set and match to the conservatives.

Lambeth 1:10 is, like all conference decisions, merely advisory. It expresses the mind of the bishops of the Anglican Communion – or at least of a large majority of them – but it does not have the force of command over the autonomous provinces and it clearly was not accepted by a substantial minority.

All of that has not prevented the conservatives and Evangelicals from claiming Lambeth 1:10 as Holy Writ ever since, just as *Issues in Human Sexuality*, the bishops' statement of 1991, is held to be the established policy of the Church of England, despite George Carey's assertion that it was 'not the last word' on the subject.

Although they might claim now to hold the voice of orthodoxy, some of the Third-World bishops had a provocative way of showing it. In 2001 two of them, Emmanuel Mbona Kolini, Archbishop of Rwanda, and Datuk Ping Chung Yong, Archbishop of South East Asia, turned up in Denver, Colorado, to consecrate four rebel conservative American bishops in opposition to the Episcopal Church and in defiance of pleas from George Carey.

Such gestures are worth remembering when Evangelicals complain that the US church has defied the rest of the Communion in deciding to consecrate a gay bishop, or when they claim that it is the liberals, not themselves, who are being provocative and departing from hundreds of years of tradition. In a church where bishops have diocesan authority, it is the conservatives who have led the way to schism.

Lambeth taught the conservative Evangelicals that they could prevail. And, having won, the traditionalists were not going to release their prize. It was to be a club with which to beat down any further change or liberal challenge.

9

THEN CAME ROWAN

'The only sixpenny article in a penny bazaar.' (Winston Churchill on appointing William Temple as Archbishop of Canterbury, 1942)

Early in January 2002, after 11 years in the job and three years before his due retirement age, George Carey announced his decision to step down the following November. He called his staff together at Lambeth Palace one Monday morning to break the news, only slightly pre-empted by the fact that it had already been disclosed by the national press the previous day. Due tributes to the 103rd Archbishop's 'widely perceived accomplishments and achievements' followed before, within moments, thoughts turned to his successor.

The likely front-runners were fairly obvious in an undistinguished field. David Hope, the Archbishop of York, was not interested in the move and was only five years younger than George Carey. He rather understandably fancied retiring to his beloved North Yorkshire and perhaps helping out in a local parish rather than acquiring the pomp and circumstance of Canterbury.

That left Richard Chartres, the Bishop of London, Runcie's former chaplain, a witty, avuncular figure. He, however, had made little secret of his distaste for the tedium of Synod and church business. Furthermore he was not very keen on ordaining women. The leading Evangelical candidate was Michael Nazir-Ali, the Pakistan-born Bishop of Rochester, an ascetic figure with mutton-chop whiskers, fiercely ambitious and with a high regard for his own intellectual abilities. Two alternatives could have been Christopher Herbert, the Bishop of St Albans, a genial diocesan, and Michael Scott-Joynt, the Bishop of Winchester, rather older than the others and an establishment figure of stately pomposity.

Several of these – and some others – fancied their chances as the tortuous, discreet and highly confidential process of selection proceeded that summer. Nazir-Ali in particular was perceived to be so keen that he all but capsized his chances by making sweeping charges of racism and prejudice in the Church of England – an odd and rather unfocused (and unsubstantiated) allegation given his previous career trajectory. On the morning Carey announced his retirement, a member of his staff at Lambeth Palace chortled during the course of a telephone conversation that he expected the Bishop of Rochester was already on his way round to measure up the fixtures and fittings – only to glance up and see the man himself standing enigmatically in the doorway. Nazir-Ali had in fact come to attend a meeting.

And then there was Rowan Williams, the Bishop of Monmouth and Archbishop of the Church in Wales. It was a measure of his perceived abilities and perhaps the thinness of the field that he was immediately seen as a possible candidate even though he was not even an English bishop. He had indeed been turned down by George Carey for the bishopric of Southwark only three years before on the grounds that he had not been prepared to give his whole-hearted support to the now-cast-in-concrete *Issues in Human Sexuality*. He was undoubtedly a hairy rather than a smooth man too: with his grey, tousled hair, straggly beard and flyaway, quizzical eyebrows he even looked like an Old Testament prophet.

Williams, the son of a Swansea engineer, was an attractive figure though, with an aura of spirituality. That was something the church had been looking for ever since it had cottoned on to the fact that the late Catholic Cardinal Basil Hume was widely perceived to be a holier figure and a more inspiring national spiritual leader than the worldly-wise, managerial men who were the established church's own archbishops.

Furthermore Williams spoke well, in a sonorous Welsh accent, was a prolific writer, a poet, linguist and extremely brainy, having been a theology professor at Oxford at an unusually early age. Despite these drawbacks, he was an approachable and genial figure, seemingly as at home talking to a primary school class as delivering a lecture on his doctoral subject, the early twentieth-century Russian theologian Vladimir Lossky.

Appointing Williams would be a leap of faith: he would be the first Archbishop of Canterbury to come from outside the Church of England since Cardinal Pole in the reign of Bloody Mary 450 years before and, at the age of 52, the youngest archbishop since Charles Manners Sutton in the early nineteenth century. He would also be the first archbishop for 130 years to have school-age children at Lambeth Palace. If he stayed the course, Williams could be archbishop for almost 20 years, longer than any of his predecessors for nearly a century. That would be a very long time to be stuck with someone the church, or factions within it, did not like or would not follow.

There were indeed reservations. He had never really served his time in a parish and had been a bishop in one of the smallest dioceses and, briefly, archbishop of one of the smallest provinces in the Anglican Communion. Despite his academic background at both Cambridge and Oxford, his reputation as a theologian and his marriage to the daughter of a bishop – a theologian in her own right – he was an outsider. And he also had a reputation as a bit of a lefty. Hadn't he once, in 1985, been arrested on a CND demo after scaling the perimeter fence at RAF Alconbury in Cambridgeshire?

But the most serious charge against him as far as some Evangelicals were concerned was not the fact that he had once toyed with becoming a Roman Catholic, nor even that he had left the Welsh Presbyterian Church of his childhood, eventually to become a socially progressive Anglo-Catholic. This only caused unease. What alarmed them most was that he had written and spoken tolerantly on the gay issue.

The Michael Harding Memorial Address, named in honour of Richard Kirker's dead partner, was delivered in 1989 when Dr Williams was Lady Margaret Professor of Divinity at Oxford, three years before he ever became a bishop. Wrapped up behind the lecture's generally sunny tone and some characteristically densely expressed ideas, is a deeply subversive and unwelcome message for those who insist that sex can take place only within heterosexual marriage. Most of them would never have heard of it until Williams hovered on to the radar screen as a possible candidate for Canterbury. It had certainly never caused controversy.[1]

The Lady Margaret Professor expatiated at some length on the 'irredeemably comic' nature of sexual intimacy with 'so many opportunities for making a fool of yourself'. But he claimed that this was a necessary part of human relationships, a willingness to surrender oneself to one's partner. Insistence on domination in a relationship, which could just as easily occur between heterosexuals, could be considered a perversion just as much as rape or paedophilia. Indeed conventional heterosexual morality could be limiting in the development of relationships precisely because it was legally sanctioned and therefore did not always appear to require a deeper exploration of the partnership: 'If this blessing [of sexual unions] becomes a curse or an empty formality, it is both wicked and useless to hold up the sexuality of the canonically married heterosexual as absolute, exclusive and ideal.'

Williams added bluntly:

An absolute declaration that every sexual partnership must conform to the pattern of commitment or else have the nature of sin and nothing else is unreal and silly. ... Much more damage is done to this by the insistence on a fantasy version of heterosexual marriage as the solitary ideal, when the facts of the situation are that an enormous number of 'sanctioned' unions are a framework for violence and human destructiveness on a disturbing scale: sexual union is not delivered from moral danger and ambiguity by satisfying a formal socio-religious criterion.

The address argued that celibacy was not the only acceptable lifestyle for the homosexual:

> Anyone who knows the complexities of the true celibate vocation would be the last to have any sympathy with the extraordinary idea that sexual orientation is an automatic pointer to the celibate life; almost as if celibacy before God is less costly, even less risky, for the homosexual than the heterosexual.

He argued that in the Bible Jesus and St Paul both discussed the idea of marriage without arguing that it should be for procreation:

> In other words, if we are looking for a sexual ethic that can be seriously informed by our Bible, there is a good deal to steer us away from assuming that reproductive sex is a norm, however important and theologically significant it may be. ... If we are afraid of facing the reality of same-sex love because it compels us to think through the processes of bodily desire and delight in their own right, perhaps we ought to be more cautious about appealing to Scripture as legitimating only procreative heterosexuality.

> In a church which accepts the legitimacy of contraception, the absolute condemnation of same-sex relations of intimacy must rely either on an abstract fundamentalist deployment of a number of very ambiguous texts or on a problematic and non-scriptural theory about natural complementarity, applied narrowly and crudely to physical differentiation without regard to psychological structures.

It is difficult to think of a more courteous assault on the arguments put forward by Evangelicals to justify their view that homosexual practice is wrong. Despite occasional calls for recantation and repentance, it remains a speech that Dr Williams has never repudiated. Perhaps it was just as well that at the time he made it he was not exactly a prominent public figure and that *Issues in Human Sexuality* had yet to be published in all its mighty totemic significance to the conservative faction.

There were a couple of other, scholarly, forays into the issue, among them a chapter in a book drawn up by Evangelicals reflecting on the St Andrew's Day statement of 1995, so Williams could scarcely be accused of keeping his views hidden from those likely to be most troubled by them. In the essay, 'Knowing Myself in Christ' from the book *The Way Forward?*, he presciently argues that it is 'depressingly easy to make this or that issue a test of Christian orthodoxy in such a way as to make wholly suspect the theology of anyone disagreeing on the issue in question. ... The possibility is neglected that Christians beginning from the same premises and convictions may yet come to different conclusions.'[2]

The essay goes on to ask:

> In what sense does the Church actually proclaim good news to the homosexually inclined person who does not see their condition as a mark of rebellion or confusion? They are told they are to be tolerated, even respected; but their own account of themselves before God is not to be recognized. I am not talking here ... about what any self-described homosexual *does*, only about their understanding of their own condition. ... If you do not accept that homosexual desire is itself a mark of disorder, can you confidently say that the presence of this desire must always be a sign that sexual expression is ruled out?[3]

These are questions that Evangelicals do not consider worth asking, let alone providing answers to because they see them as beside the simple, Biblical, point. In a recent critical review of Williams's writings on homosexuality, Dr David Hilborn, head of theology at the Evangelical Alliance, describes them as 'both morally and hermeneutically flawed'.[4] Just because God is gracious and wants a relationship with us, he says, does not mean we are excused from repenting of what He has revealed and defined as wrong – though that is not something Williams has ever denied. Therefore, the assistant curate of St Mary's Acton says that the Archbishop's writings are 'exegetically partial, theologically elliptical and ethically contentious'.

Rupert Shortt, a former pupil, in his introductory study about Rowan Williams, published in 2003, says: 'His private view remains that an adjustment of teaching on sexuality would not be different from the kind of flexibility now being shown to divorcees who wish to remarry, or the softening in the sixteenth century of the Church's total opposition to borrowing with interest, or the nineteenth- and twentieth-century shifts of view on subjects like slavery and eternal hellfire.'[5]

Unlike some, Williams did not have an obsession with homosexuality. As Barry Morgan, the Bishop of Llandaff and Williams's successor as archbishop, said: 'I have been on the bench of bishops in Wales with him for a decade and I have never heard him mention homosexuality. God preserve us if we choose an Archbishop of Canterbury because of his views on just one topic.'[6]

The deliberations of the Crown Appointments Commission ground extremely slowly for about six months but it was increasingly clear that Williams was being seriously considered and was probably the strongest candidate. The Commission does not do anything so vulgar as to require applications or formally interview candidates, but its 13 members, lay and clerical, from the Canterbury diocese and from the bench of bishops, took soundings before retreating into two days' sequestration in early summer to discuss and pray about who should be chosen. In this they were advised by William Chapman, the prime minister's appointments secretary, responsible for a wide range of patronage in the established church, Tony Sadler, the Archbishop's appointments secretary, and by John Peterson, the American Episcopalian, who represented the worldwide Communion in his capacity as secretary general of the Anglican Consultative Council.

Nazir-Ali was still perceived to be a strong candidate, particularly by Evangelicals, partly because his name might appeal to a prime minister anxious to demonstrate the British establishment's multiracial character. But there was a tradition that an Evangelical archbishop should be succeeded by an Anglo-Catholic one and it was clear from an early stage that Williams was likely to emerge as the favoured candidate, even though Evangelicals were well represented on the appointments commission. Two names, with the preferred candidate starred, are submitted to the prime minister, who makes his selection and then submits the name to the Queen – always supposing the candidate is agreeable to being chosen. The sovereign, as supreme governor of the Church of England, theoretically has the last word, although all she ever does is endorse her first minister's decision. Mr Blair, his official spokesman said, was not going to relinquish this particular piece of patronage: he was an anti-disestablishmentarianist.

There was never any question in Downing Street's mind that Williams was the outstanding candidate, nor was there any serious consideration of anyone else. Tony Blair was impressed by the Welsh primate as by nobody else on the list. In late July, Williams, with his wife beside him, appeared diffidently before the media at Church House and professed publicly his willingness to be archbishop: 'I hope with all my heart that I can serve to nurture confidence and conviction in our church and to help Christian faith to recapture the imagination of our people and our culture,' he said.

'I have to go on being a priest and bishop, that is, to celebrate God and what God has done in Jesus and to offer in God's name whatever I can discern of God's perspective on the world around – something which involves both challenge and comfort.'

For good measure the new Archbishop added a few words of warning on the looming Iraq conflict. Williams said he would only support military action if the United Nations sanctioned it first. He was not to know, though he might have guessed, that the prime minister would show as much sublime indifference to his Archbishop's reservations as he did to those of most of the rest of the country. The Archbishop did not even have the power to irk, as once Runcie had irked Thatcher.

Instead the rumblings were from another front, from pressure groups within the church. They had previously remained fairly quiet during the selection process, but made up for it as autumn drew on. The running was made by the conservative Evangelical groups, the Church Society and, inevitably, Reform, which both engaged in a shrill and unproductive campaign against the new Archbishop, accusing him of unsoundness on homosexuality in particular and Gospel teaching in general. It was highly political and, if the intention was to persuade Williams to step down, it was entirely unsuccessful. But if the purpose was to send up a storm warning to the wider Evangelical community, it had much more success. It was a shot across the Archbishop's bows. While many Anglicans - including many Evangelicals - welcomed the appointment as an inspirational and imaginative one, others had private doubts, sedulously stirred by the pressure groups.

The tactics were extraordinarily, even shockingly, churlish. Probably no new leader of the modern Church of England had ever faced such truculent opposition. Williams's acknowledgement that he had once knowingly ordained a homosexual - made in a newspaper interview - was pounced upon as if he was the only bishop ever to have done so. (Carey would later admit to having consecrated two gay, though celibate, bishops, without comparable censure.[7]) His position as one of the founders of the Affirming Catholicism network - an organization of progressive Anglo-Catholics founded by liberal clergy in the early 1990s in support of the ordination of women - also made him a figure of suspicion on several counts.

And the Welsh Archbishop's attendance at the Welsh eisteddfod, a nostalgic occasion before he left the principality to take up his new job, where he was awarded a bardic honour in recognition of his poetic abilities, was also seized upon. *The Times*, either mischievously or obtusely, chose to describe the gathering as a pagan ceremony rather than a cultural one. The photographs of Williams in his bardic robes complete with funny headdress were assiduously disseminated by conservative Evangelicals to developing-world bishops who duly registered consternation. Rowan Williams was furious at the misrepresentation of a perfectly innocent gathering - and at the deliberate and cynical misinterpretation of his presence there.

Before long, Williams's theological writings were also being pored over and pronounced deficient, usually by scholars rather less distinguished than himself and sometimes with a disingenuousness that was either perverse or dishonest.

By September 2002, the tiny Church Society, founded in 1835 and operating out of a building in Watford, was ready to pronounce Williams a heretic – an unprecedented and insulting charge to level against an archbishop in the modern church. The Society, which claims to be the oldest Evangelical group of its kind in the world, has a distinctly Fundamentalist tinge and is on the far-right, Calvinist wing of the Church of England both politically and theologically, rancorous and permanently shocked by anything progressive that has happened in church or state since about 1700. Indeed some of its governing council have grown so dissatisfied with the Church of England that they have left it altogether for more congenial, ideologically purer fringe groups. The body nevertheless still claims a place as of right on the executive committee of the umbrella body, the Church of England Evangelical Council (CEEC). The Society is in decline, claiming a membership of only a thousand, many of them retired clergy.

An indication of why some brighter, younger members of the Evangelical movement were pressing by the autumn of 2003 for the Society to lose its seat on the CEEC[8] was contained in an editorial in the winter edition of the Society's quarterly publication *Churchman*. The periodical's editor, Gerald Bray, an Englishman, former Oak Hill-ite, ordained cleric of the Church of England and professor of divinity at a university in Birmingham, Alabama, penned the piece which managed to be extraordinarily insulting to black church leaders while suggesting they might be the alternative for traditionalist Episcopalians who could not stomach an openly gay bishop. Bray thundered: 'Faced with a choice between a white American homosexual bishop and a black-skinned African archbishop, there has been no hesitation – Rwanda has won hands down. The celebrant may look more like the church janitor than like any of his worshippers in the pews, but it does not matter.'[9]

The Society also brayed in a fortnightly periodical called the *English Churchman*, a newspaper with a minuscule circulation and a tendency to refer to the pope as the antichrist. Many of the paper's readers and some of its editorial staff had left the Church of England to set up a small fringe organization called the Church of England (Continuing) in disgust at the main church's dangerous liberalism. One of their icons is the Rev. Ian Paisley, for his religious as much as his political philosophy.

Such was the paper's antipathy to Dr Williams, its inability to detect any goodness in him at all and its determination to disagree with anything he might say on any subject whatsoever, however cogent, that it would soon be describing him as the 'Arch-heretic of Canterbury'. When he ventured to suggest that attitudes to some things that the Bible had once commended, such as slavery, had changed over time, the *English Churchman* promptly published an article arguing that the form of slavery advocated in the Old Testament had, in fact, had some beneficial effects that those living in poverty today might appreciate. It had been 'a form of social security for which many starving people today would be grateful'.[10]

In an effort to mollify the Fundamentalists and convince them of his bona-fides, Williams invited the Church Society's executive to lunch and also corresponded with the leaders of Reform. He might have spared his hospitality. In an editorial prior to the meeting, the *English Churchman* argued:

> It is not enough to tell [him] that he should be silent about his views; it is not enough to tell him he shouldn't rock the boat ... he must be told he is in error. He must be told he is a false shepherd of his sheep; he must be told to repent his views. Let the Word of God be brought before him. 'If any man preach any other gospel unto you than that ye have received, let him be accursed.' (Galatians 1:9). ... The utter seriousness of the matter demands confrontation.[11]

The Rev. David Phillips, the Church Society's director, said: 'Our fundamental concern is whether he is prepared to live by the teaching of scripture. ... At the very least his views about sexuality are a matter of gross error. There are folk who wonder what is the point of staying in the church and there are days when I feel that too.'[12]

Phillips admitted that he found the Archbishop's writings 'extremely difficult to penetrate'. Some of those expressing reservations – and certainly many of the flock they were hoping to influence – had not troubled to make the effort.

This sort of apocalyptic language, as if the church had suddenly appointed a pagan to lead it, might have been merely risible – indeed it is pretty hard for any non-fanatic or outsider to begin to understand or appreciate – but it fed into more mainstream organizations. Richard Chartres, the Bishop of London, who had said he thought Rowan Williams was being 'too damn Christian' in seeing them, added: 'I find these splinter groups' attitudes pretty horrifying but I am worried that they are stoking the fires. I don't think Rowan should have met them and given them dignity and significance.'

Rowan Williams certainly tried to appease the irreconcilable lobby. In an early letter to the bishops of the Church of England he stated that, whatever his personal views, he would uphold the policy laid down in *Issues* and that he would not again knowingly ordain a gay priest. Later, during his last diocesan conference in South Wales, the former Oxford divinity professor insisted that he believed in the Bible:

I have always been committed to the church's traditional teaching on adultery and sex before marriage. It seems obvious to me that if we are to show God's costly commitment in all areas of our lives, this applies as much here as elsewhere. We may want to be compassionate and realistic with people coming from a setting where these ideals are remote or completely unintelligible, but the last thing I'd want to do is to weaken the challenge and excitement of the traditional view that says we can and should demonstrate God's faithfulness in our bodily lives and that this is the meaning of Christian marriage.

For all their huffing and puffing, the conservatives failed to find a concrete example of heresy in anything Williams had written. There were no 'conjuring tricks with bones', no denial of the Resurrection or the miracles, no downplaying of the divinity of Jesus Christ. The most they managed to uncover was a slightly overblown rhetorical analogy to Christ as a handicapped child. The reason for this was something they entirely and consistently failed to acknowledge - that although Rowan Williams is socially and politically of the moderate left, he is an orthodox, even traditional, theologian, entirely lacking the flights of speculation of a Spong or a Jenkins. His political views are informed by his theology.

Just a week before the Archbishop's confirmation, in December 2002, the conservatives played one last shot. At a press conference at All Souls, Langham Place - John Stott's old church - they released a statement which, while it did not mention Williams by name, was pretty clearly aimed directly at him; otherwise there was no real reason why it should have been issued at the time it was. It stated the traditional line that the Bible contained all that was necessary for salvation and that its guidance was entirely relevant to all sexual relationships:

> If ... norms of marital faithfulness are not upheld, social cohesion and sense of belonging begins to unravel, with consequential threats to individual happiness, children, health, community harmony and social well-being. We find no other model of personal faithfulness is permissible as an alternative to marriage. ... Biblical norms of sexuality and sexual relationships are first-order issues.

The statement had been signed by one English diocesan bishop, Graham Dow of Carlisle, by the Archbishop of Nigeria and by three other archbishops from the developing world. On the platform were David Phillips of the Church Society, David Banting of Reform, Chris Sugden of the Oxford Centre for Mission Studies and, as chairman, Andrew Carey, the journalist son of the former archbishop. Carey sat, complacently listening to statements attacking his father's successor. At the very least, he must have known that it associated the family name with the Fundamentalist irreconcilables before Rowan Williams had even moved in to Lambeth

Palace. Aligning himself so publicly with the most vociferous of the new Archbishop's opponents so soon after his father's retirement could only send a clear message that the Careys thoroughly disapproved of the choice of George's successor. Chairing such a meeting was ill-advised.[13]

Sugden admitted that the statement would indeed be seen as an attack on the new Archbishop, adding: 'We should always listen to others but there is such a thing as the mind of the church which does not change.' Banting told me at the meeting that Reform felt they could not believe a word Dr Williams said.

It was no wonder that Williams admitted that he had been taken aback by the ferocity of the personal attacks upon him. 'I think I have learned quite a bit about the church that I didn't really know. There is a certain amount of blood on my face,' he told the *Church Times*.[14] His staff reported that while all archbishops receive hate mail, his was already more than his predecessors had been accustomed to. They did not show him the worst of it, and kept from him the package of dog excrement that someone sent.

Phillips defended the robustness of the Church Society's criticisms, saying it was all part of the ongoing debate and only to be expected. He added smugly: '[Some] have apparently said that he is a false teacher. If that is their conviction, why is it offensive to state it? If Christian leaders contradict the teaching of the Bible then they are teaching falsehood.' A spokesman for Reform added: 'We want repentance. We want him to repent. We don't want to mollify things. The authority of the Bible is at stake.'[15]

Nevertheless some Evangelicals were troubled by the virulence of the hostility. Dr Philip Giddings, later to be instrumental in leading the opposition to the appointment of the gay Bishop of Reading, Jeffrey John, told me: 'Some disgraceful things were said. Sometimes your apparent friends are more of a problem than your enemies. Some Evangelicals can come across as extremely negative.'

What was also noticeable was the silence of the bishops of the Church of England. Only Richard Harries, the Bishop of Oxford, spoke up in Dr Williams's support. The rest kept quiet and offered him no public defence. One of the bishops who had been in the running for Canterbury said to me that it would be 'inappropriate' to intervene to assist or defend a newly appointed bishop and that he would have to make his own way. There was a sense in which Rowan Williams was a resented outsider, left to sink or swim. Meanwhile the bishops were either pusillanimous or reluctant to challenge the conservative Evangelicals too openly for fear of causing trouble in their own dioceses.

This internal squabbling contrasted with the public acclaim with which Dr Williams was greeted in the media and from outside the Church of England and appeared all the more sour and mean-spirited because of it. He was widely feted and eulogized. The tabloids fastened on his stated enjoyment of *The Simpsons* television cartoon series ('*The Simpsons* is one of the most subtle pieces of propaganda around in the cause of sense, humility and virtue') and of the lampoon of Irish Catholic priests, *Father Ted*, whose accents Williams would quietly imitate during tedious meetings. Despite the depth of his spirituality and learning, the wispy beard and the suspicion that he was the sort of chap to wear open-toed sandals, he seemed like a good bloke really. He even consented to be photographed smiling on receipt of the *Sun*'s present of a pile of *Simpsons* memorabilia. Even the newspapers most suspicious of him, such as the *Daily Mail*, were inclined to give him a chance – after all, they had been calling for a 'real' Christian to lead the Church of England for decades.

Williams was given the chance to deliver the Richard Dimbleby Lecture before an invited audience, on BBC television, an address which was pronounced a success largely because of its impenetrability, and – the ultimate accolade – he was invited on to BBC Radio's *Desert Island Discs* for its Christmas edition. His choice of music, Bach, Vaughan Williams and the Incredible String Band's 1960s hit 'The Hedgehog Song' was also seen as proving him to be someone in contact with humanity. He told the programme's interviewer, Sue Lawley, that gay priests were not on his agenda as a campaigning issue:

> It is certainly no part of my programme to change this, or even to push it as a matter of discussion, but there it is, on the table, and we have to think about it without too much rancour, too much prejudice or too much fear. It comes to an issue about the significance of the Bible and the authority of the Bible. And it is not for many people primarily about sex, it is about what you think of the authority of the Bible.

The orthodox Archbishop chose the Authorized Version of the Bible to be marooned with on his desert island.[16]

Slowly the wheels of the Church of England's appointments procedure ground onwards. In December Williams was formally arraigned before a bench full of his fellow bishops at St Paul's Cathedral as their 'right trusty and well-beloved brother' to be confirmed as the 104th Archbishop of Canterbury. The bishops solemnly denounced as contumacious anyone opposing his appointment, but David Hope, the Archbishop of York, mindful that some Evangelicals had warned they might disrupt the service, and having announced that all opponents of the election would be given an opportunity to object, proceeded immediately without a pause to declare that, as they had not done so, they had missed their chance. It was the sort of picturesque flummery, with bishops in scarlet robes and lawyers in wigs and the fiction that the Archbishop had been chosen by God rather than the prime minister, to brighten a winter's day in London. Williams himself had denounced that sort of ritual in an interview the week before as 'profoundly anti-Christian ... about guarding position, about fencing yourself in'.[17]

Then, two months later, on an early spring day at the end of February in Canterbury, the Archbishop was finally enthroned in his cathedral church, on the thirteenth-century stone throne of St Augustine, having kissed the fourth-century copy of the Gospels first sent to England 1,600 years before by Pope Gregory the Great. The cathedral rang with the ecstatic chants of a group of African singers, dancing to the beat of drums and then echoed to the sonorous Welsh anthem 'Cwm Rhondda'. It was filled with bishops, archbishops, Catholic prelates and Orthodox patriarchs, Muslim imams and by a congregation of political leaders led by the prime minister, as well as ordinary citizens of the diocese of Canterbury. They heard the Archbishop, his grey hair awry, sweat pouring down his forehead, speak of the need for tolerance in his fractious church: 'We have to learn to be human alongside all sorts of others, the ones whose company we don't greatly like, whom we didn't choose, because Jesus is drawing us together into his place, his company.'[18]

Outside the medieval gate of the great cathedral a small group of demonstrators had gathered, penned in by the police in front of a coffee shop and opposite a much larger flock of demonstrators out to lobby the prime minister against war in Iraq. The small group of the faithful were from the Church of England (Continuing). 'We think Rowan Williams does not believe in the gospel. He is unfaithful to the doctrines of the Church of England, We are concerned for its future. It is in tremendous decline, Liberalism and Anglo-Catholicism is rampant,' the Rev. Andrew Price of Wimbledon declared, his lip curling ostentatiously at the thought of talking to someone from the *Guardian*. But it was not his day – so few of them have been. That belonged instead to the bearded priest, dressed in gold and yellow, who was finally becoming bishop of the diocese of Canterbury, primate of the Southern Province, primate of All England, Archbishop of Canterbury and leader of the worldwide Anglican Communion, sitting uncomfortably on the ancient stone throne inside the building.

10

DOCTOR JOHN

'We are not wholly bad or good,
Who live our lives under Milk Wood,
And Thou, I know, wilt be the first,
To see our best side, not our worst.'
('The Sunset Poem of the Rev. Eli Jenkins', from Under Milk Wood by Dylan
Thomas)

T he first few months of Dr Williams's time at Canterbury contained
glimpses of what might be on the occasions when he was allowed
to be a simple priest. There was the Maundy Thursday washing of a
dozen parishioners' feet at the cathedral, a quiet and moving service but
one which Williams's predecessors had never stooped to since the Reformation. It had been warned against by the Archbishop's senior adviser at
Lambeth Palace, a surprisingly charmless former middle-ranking BBC
journalist appointed by Carey, named Jeremy Harris. He thought it was
inappropriate. Fortunately, his advice was ignored. Williams was surrounded by staff who were Carey appointees, rather than men and women
who were his own choices, sympathetic or even necessarily personally
congenial to him. He was reluctant though to get rid of them and indeed,
as an outsider, relied on their guidance. On this occasion, however, his
own instincts were best. The young daughter of the cathedral choirmaster
giggled as the Archbishop kneeled at her feet with his bowl and flannel
and he smiled encouragingly up at her. The picture of the humble Archbishop filled the next day's front pages in a way George Carey had rarely
managed.[1]

Then there was the Sunday on which he performed an unexpected
christening. Williams had told his diocesan staff that, as often as he could,
he would like to visit an ordinary parish church in the Canterbury diocese, preferably one which had been undergoing difficulties. Arriving
unannounced, he would either take the service or give the sermon. On
one of these occasions, he dropped in on a parish church on the fringes of
Maidstone where the vicar had been extremely ill with cancer. Afterwards

they retired to the vicarage for a chat and were interrupted by a knock on the door. One of the church wardens appeared, apologetically saying that a family had turned up to have their new baby christened. It had been booked but the vicar had forgotten. He was tired after the service and so the Archbishop volunteered to go back to the church and conduct the christening for him. He was getting back to being an ordinary priest again. He did not tell the family who he was and they did not recognize him. Much enthused and cheered, Rowan Williams returned home, feeling he had performed a useful function.

These times were rare. Although the Evangelicals had quietened for a while following Williams's enthronement, attitudes among conservatives towards him were still deeply suspicious. The organizers of the largest Evangelical Congress for 16 years, due to be held in Blackpool in September, were divided over whether the head of the Church of England should be invited at all, even to lead them in their prayers. They felt he certainly should not be entrusted with an address. The Archbishop's predecessors, Michael Ramsey and Robert Runcie – neither of them remotely Evangelicals – had both attended previous conferences without objection, but it took several meetings before the organizers of the National Evangelical Anglican Conference voted that they would tolerate his brief presence among them. It was a demeaning experience for both the Archbishop, who must have been growing used to slights from Evangelicals by now, and for the Evangelical movement itself, unable unreservedly to extend a welcome to him. Even then, the Church Society and Reform both said they could not encourage their members to be present.

Nevertheless in the spring of 2003 there must have been grounds for optimism at Lambeth Palace that the storm over the Archbishop and the homosexuality issue was dying away. The horizon was clear, Dr Williams was widely accepted, even enthusiastically so in much of the Church of England, and there could be hopes that there were more tranquil waters ahead. In the USA and Canada there were moves to consider authorizing same-sex blessings for gay couples, but there had been such intentions for some time and there seemed no immediate cause for concern.

In late May 2003 the primates of the worldwide Anglican Communion retreated to Gramado in southern Brazil for one of their regular gatherings. According to one who was there, Rowan was the star, hugely impressing his new colleagues when leading a seminar on the Gospel of St John. But inevitably homosexuality was one of the issues discussed together with its corollary, same-sex blessings, and, at the end, the archbishops issued a unanimous statement. 'The question of public rites for the blessing of same-sex unions is still a cause of potentially divisive controversy. The Archbishop of Canterbury spoke for us all when he said it is through liturgy that we express what we believe and that there is no theological consensus for same-sex unions. Therefore we as a body cannot support the authority of such rites.'[2]

Two days later, in a diocese in the far west of Canada, a pair of middle-aged men walked self-consciously down the aisle of a church to the strains of the Hallelujah Chorus and a new crisis was sparked. Michael Kalmuck and Kelly Montfort, partners for 21 years, may not have known it, but their action and that of their female priest, Margaret Marquardt, seemed like a deliberate snub to the archbishops.

The decision of the diocese of New Westminster to proceed with a rite of same-sex blessing occurred by chance at the same time as the primates' meeting. Consideration of such a service had been under way in the diocese, which centres on the city of Vancouver and its hinterland in British Columbia, for some years and had caused much local controversy. It was a change that had been pressed for by some urban churches in the west coast conurbation, which has a large gay community, and had been opposed by a handful of suburban Evangelical parishes, several of them with a large expatriate Asian population. Perhaps unsurprisingly, the leadership of the revolt came from a group led by a Sydney-trained Jensenite clergyman and the former British army chaplain and Reform member Paul Carter.

Michael Ingham, the local diocesan bishop who had been in post for ten years, was one of the rising stars of the liberal Canadian church, but the issue had predated his arrival. Candidates for the bishopric had been asked in 1993 whether they would uphold the Canadian House of Bishops' guidelines on the subject – broadly in line with the Church of England's – and Ingham for one had said that while he would, he would also work to change them.

Thereafter, in response he says to parish pressure, the Bishop inaugurated a discussion across the diocese about whether there should be some sort of service for same-sex couples. A debate on the matter had even been organized between Jack Spong and John Stott. The Bishop had also set up a canonical commission to see whether such a service could be authorized independently by a diocese, which had concluded it was up to the Bishop and the synod to decide, for there was nothing in Canadian canon law to stop them doing so. Next, a liturgical commission had been set up to decide what such a service should be like. Ingham insists that its brief was not to create a liturgy that sounded like a marriage service and that when it did so, it was asked to try again.

The Bishop says that some parishes – nine out of 80 in the diocese – were firmly opposed and that when he tried to draw them into a dialogue they refused to participate. He offered them the services of a conservative mediator, William Hockin, the respected and conservative Bishop of Fredericton, but was rebuffed. It seemed they wanted a confrontation with their liberal diocesan. They said they wanted an alternative bishop with full authority to minister to them directly but Ingham would not go that far because that would be an undermining of Episcopal authority. At every step the diocesan synod approved what was being done and the national church was kept informed. 'I am angered by the idea that I have bullied the diocese,' Ingham said. 'As if I could lead a synod of 400 people by the nose.'

At its synod in June 2002 the diocese voted heavily in favour (by 215 to 129) of a motion allowing those parishes that wished to offer same-sex blessings to be able to do so. It was not something any priest or church would be required or even expected to do. Each parish would have to vote on the issue before going ahead and there was a conscience clause for those clergy who did not wish to conduct such services. The traditionalists were in a minority for the first time and walked out. 'I saw anger and dismay on their faces. I tried to be conciliatory and asked to meet them to discuss how to keep them within the family. There was a guarantee that no one would be discriminated against for saying no. I have continued to ordain and appoint clergy who are opposed to same-sex blessings,' said Ingham.

Instead the rebel parishes, led by the parish of St John, Shaughnessy – which had long withheld funds from the diocese – found that the Diocesan Bishop of the Yukon, Terrence Buckle, a solid Church Army Evangelical, was ready to offer his oversight to them. Ingham is scathing about him: 'He's not very bright and he's easily manipulated, that's why they wanted him,' he said. 'Buckle's only got half a dozen parishes in his own diocese so after he's rung them all up a few times and it's got to Tuesday, he's got nothing left to do with himself for the rest of the week.'

This really was quite a declaration of war by a fellow bishop in support of the rebel parishes and it was a move that both George Carey and Michael Peers, the Canadian primate, had asked the churches not to make. Carey while still archbishop, had written to them in 2002 saying that although the diocesan synod's decision threatened the unity of the church, it was best to 'speak the truth in love' to one another: 'we do so most effectively by standing our ground in continuing dialogue and ongoing fellowship with each other, not by walking away.' Peers said: 'You don't build dioceses within dioceses.'

The 700,000-strong Anglican Church of Canada was deeply riven by its differences while trying to maintain a façade of unity. The metropolitan bishops with urban dioceses were broadly sympathetic to Ingham. Some, such as Toronto and Niagara, were contemplating introducing similar services themselves. Peers himself, a close friend – Ingham had been his chaplain until being appointed to New Westminster – was also supportive. But the bishops of the huge, underpopulated, agrarian, maritime and Arctic dioceses were much more hostile. The split was about two-thirds to a third, supportive of the diocese's introduction of the rite.

At Gramado, Peers tried to soften the final statement from 'cannot support' to 'cannot recommend'. Although his fellow primates assume he must have known what New Westminster was about to do, he did not let on to them. They received the unwelcome news of Michael and Kelly's little service just as they were arriving home three days later. It has some claim to being the wedding of the year.

Ingham had that weekend authorized the implementation of the service that had been agreed in principle at the previous year's synod. Even he was taken aback, however, by how quickly Ms Marquardt went ahead with the ceremony, within 48 hours. She did not inform the Bishop that she would be doing it, and, much worse, she introduced an element that was specifically excluded from the authorized rite, an exchange of rings. This made the service altogether much too much like a wedding, something that opponents of such services have always maintained is exactly what they will become. The happy couple pledged themselves to a relationship exclusive of other partners 'with the expectation of permanence'.[3]

Ingham said: 'It surprised me how quickly Margaret put together the first service. I thought, my God, that's indecent haste. She didn't tell me about it and she didn't have to, although it would have been nice. Then there, all over the papers the next day were pictures of Kelly and Michael holding up their rings. My diocesan chancellor told me I should have disciplined her for allowing it.'

Rowan Williams issued a statement expressing sorrow, rather than anger: 'In ignoring the considerable reservations which have been repeatedly expressed, most recently by the primates, the diocese has gone significantly further than the teaching of the Church or pastoral concern can justify and I very much regret the inevitable tension and division that will result from this development.'[4]

But it was too late. The damage had been done. Since those nuptials at St Margaret's Church, there have been only two other such services in the diocese, but one was quite enough for the rest of the worldwide Communion.

By then a much more immediate crisis was beginning to swirl through the Church of England. Ten days earlier, with very little fanfare – a deliberate policy by the diocese – Downing Street had announced, with the endorsement of the Queen, that the chancellor and canon theologian of Southwark Cathedral in south London, Dr Jeffrey John, had been appointed as the next Suffragan Bishop of Reading, one of three junior bishops in the diocese of Oxford. The Reading suffragan's area is essentially Berkshire, 30 miles west of London, and runs along the Thames and Kennet valleys. It is an area of prosperous towns such as Reading and Newbury (where the author of this book grew up), high-tech computer industries, large farms, affluent and pretty villages, booming house prices, white-collar commuters and horse racing. Dr John, who was aged 50, with his gifts as a speaker and theologian, on the Anglo-Catholic wing of the Church of England, was thought to be ideal. He was pictured smiling happily in a local church. The one thing that wasn't mentioned was that he was gay and that, while he had been discreet about his private life, he had made no secret of his view that the church should adopt a more liberal attitude to the gays in its midst, ordaining them and blessing same-sex partnerships.

Dr John was in many ways similar to Rowan Williams – indeed in some ways the attack on him was a scarcely veiled assault on the Archbishop. Both were scholarship boys from South Wales who had gone to Oxbridge and had successful careers as theologians. The Canon of Southwark was highly regarded for the power and cogency of his preaching and for his success at what the church today calls 'mission' in south London. And he was ambitious. Reading was the third bishopric he had been considered for; he had previously been rejected for a suffragan bishopric in the diocese of Europe and, ironically, for Monmouth, which Rowan Williams had just vacated and to which the ascetic bachelor Bishop of Reading, Dominic Walker, had just been appointed.

Richard Harries, the Bishop of Oxford, who had chosen John, also knew that he was gay. So did the advisory committee that had interviewed the candidates for the post and the neighbouring suffragan bishopric of Buckingham, which was also vacant and to which John might alternatively have been appointed. Furthermore Rowan Williams, the Archbishop of Canterbury, also knew that Dr John was gay. The two men had been colleagues for many years. A decade earlier they had helped establish Affirming Catholicism, the pro-women, socially liberal Anglo-Catholic group. They had even gone to Lambeth Palace to lobby George Carey on the issue of homosexuality. During that meeting Williams had gone so far as to ask Carey rhetorically: 'Who bears the cost?' when discussing the church's attitude to gay clergy.

Bishop Harries, who for the previous decade had chaired the House of Bishops' working party on sexuality – essentially looking into the gay issue – was suspected by Evangelicals of pushing the appointment through to test the boundaries of acceptability within the Church of England. But he told me:

> That's absolute nonsense. I have never been a campaigner on this issue. It would have been quite improper of me to express a point of view in that way. It was an issue of principle: Jeffrey John was the best person for the job.

> Actually I was very reluctant to include Jeffrey John on the list of candidates at first. His homosexuality was a major factor to consider. We had drawn up the job descriptions for both suffragans and sent them to Tony Sadler, the Archbishops' appointments secretary, and he sent us four names for each vacancy with a starred name for each as potentially the best candidate. Jeffrey John was the starred name. He was the person who most obviously fitted the bill for Reading. I was looking for someone from a Catholic tradition with a proven track record of mission. I looked very carefully at the references to his lifestyle.

There were 90 possible names for the two posts, whittled down eventually by the Bishop's advisory committee, which was made up of the chair of the diocesan House of Laity, the two archdeacons for the areas under consideration and Dr Philip Giddings, a politics lecturer at Reading University, a senior lay Anglican, member of the General Synod, member of the Archbishops' Council, the church's executive body established by George Carey, member of the Crown Appointments Commission's review group and, more to the point, a committed Evangelical.

Jeffrey John was one of four shortlisted candidates. Harries rang Rowan Williams to discuss the appointment and asked him whether he would be prepared to consecrate Dr John if he was appointed. The Archbishop said yes.

The four candidates were called in to give presentations, each asked to select one of the two vacancies and discuss how they saw the role of bishop and how they would go about energizing the church locally. All four chose Buckingham. This, says Harries, was a much more transparent way of conducting the search for a suffragan than is usually the case. Jeffrey John's presentation was said to be excellent and he was the Bishop's choice. Harries rang Lambeth Palace again and for a second time the Archbishop made no objection to the appointment. Only Philip

Giddings raised reservations, saying there would be a strongly negative reaction from conservative Evangelicals.

Giddings knew all about Jeffrey John. He told me:

> He was a member of the General Synod standing committee and I had met him a couple of times. I was aware of him and aware of his views. And I was aware of the way in which a great number of people would react against his being nominated. His name was added to the list at the last moment. Bishop Richard made the nomination, which was a serious error of judgement on his part. I pointed out that it would be extremely damaging to the Archbishop of Canterbury. His views were known to be similar to John's and that was why people had been opposed to his nomination. I didn't know of the long-standing friendship between them.

But Harries says:

> Philip Giddings did not express a strong personal view. He did not indicate that he would oppose the appointment publicly afterwards, but obviously he was not happy. He came out much more strongly later than he anticipated at the time.

> I knew Jeffrey John had won the respect and trust of Evangelicals in the diocese of Southwark. I had a letter from an Evangelical incumbent in the diocese there and a very moving tribute to Jeffrey's abilities from the previous bishop of Southwark who had appointed him a canon of the cathedral. I did think that, given two years in the Episcopal area of Reading, he could win people over.

Dr John was required to give an assurance about his current lifestyle, saying that although he had a male partner, also a priest, of many years' standing, he had lived a celibate lifestyle for more than a decade. He further gave assurances that he would support the church's position as outlined in *Issues in Human Sexuality*.

While John had been discreet about his own sexuality, he had written about homosexuality several times in the past, had contributed to the collection of prayers for homosexuals and had, like Rowan Williams, written a chapter for the book on the Evangelicals' St Andrew's Day statement called *The Way Forward?*, in which he had argued in favour not of gay marriages but of the blessing of same-sex couples. It added:

> As things now stand in the Church of England, a priest or bishop who has been divorced and remarried (even more than once) is considered more ac-ceptable than a priest who has remained faithful to one person of the same sex for a lifetime. ... It is hard to avoid the conclusion that popular prejudice and politics count far more in determining these attitudes than genuine scrip-tural or theological considerations. ... Enforced celibacy for homosexuals is

widely conducive to personal disintegration and loneliness, punctuated by more or less frequent lapses into promiscuous and furtive sex with all the spiritual damage and degradation it entails.[5]

You don't have to be much of a detective to guess the author's sexuality from such statements, but there the issue might have languished, for Evangelicals could scarcely out a man who had not outed himself and furthermore had given assurances about his sexual life. But John had form, in the shape of a much more personal and outspoken assault on the church's position during a speech to a private conference at Keble College, Oxford, five years before. It had already been removed from a website, where it had reposed in obscurity since 1998, but it was too late. Some Evangelicals, alerted to his appointment, had got hold of the text. And they were ruthlessly prepared to use it against him.

They gave it to Jonathan Wynne-Jones, a young journalist on the Evangelical *Church of England Newspaper*. Wynne-Jones is the son of the vicar of Beckenham, a senior member of the governing council of the Church of England Evangelical Council. He shared the story with Jonathan Petre, the religious correspondent of the *Daily Telegraph*, who shared it with the conservative newspaper-reading nation the following week. Petre had known of Jeffrey John and written about his views some years before, but it was the publication of his speech that alerted the wider Evangelical community and caused consternation first in the Oxford diocese, then throughout the rest of the country and, very soon thereafter, across the Anglican Communion. The Bishop of Oxford had not reckoned with that and the strategy of downplaying the significance of the appointment began to fall apart.

John had said to an Affirming Catholicism conference that from the time he had been a teenager he had been told by Anglo-Catholic clergy privately that if you were not celibate, you should avoid promiscuity, find a partner and live as discreetly as you could. At theological college in the mid-1970s, 'when I began the relationship I am still in, I went along to the principal to own up and asked if I should leave. To my astonishment and joy he congratulated me.' The newspaper did not say so until the following day, but the principal of St Stephen's House, Oxford, during Jeffrey John's time there was David Hope, now Archbishop of York. John's relationship with his partner had lasted 27 years, longer than many church-blessed marriages.

John had gone on to say that such truths about gays in the clergy had to be kept 'within the Catholic clerical club where gay relationships were entirely normal and still are'. More damagingly he had gone on bluntly to attack both the 1998 Lambeth Conference and *Issues in Human Sexuality*. He had said:

> We are now in a genuinely evil situation which has arisen directly from a collective decision to collude in a lie. I do not only mean the collusion of bishops: to some extent we have all succumbed to it. ... Nevertheless it is disappointing that so few have summoned the moral and intellectual strength to cut through it – or even want to.[6]

This gave the Evangelical opponents of John's appointment in the Oxford diocese all the ammunition they could possibly want: an admission of a lengthy and on-going same sex-relationship and an attack on the church's policy as 'evil'. The one added fuel to the other, for the Evangelicals could draw florid attention to the hypocrisy of publicly upholding a policy that the bishop-to-be did not believe in (never mind that many other more senior bishops felt much the same) while insinuating both that the new Bishop had outed himself and that he was flouting the very same policy in his private life. And of course he was gay, which was disgusting in itself. Evangelicals immediately started trawling through London electoral registers to see whether John was telling the truth about his current chastity or whether he was living with his partner.

Some Evangelical opponents in the Oxford diocese mobilized fast. A number of leading clergy in Oxford itself pronounced themselves unhappy, and the leadership of the Oxford Centre for Mission Studies popped up to offer its good offices in alerting its network of Evangelicals around the world. The leadership of the group was largely self-nominating. and when they claimed hundreds of followers within the diocese it was not always clear whether all were equally fervently in their camp or not. Certainly the Bishop believed that their number included some clergy who had merely expressed unease and who were susceptible to being won round. Philip Giddings was enlisted as the most plausible spokesman for the group, being a layman living in Reading rather than an Oxford cleric.

But more national figures were being stirred up too: Graham Dow, the Bishop of Carlisle, broke collegial ranks at once to express his deep concern at the appointment which, he said, had 'broken the period of serious discussion and reflection' on homosexuality, as though either had actually been going on. Paul Gardner, the Archdeacon of Exeter, a leading Evangelical and chairman of the Church of England Evangelical Council, also weighed in: 'The appointment of a bishop who has openly stated that he has been in a long-term homosexual relationship is breath-taking and unless there has been clear repentance he should stand down for the sake of the church and its unity,' he said.

Dow was an interesting character, a former Oxford college chaplain, the man who indeed 30 years before had prepared the undergraduate Tony Blair for confirmation. He is a man who believes in the very real and immediate presence of devils. Even his friends such as the Bishop of Winchester start to edge away at this point, but he is the author of a slender pamphlet which is his great contribution to theology. Penned in 1991 when Dow was working in Coventry, the opus *Explaining Deliverance* contends that many people are inhabited by demons – 'I now believe that such spirits are widespread' – and offers a handy guide on how to spot Satanic possession before preparing to exorcize it. Signs such as inappropriate laughter, inexplicable knowledge, a false or artificial smile, Scottish ancestry or relatives who have been miners or even 'repeated choice of black for dress or car; markedly unrestful colour schemes for dress or house décor' can all be dead giveaways. (Even the prime minister himself might prove susceptible on some of these counts.) And of course, devils enter through the openings of the body: 'most spirits leave through the mouth; some leave in the way they came, for example, through the eyes, the sexual orifices or the fingers.' It is an oddly threatening and dark-clad world that the Bishop of Carlisle inhabits.[7]

But he was zealous in mobilizing other bishops in his support. This, a few days later, produced a letter which nine diocesans and seven suffragans would sign in opposition to the appointment. Among those signing were Michael Nazir-Ali, the Bishop of Rochester, and Michael Scott-Joynt, Bishop of Winchester – not an Evangelical himself but an old friend of Dow's – both of whom had been potential rival candidates to Rowan Williams for Canterbury the year before. Most of the signatories, but not all, were conservative Evangelicals. Concern about the appointment did spread more widely across the church, though it was the Evangelicals who made the running. The other diocesan signatories were the Bishops of Liverpool, Chester, Bradford, Exeter, Southwell and Chichester. Two further diocesans, the incoming Bishops of Bristol and Durham, supported the letter but did not sign it because they had yet to be formally enthroned.

It was useful to have so senior a bishop as Scott-Joynt on board, as the fifth-ranking cleric in the Church of England and, moreover, not one of their tribe. It was just as convenient to overlook the fact that he had piloted through General Synod the year before the relaxation of the traditional ban on the remarriage of divorcees in church services: divorce, of course, being just as heavily condemned by Biblical injunction and by conservative Evangelicals as homosexuality, but somehow now less important to an institution seeking to maintain its share of the national matrimonial market.

The Bishop of Winchester was genuinely aggrieved at Jeffrey John's appointment because of the effect he perceived it would have on the church's mission in Africa – homosexuality in the Thames Valley somehow being much more important as a sin and an impediment to the Christian mission than polygamy and genocide in the Dark Continent.

The letter, written by Dow, praised Dr John's 'many admirable qualities' before adding: 'the issue is what is acceptable sexual behaviour in God's sight.' It stated: 'But it is the history of the relationship, as well as Dr John's severe criticism of orthodox teaching, which give concern.'[8] Presumably this was a reference to his contribution to *The Way Forward?* book, which had deliberately sought a range of contributions to the debate including from Rowan Williams, rather than John's attack on *Issues*, which was a policy document. The same bishops could have levelled the same charge at their new Archbishop.

The letter added unctuously: 'We value of course the gift of same-sex friendship and if this relationship is one of companionship and sexual abstinence, then, we rejoice.' This was precisely what Dr John had told the Bishop of Oxford – something that the Bishop of Carlisle had evidently failed to ascertain in his breathless haste to circulate the letter – and when it was pointed out, the bishops changed their tune: not to pronounce their satisfaction at the assurance, nor indeed to rejoice, but to assert now that Dr John had been insufficiently penitent of his previous behaviour and that he needed publicly to repent as well – not something any of them had ever been called upon to do for their past misdemeanours and trespasses as a condition of becoming a bishop.

Repent was something Dr John could not do, as his opponents well knew, not only because he clearly did not think his partnership was wrong, but because to do so would be demeaning and undermining of his entire future ministry. Instead he gave an interview to *The Times* in which he spoke of the relationship and of his discomfort at being forced publicly to reveal its details, an exercise thrust upon him by the vengeful Evangelicals. He felt uncomfortable in the role of pioneer: 'It is not a role I have set out for myself. I do not like it. I have a thin skin. I find all this extremely difficult. ... I did not apply for the job.'

The Canon was clearly deeply unhappy. He felt tempted to withdraw:

There are two conflicting things here. It is terrible to feel that I am a cause of division and fragmentation. My instincts are very much those of a Catholic, looking to the whole church and the unity of the church. But at the same time I have received huge numbers of messages of support, people saying:

'You have to go ahead with this for us'. I have become a symbol of hope for
an awful lot of people. It feels like a terrible burden to have ... either way,
people will be hurt.[9]

He asserted that he had never campaigned on the issue of homosexuality
and said he had never lived with his partner. But he was not going to
resile from it either:

It has not ended. It is perfectly clear that the relationship is going to last. It is
a permanent thing. That must not be denied ... it is for life. We have been together for 27 years and we will remain together. But the relationship has not
been sexually expressed for years.

Dr John said he would like the church to bless covenanted, permanent
relationships, but he had never performed the service for anyone else,
would not do so and appreciated that there was no consensus on the issue
within the church. He had battled with his homosexuality:

I was conscious of it from quite an early age and that it was probably going to
bring problems. I certainly resisted and fought it. I wrestled hugely with it and
prayed about it, as I think so many gay people do. ... It seemed there was a
private morality, a Christian one, but one that could never be talked about
openly. ... There have been centuries of double thinking. ... I think the current discipline cannot hold for long because it penalizes honesty and
openness. Gay people are now frightened to come forward for ministry.

There was a tense atmosphere by now. Bishop Dow went on the BBC's
Newsnight programme where he suddenly started expiating on gynaecology,
to the gasped surprise of the presenter: 'It's, well, in a way obvious that the
penis belongs with the vagina and this is something fundamental to the
way God has made us. Sexual intercourse is a lovely sign of the lifelong
bond of marriage.'[10] Meanwhile Winchester appeared on the BBC's *Today*
programme to blame John for the whole thing: 'I think it remains to be
seen whether the appointment will go ahead. The responsibility, which I
greatly regret, for that decision probably now lies with Dr John,' Scott-
Joynt asserted, apparently forgetting that the Canon had never applied for
the job in the first place (though he was not averse to taking it).

One bishop signatory told me:

The letter was led and written by Dow, who was the ring-leader. The wording
was not satisfactory, but it was not changed. He recruited Scott-Joynt, who recruited another non-Evangelical. We thought the letter was needed to set the
ball rolling, to show that Evangelicals were not going to roll over on the appointment and that there was concern. Dow's performance on *Newsnight*
though caused despair. I was watching and thought, 'phew, he's got through

it' and then there was a pause and out it came, breaking the first law of media presentation. It was quite awful.

Scott-Joynt told me: 'Graham knows he made a mistake. He also knows what I thought about it because I've told him. I've known him for 37 years. You can't condemn a man for one mistake.' When I pointed out that the bishops were condemning Jeffrey John for remarks made once in a private meeting years before, the Bishop of Winchester harrumphed that that was *quite* a different matter.

The bishops' letter infuriated Richard Harries as an open and unprecedented breach of collegiality and an intervention in another diocese's affairs. It exasperated other diocesan bishops who held more liberal views on the issue as well. They raised an alternative letter, supporting the appointment and signed by eight diocesans. This was organized by Peter Selby, the Bishop of Worcester. The other signatories were the Bishops of Hereford, Leicester, Newcastle, Ripon and Leeds (who would soon be expressing his desire to authorize gay blessings), St Edmundsbury and Ipswich, Salisbury and Truro. The letter criticized the 'serious and unwanted pressure' which had been applied to Dr John and promised support both to him and the Archbishop of Canterbury.[11] But the group's members, unlike their opponents, were more reticent about coming forward. When the Bishop of Salisbury was also offered a chance to appear on *Newsnight* he at first accepted and then pulled out at the last moment.

The crisis had smoked out 17 of the 44 diocesans to declare their positions and, although the rest kept their heads down, the atmosphere on the bench of bishops was by now poisonous. It would boil over in acrimony and accusations at the bishops' next monthly meeting. 'There was absolute fury in the House of Bishops,' says Harries. Prebendary Richard Bewes, of All Souls, Langham Place, admitted in a letter some months later: 'Michael Nazir-Ali told me that it really cost, for them all to make that stand. I heard Peter Forster [Bishop of Chester] say the same thing.'

Both sides were now into a numbers game. The Oxford Evangelicals claimed that 80 of the diocese's 800 clergy and 20 leading lay figures were resolutely opposed to the appointment going through, but the Bishop's party claimed that 100 clergy had come forward to support Dr John. When Richard Thomas, the diocesan press officer and himself a Wycliffe-House-trained Evangelical, bumped into a group of the leading opponents at Church House during the crisis, they furiously berated him for suggesting that they did not have majority support, or that some Evangelicals actually supported the appointment. He was shaken by what happened, feeling physically intimidated, believing the group to be both bullying and manipulative, and he subsequently severed his previously close connections with them as an adviser to the Oxford Centre for Mission Studies. He said:

> A certain group within the church wanted to get its own way. The public face was theological but actually the methods used showed that it was all about power. I am sceptical about how much support they really had. It was usually difficult to get the names being claimed as supporters of this group and what was certainly true was that very few people were prepared to say what they truly believed for fear of being clobbered by some group. We need to move away from this culture of fear.

A friend of Michael Brierley, Harries's chaplain, told him that he had been rung up by his old tutor at Wycliffe Hall, for the first time since his graduation years before, to ask if they could count on his support.

The Bishop of Oxford was receiving hate mail (and the now seemingly obligatory dog excrement). Eventually his office would receive more than 3,000 communications about the appointment, two-thirds of them supportive. By the end of the first week of July, 2,334 letters had been received, 789 negative and 1,545 positive. Support for Jeffrey John's appointment came from 517 clergy and 1,028 laity, including 38 MPs and five peers. There were also supportive messages from one archbishop (Ndungane of Cape Town), 16 diocesan bishops, nine suffragans, eight deans, five archdeacons, 15 university chaplains, 16 professors of theology and 14 area deans.[12]

Among other communications was one from the wife of John Staples, the vicar of Tidmarsh, the little village outside Reading where the suffragan bishop has his residence. Staples himself had made it clear that he was not happy about the appointment, but his wife went somewhat further. She wrote a letter to Dr John saying that, unlike his predecessors, he would not be welcome to park his car in the vicarage drive, presumably for fear of perverting the petunias.

Harries thought he was winning the argument, though actually the picture was mixed. A meeting of local clergy in St Nicolas Parish Church in Newbury had not been a success and there were some senior staff with doubts about the appointment as well, in particular the Archdeacon of Berkshire, Norman Russell, who believed he had been misled.

By now some members of the Anglican worldwide Communion were weighing in. The first was Nigeria's Archbishop Akinola who rapidly cornered the market in vehemence and bigotry, saying the appointment of the Bishop of Reading showed that God's church was under Satanic attack. He added: 'I cannot think of how a man in his right senses would be having a sexual relationship with another man, it is so unnatural, so unscriptural. This is unheard of ... and not what we can tolerate.'[13]

He and Jensen of Sydney immediately threatened to split the Communion if the appointment was not rescinded. This was actually easier said than done, as they probably knew. Since the appointment had been formally announced on the Queen's behalf, there appeared to be no way of preventing it going ahead. Her Majesty, after all, had found no fault with Dr John, nor had Downing Street – and nor had the Archbishop of Canterbury.

Tony Sadler, the Archbishops' appointments secretary, unprecedentedly on the record, told the *Sunday Times* that he had put forward 'seven or eight names', adding: 'My understanding is that we are not in the business of discriminating on the grounds of sexual orientation. I put Jeffrey's name down on my list because his gifts and experience fitted the job description.'[14]

By now though pressure was mounting for Williams, hitherto silent, to intervene. He duly materialized in the front garden at Lambeth Palace the following day to read a letter he was sending to all 116 bishops pleading for calm. It was characteristically opaque, so much so that its meaning was interpreted entirely differently by several of the newspapers that reported it. It said:

> It would be a tragedy if these issues in the Church of England and in the Communion occupied so much energy that we lost our focus on the priorities of our mission, the priorities given us by our Lord. What we say about sexuality ... is a necessary part of our faithfulness, but the concentration on this in recent weeks has had the effect of generating real incomprehension in much of our society in a way that does nothing for our credibility.[15]

It acknowledged that the concerns about the appointment were 'theologically serious, intelligible and by no means based on narrow party allegiance or on prejudice'. The statement called on the diocese to be allowed to sort out its problems for itself: 'It is not for anyone outside the diocese to override or pre-empt what is obviously a painful and complex process' – something that was indeed going to happen in the coming days. Crucially the Archbishop did not say he would intervene to prevent the appointment going ahead.

It was all too late, invoking the Almighty or appealing to the church to pause and think about the spectacle it was making of itself. Rod Thomas, the spokesman for Reform, said: 'We have a great deal of sympathy with the appeal for calm and serious reflection, but it is difficult to be reassured because at the moment the appointment still stands.' Bishop Harries was also dug in: he went on that night's *Newsnight* programme to say that if an abstinent gay person could not be welcomed then 'frankly there's no hope for gay and lesbian people in the life of the church'.

It was at about this time that Jeremy Harris, the nearest Lambeth Palace had to a spin doctor, produced an internal memo discussing how the Archbishop might distract the media's attention from the gay row by means of 'alternative attractive stories' such as delivering a reading of his own poems, making a high-profile intervention in a House of Lords' debate or announcing a new theological prize. The issue of homosexuality, it suggested, 'had to be managed in media terms by seeking to take the sting out of it and displacing it in the public mind'.

Some hope. The memorandum was off-beam and inadequate. This was the calibre of advice Williams was receiving. The memo appears not to have been acted upon - in any event no poetry reading took place and no prize was announced - and the media was not likely to be distracted so easily. The main story needed no poetry.

Far from pausing for calm reflection, the leaders of OCMS now organized a meeting in Oxford attended by several bishops and by Drexel Gomez, the primate of the West Indies. For a non-partisan body the Oxford Centre and its personnel were certainly heavily involved on just one side. Among those attending were representatives of Reform, the Church of England Evangelical Council, the New Wine Charismatic movement and the conservative American Anglican Council. Two of the bishops were retired, but present were the Bishop of Dallas, Lewes's Wally Benn and Michael Hill, consecrated only the weekend before as Bishop of Bristol. Gregory Venables, Archbishop of the Southern Cone, was for once not present, but sent his support.

The meeting issued a statement warning that those attending would refuse to recognize not only Jeffrey John's authority if he was consecrated but that of any other bishop who backed him. Since Rowan Williams was due to conduct the consecration at Westminster Abbey on 9 October, this had potentially serious consequences. It added that the homosexual issue had been 'definitively' settled at the Lambeth Conference - something that would have been news even to George Carey, since the motion had proposed setting up a commission to study the issue - and said that Dr John's appointment disrupted the unity of the Communion - though only they themselves were threatening to disrupt it - and flouted mainstream Anglican teaching.

Richard Harries was still attempting to hold the line in the diocese of Oxford. He estimated that, far from representing a united view of all the major parishes, as the Evangelicals were claiming, they represented only a small, and diminishing band led by self-appointed leaders: in Reading itself, Greyfriars, attended by Dr Giddings, and Arborfield, the bleak village incorporating an old army camp south of the town and in Oxford the big city centre Evangelical churches of St Ebbe's and St Aldate's. What he had not anticipated though was the pressure mounting from the developing world, sedulously fostered by the Oxford Centre for Mission Studies, whose leadership was absorbed full-time in the most partisan way with the issue. 'They took control and appointed themselves spokesmen for it. It was all probably slightly spurious because not everyone, even within the Evangelical community, felt the same way that they did,' said Harries. The OCMS certainly had no intention of heeding Dr Williams's plea for the diocese to sort the matter out for itself. Email technology made immediate communication and rapid responses possible.

It was the international threats, especially from Africa, that were mounting. Akinola popped up on the BBC to threaten: 'We are Bible-loving Christians ... we would sever relationships with anybody, anywhere. ... Anyone who strays over the boundaries we are out with them. It is as simple as that.' He perhaps did not observe the waspish letter from the Rev. Mark Williams in that day's Church Times. Williams, who knew Nigeria and shared a parish there, pointed out that local tribal practices of polygamy and child sacrifice appeared to be going uncondemned by the Archbishop (or, he might have added, his supporters in England). Williams added: 'The Archbishop's faithfulness to scripture at home is far more a cause for question and concern than anything going on here or in Canada. ... We cannot be held hostage to such double standards.'[16]

The international pressure was growing even as domestic pressure appeared to be waning. With the Church of England's General Synod looming at York in a fortnight's time, the Evangelicals gave up their plans to press for an emergency debate. In the event they would not have needed one for, a week before the representatives were due to gather, Rowan Williams pulled the plug on Jeffrey John.

On Friday 4 July the Archbishop received a petition from church figures, mainly from Oxford. Later that day he consulted by telephone a number of bishops, though apparently only those, like Scott-Joynt, opposed to the appointment going ahead. Then he telephoned Richard Harries, calling him to an early meeting at 8 a.m. the following morning. At the same time, Jeffrey John was telephoned by Lambeth Palace staff telling him to report, not to the Palace itself but to a rendezvous nearby.

He was asked to wear civilian clothes, apparently out of fear that the meeting might be observed. Smelling a rat, the cleric turned up to meet the Archbishop in his dog collar and was escorted across to the Palace.

The only way of preventing the new Bishop of Reading from proceeding to his exalted post was for him to resign it. Dr John had therefore to be persuaded by his old friend and colleague in Affirming Catholicism, the Archbishop.

Harries thought his appointment with Dr Williams was just a consultation exercise, to find out the latest state of opinion in the diocese. When he arrived, however, he was ushered into the Archbishop's first-floor study at the head of the grand staircase to be told that Williams had decided the appointment could not go ahead.

> I had no idea that it was coming. I thought we were going to see how to handle the issue. Rowan made absolutely clear to me that he had made an agonizing decision, which was very hard for him to make because he agrees with Jeffrey John's views and Jeffrey John was a very old friend. He had agonized long and hard and there was nothing we could say to change his mind.

There was little discussion of the decision itself. What took the time was the letter of resignation that Dr John was required to sign. He disagreed with the draft that was presented to him for signature and made clear in his statement that the decision had been forced upon him. Jeffrey John had not intended to pass up the appointment. He was too ambitious for that. He still wants a bishopric and knows that his talents merit one.

At one point in the morning, John's own bishop, Tom Butler of Southwark, got wind of what was happening and telephoned to ask to attend. Butler was not particularly sympathetic to the Canon – in fact the two had never got on – but he wanted to be present. He was refused permission but did speak to Jeffrey John by telephone. He urged him not to resign, support for which the Canon was personally grateful.

By lunchtime the meeting was over. Dr John's letter of resignation to Bishop Harries stated: 'It has become clear to me that in view of the damage my consecration might cause to the unity of the church, including the Anglican Communion, I must seek the consent of the crown to withdraw.'

In his own, lengthier, statement, made on the following day, the Archbishop said disingenuously that John had announced his intention of withdrawing: 'The road that has led him to this point has been extremely arduous and I must pay the warmest public tribute to the dignity and forbearance he has shown throughout, often under the most intrusive and distasteful personal scrutiny.'[17]

Once again the Archbishop called for an opportunity to pause for thought and reflection:

> We have to grasp that Canon John's appointment has brought to light a good deal of unhappiness among people who could by no means be described as extremists. ... They are convinced that there is a basic issue at stake relating to the consistency of our policy and our doctrine in the Church of England. ... Such unhappiness means that there is an obvious problem in the consecration of a bishop whose ministry will not be readily received by a significant proportion of Christians in England and elsewhere.
>
> Let me add that some of the opposition expressed to Canon John's appointment has been very unsavoury indeed. A number of the letters I received displayed a shocking level of ignorance and hatred towards homosexual people.

Jeffrey John retired 'battered, devastated and bewildered' at the bolt from the blue. Richard Harries felt similarly: 'I was shell-shocked, angry - no, depressed - drained and disconsolate.' It was a sad group that gathered at his home that evening. His chaplain, Michael Brierley, took a bottle of wine round so they could drown their sorrows. Harries says: 'It still seems to me it was quite wrong for the church to discriminate. Jeffrey John had all the kinds of gifts we were looking for and a number of dioceses would benefit from having them now.'

The following morning, before the statements were released, the *Sunday Times* carried a story in which George Carey conceded that he had ordained two bishops knowing them to be gay, though celibate. Jeffrey John immediately rang Lambeth Palace to speak to the Archbishop. It was not too late: word had not got out. He wanted to rescind his resignation. He was told by Jeremy Harris, whom he eventually reached, that the Archbishop was unavailable and anyway the Carey story was wrong. Some minutes later Jonathan Jennings, having been alerted by Harris, telephoned John and repeated that the Carey story was false. He nevertheless promised to relay John's message to the Archbishop before the withdrawal was announced. He never did and a few hours later, in time for the Sunday lunchtime news bulletins, the resignation was announced.

In response Tom Butler, the Bishop of Southwark, said: 'Jeffrey John would have brought many gifts to the diocese of Oxford had he taken up his appointment. ... He has my prayers and support.'

The Evangelical community issued statements applauding Jeffrey John's decision, praising his integrity and courage and deploring the exposure of his private life, which they themselves had previously been so assiduous in disseminating. They tried hard not to gloat. Joel Edwards,

general director of the Evangelical Alliance, said: 'We are grateful to
Canon Jeffrey John for exercising sensitivity in this matter and we are
relieved that his actions have averted a situation which may have had
catastrophic consequences for unity within the Anglican Communion and
for Christian witness in the United Kingdom. I think it is sad he was put
in this position.'

The most vocal critic of the decision was Colin Slee, the Dean of
Southwark, one of the Canon's strongest supporters, who would soon be
writing angry letters to the nine diocesans telling them exactly what he
thought of them. 'You can take it that he was bounced. This stinks to high
heaven. There is no way that he has resigned voluntarily. He is in agony,'
he said. 'The people talk of empty churches. Empty churches may well be
empty because of the image that we are presenting of narrowness and
bigotry and prejudice.'

Liberals, not least among the gay community, felt betrayed by an
archbishop in whom they had deposited such hopes for a change in
church attitudes. The word 'betrayal' was in the air, together with a warning that if Rowan did not know who his friends were he might find
himself abandoned when he needed their support. They believed he had
been bounced by the vociferousness and vehemence of the Evangelicals'
campaign.

In the Oxford diocese itself, there were hundreds of messages of support for the deposed cleric, rather more perhaps than the number of
signatures his opponents had ever secured. Among them were the two
Labour MPs for Reading, the area's Conservative MPs and, possibly more
surprisingly, the lord lieutenants of Berkshire and Oxfordshire.

A few days later in a letter published in the *Reading Chronicle*, Dr John
thanked them all for their support. He made clear that he had been forced
to step down:

> I have received literally thousands of messages, including many hundreds
> from the Reading area. The overwhelming majority have been friendly and
> supportive. ... This avalanche of kindness has left me all the more saddened
> and disappointed that I cannot now come to serve you as your bishop. ... I am
> more sorry than I can express that in the end the chance [to prove myself] was
> taken away.[18]

✠ ✠ ✠ ✠ ✠

Why did Rowan Williams make his decision? Six months later he told me:

> There were three reasons. I had understood the diocese was more behind the
> appointment than seemed to be the case. Secondly, there was the public dis-

agreement in the House of Bishops: if the bishops are divided over welcoming a new member then that does make one scratch one's head. Thirdly, there was the international dimension, which was very complex and quite fragile. When a third-world diocese says it cannot remain in fellowship, that is a cost to both sides. But it was a very hard decision to have to take. Yes ... yes ... yes.

The resignation allowed the following weekend's Synod to go ahead unhindered, though it left a heavy cloud hanging over the gathering. The authorities made clear that they did not want a debate on the issue of the moment. It would all be far too early. Maybe the next meeting in February would be better. Someone with a subversive sense of humour chose the Victorian hymn 'There's a Wideness in God's Mercy, Like the Wideness of the Sea' by F.W. Faber as one of the anthems at the Synod's Sunday morning service in York Minster. It has the refrain:

We make His love too narrow
By false limits of our own;
And we magnify His strictness
With a zeal He will not own ...
If our love were but more simple
We should take him at His word;
And our life would be all gladness
In the joy of Christ our Lord.

If Evangelicals were notable for their sense of irony they might also have spotted the Gospel reading concerning Salome's demand for the head of John the Baptist and the choice of a prayer written by Michael Vasey, the gay Evangelical theologian.

Otherwise the only unscheduled intervention to the Synod's proceedings was by Peter Tatchell, making his inimitable contribution by invading the stage at the university's central hall and haranguing the Archbishop of York. Tatchell had his say, to an emptying hall and then, having run out of things to add, left to be interviewed outside by television reporters. Outside the hall a more dignified group of gay Anglicans, including clergy, held up banners saying 'Here We Are – Get Over It' and 'What a Friend We Have in Jesus'.

The bishops remained in some disarray. Michael Scott-Joynt, the Bishop of Winchester, found himself in difficulties during the Synod's question-time session when asked whether he still believed that homosexuality was a sin. He would not say, resorting instead to reading from *Issues in Human Sexuality*.

His brother bishop John Gladwin of Guildford was more forthright in answering a question from Reform's David Banting who had protested at being called a homophobe just because he did not like homosexuality. 'I have been in conversation with clergy, struck by the fact that a number of them are angry, some are confused, many are depressed and some are frightened. I think there is a duty on myself and my colleagues to recover lost ground in relation to their pastoral safety and care,' Gladwin said with some asperity. The two men would soon have the opportunity of closer acquaintance as Gladwin had just been appointed Bishop of Chelmsford, the diocese in which Banting has his parish and where he vets speakers for their suitability to address his tender flock.

On the fourth day of the Synod, Rowan Williams addressed the gathering for the first time, although he had preached a sermon on the theme of unity at the Minster service. He was greeted with some relief and a wave of near-adulation. Members wished to register their support and sympathy and gave him a standing ovation. Williams addressed the issue directly:

> These levels of fear and distrust on both sides are cause for grief and repentance. If all the pain of these weeks can in some way prompt us to see more clearly what we do to each other, why we threaten each other so, we shall have grown a little into the space God has made. ... Everyone believes they are a persecuted minority. It is not a situation that encourages easy and honest communication ... it cries out for scapegoats.

Amid the applause at the end, the Reform leaders sat ostentatiously on their hands, like stern Puritans among the clamorous mob. 'We feel we represent the silent majority of the church, who are still essentially orthodox, conservative and not always very articulate,' sniffed David Banting afterwards. 'The archbishop only has to walk on a stage and people applaud him. I don't want to lionise him.'[19]

A few weeks after the crisis, Jeffrey John quietly contacted Lambeth Palace again. He wanted to discuss his future in the church, indeed whether he had one at all, and wondered if he could speak to the Archbishop. He was told a meeting could be arranged if he was prepared to wait. The Archbishop was busy. Perhaps he could be fitted in in a few months' time. Jeffrey John accepted the arrangement meekly, but the Palace's attitude infuriated his partner who himself called Lambeth a few days later. He told them that Jeffrey was devastated and needed to speak to the Archbishop to obtain spiritual advice from him. If Rowan Williams was that uncaring, perhaps he would go to the media and tell them what the Archbishop's pastoral care was really like. After that, an appointment was arranged within a few days.

The meeting was private, so who can say what really occurred? It must have been deeply uncomfortable for the Archbishop. If Jeffrey John had used the same ploy as Williams himself had once adopted when they had gone together to see George Carey about the gay issue and asked the 'who bears the cost?' question, it could scarcely have been more pointed.

At the end of the interview the Archbishop apparently asked to pray with the Canon and fell to his knees, requesting his blessing, which the surprised Dr John bestowed. There were some in his position who might have thought twice about doing so.

At the York Synod, Philip Giddings had murmured that the Archbishop would need to hold talks with Dr John about the future of his ministry, but nothing came of the meeting at Lambeth Palace. Jeffrey John continued to harbour hopes for a time that he might still be considered for a bishopric. There was talk of his name being put forward for Woolwich, where the Evangelical Colin Buchanan was due to retire as suffragan. After all, Jeffrey was known in the Southwark diocese and was even liked by some Evangelicals. But the idea that Evangelicals would allow the gay canon to be appointed there or anywhere else was out of the question. Dr John was chafing with frustrated ambition but there seemed no obvious outlet for his talents within the Church of England. At the end of the year, his partner was taken to hospital with a serious stress-related illness, leaving the unhappy cleric more distressed and depressed than ever. The church seemed to have turned its back on him.

Eventually, in January 2004, the Church of England did fill the Reading vacancy with Canon Stephen Cottrell of Peterborough Cathedral, an Anglo-Catholic member of Affirming Catholicism and, incidentally, someone who had supported the appointment of Dr John. But the church had taken care to select a sport-loving father of three, a man who would be welcome to park his car in the vicarage drive.

Bishop Harries escaped the immediate fall-out of the row since he was going into hospital for a hip operation on the Monday following the meeting at Lambeth Palace. Looking back a few months later he said:

> There is still quite a bit of turbulence around in the diocese. It has been very divisive. My first instinctive reaction was to resign. I felt I really did not want to go on. But I also knew it was foolish to make a decision straight away and I let it lie for the summer. I decided to stay because we need to appoint someone for the Reading area, but the consultation was going to be different.
>
> If anything good has come out of this, it is that the nomination of Jeffrey John has shaken up middle England and forced it to ask itself where it stands on the issue of homosexuality. I think, rather to its surprise, it has come to stand with Jeffrey John. Wherever I go people tell me that it was wrong for him not to be appointed. That is perhaps a hopeful sign.

Philip Giddings says:

I said it would be very damaging to Jeffrey because he would come under immense media scrutiny and pressure and I fairly accurately predicted what would happen. ... It seems to me implausible that he could have upheld the teaching of the church when he had argued against it. It would have been unbelievable.

Others, on the liberal wing of the church, believe that the appointment was inopportune and ill-timed and has set back the gays' position within the Church of England for at least a decade. The ground was insufficiently prepared, the Evangelicals felt bounced into an appointment they did not support and the ill-fortune that Jeffrey John should be almost the first cleric to be promoted by Rowan Williams seemed to bear out all the conservative suspicions about his agenda. Conspiracy theories that the Reading decision was made to test the water can be ruled out. But the whole saga winded the Church of England badly. Gay clergy now knew that it did not pay to be open about their lives or aspirations. Rowan Williams had given a hostage to fortune. And conservative Evangelicals discovered that if they shouted loudly enough they would get their way.

In April 2004 it was suddenly announced that Jeffrey John was being appointed Dean of St Albans – one step down from a bishopric, but in charge of one of England's oldest and loveliest cathedrals. It seemed an excellent match for the canon's teaching talents, and he was warmly, even enthusiastically welcomed by both the bishop and parishioners. There could be no subterfuge about his sexual orientation this time. The bishop spoke warmly of his resilience and Christian forbearance: 'The more I prayed, the more I felt this appointment was right and good.'

The Evangelicals sat on their hands. Having said that John was unsuitable for a bishopric because of its special nature, but not that it was inappropriate for him to be in holy orders, it would have been hypocritical for them to have objected to any change of job at all. Critics had to search as far as the US to find a conservative website saying the appointment was an outrage, or to Jesmond, where the Rev. David Holloway popped up to claim, as usual, that the church was institutionalizing decadence.

Dr John announced at his initial press conference that he would not defy church policy, but added: 'I support the state and the church offering gay people a framework to live their lives within a covenant of faithfulness to each other. I don't mind whether that is called a marriage or not.' But he realized, he said, that the word 'marriage' was a 'red rag to many bulls'.

Asked what he had learned from his experience over the last year, he replied: 'The value of silence. If you had seen me in private some times this year, you would not have said I was courageous.'

11

GENE GENIE

'The legitimate powers of government extend to such acts only as are injurious to others. But it does me no injury for my neighbour to say there are twenty gods, or no God. It neither picks my pocket nor breaks my leg.' (Thomas Jefferson, Notes on the State of Virginia)

The Episcopal Church's general convention in Minneapolis was a very different event from the meeting of the General Synod of the Church of England three weeks earlier. The convention gathers only every three years, instead of twice annually. Its members tend to dress more formally even in high summer: high-necked dog collars for the clergy – men as well as women, of course – rather than open-necked summer shirts, and black polished brogues instead of the open-toed, heavy-soled apostolic sandals and socks that plod towards York and say that an English vicar is on holiday. American participants wear prominent name tags – Chuck, Bud and Doug – instead of the scrappier efforts of the Church of England. And its procedures are interestingly different in the USA, with the various constituent parts – bishops, clergy, laity – meeting separately to hold discussions and debates instead of joining in all together as in England.

There is another subtle difference too: whereas in England membership of the church is almost routine and an automatic inheritance, to be an Episcopalian in America is to have made a positive choice of denomination, often as an adult, to have bought into its ethos and the nature of its worship and to support it both wholeheartedly and financially. There is nothing perfunctory about the decision.

The Minneapolis Convention Centre may have been built in the same concrete brutalist 1960s style as York University, but it lacked the surrounding parkland greenery and the lake with ducks and geese quacking and honking on it that forms such a pleasant and vocal backdrop to the General Synod debates. Instead the convention centre was bounded on one side by a freeway and on the other by some desolate downtown blocks. Inside the centre, long corridors stretched seemingly into the infinite distance, identical doors gave on to anonymous, pastel-painted meeting rooms and the Convention's main gatherings were held in windowless halls the size of aircraft hangers.

In one of these enormous spaces, stalls had been set up. You could kit yourself out in clerical vestments, buy yourself an embroidered waistcoat, an appliquéd stole, plaster statuary, a stained-glass window or some 'venerable beads', invest in a bronze eco-niche for your ashes, visit the recovered alcoholic clergy stand or even recoil in horror at the death-row gurney complete with leather restraining straps that adorned a stall devoted to the abolition of capital punishment. Episcopalians are awash with a good-hearted view of the better possibilities of human nature.

Yet there can have been few less spiritually uplifting places in which to meet: a sound-deadening void in which everything seemed to move in slow motion. Staff wandered about like lost souls, desultorily emptying trash cans. Armed policemen sauntered in search of somewhere quiet to gossip. I passed one absorbed in a large instruction manual entitled *Sniper*. It didn't seem entirely necessary at a convention of Episcopalians, but to make sure, at the centre's entrance, there were signs saying: 'Show management bans guns in these premises'. If purgatory has a reality it may be rather like the halls of Minneapolis. In 1976, the last time the convention had gathered in the Twin Cities, it had voted to ordain women. This time it had to make a decision of similarly Bible-shaking dimensions.

The Convention lasted a fortnight and had several weighty matters on its agenda, but only one that absorbed wider attention: the endorsement of the election of Canon Robinson as Diocesan Bishop of New Hampshire. His was not the only appointment to be confirmed: those of the Bishops of Milwaukee, Montana and Florida and the splendidly named Johncy Itty of Oregon all went through on the nod without controversy or attention as that of every American diocesan bishop since the 1870s had done.

The atmosphere was like a political rally and just as closely organized by Robinson's supporters. This was a man running for office. His followers roamed the convention wearing badges saying 'Ask Me About Gene'. The man himself wore one saying 'I AM Gene'. He was certainly not retiring, touring the exhibition stands, shaking hands, chatting and smiling benignly; his partner Mark – neat dark suit, trimmed moustache – in rather self-conscious tow, and a bulky, crew-cut security man called George lurking nearby.

This was a necessary precaution, for outside on a grassy knoll opposite the conference centre stood the stern and ghastly figure of the Rev. Fred Phelps, a Primitive Baptist minister from Topeka, Kansas, his wife, some of his 13 children and a small band of acolytes holding banners and bawling messages of hate. The banners carried texts such as 'God Hates Fags' and 'AIDS is the Cure'. Through a bullhorn Phelps targeted representatives entering the building. Spying one accompanied by children, he screamed at them: 'Wha would yew take childrun into tha' house of Baal?'

Phelps himself has an obsession with homosexuality. A cadaverous figure, wearing a white Stetson, he tours America to spread his message of abomination for gays. A measure of his fury is to be found on his website (Godhatesfags.com), another in his purchase of a small piece of land in the town of Casper, Wyoming, where he hopes to erect a monument to 'celebrate' the death of a young local man named Matthew Shepard, who was gay and was beaten to death by local thugs in 1998.

It was with some trepidation that I approached a very fat woman in a T-shirt and shorts who was holding a banner and standing on the Stars and Stripes. This turned out to be Mrs Abigail Phelps. 'Any time there is a group of Episcopalians we are goin' to be there to picket them. Jesus has banned their alternative life-style,' she told me conversationally, when she learned I was not an Episcopalian. 'We want to fill up the cup of their iniquity, see?'

I diffidently suggested that it was not a very loving message and she bristled: 'It's extremely lovin' and VERY CHARITABLE,' she replied at full volume. 'Heterosexuality is the only life that has been specifically mandated by the Lord Jesus Christ. What I am showin' here is the HIGHEST FORM OF LOVE. If you see someone's goin' wrong, you point it out, don't you? That's what we're doin'.'

I asked why she was standing on the American flag. 'September 11th was A VERY GOOD DAY, in deliverin' us the message that eternal power is God's. It was God's judgement on a sinful, faggot-ridden, fornicatin' nation. It was a sign.'

As I started to edge away. Mrs Phelps called cheerily after me: 'Have a good day!'

In the ballroom of a nearby hotel, Gene Robinson was putting his case for confirmation to a committee on the consecration of bishops. In front of a large audience – there were many more watching the hearing on closed-circuit television in an overflow room – and holding his microphone like a chat-show host, Robinson insisted that he was in a 'sacramental relationship' with Mr Andrew, adding that it was a reflection of God's desire for humans to be in sexual relationships. He claimed that his example was encouraging the disillusioned to return to the church.

In attendance was his 21-year-old daughter Ella, who read out a statement from her mother, Robinson's former wife, which comprehensively
disavowed the claims that he had deserted his family.

> This simply is not true. ... We truly have honoured the vows we said to love
> and honour each other. ... We have never made an important decision about
> our daughters without being in touch and doing it together. ... All of the spe-
> cial events that make for 'family' were planned and carried out by both of us.
> ... Our lives together both married and divorced have been examples of how
> to deal with difficult decisions with grace, love, integrity and honour. He is
> worthy of your affirmation. His charisma will draw in many more people to
> the church than will leave due to his sexuality. He will be a truly great bishop.[1]

'Give me a moment here,' said Robinson, wiping away an emotional tear.
'I think God is doing a new thing here. He is telling us that he wants gay
and lesbian people to be included. He wants them to know he is including
them in his embrace.'

His was not the only emotion: 'I love you, Gene. This is painful, but
we cannot so significantly depart from the teachings of the church without
consequences,' said Bishop Keith Ackerman of Illinois.

By this stage it was thought that Robinson had enough votes in the lay
and clergy houses of the convention to win affirmation, but it was less
clear that he had enough support in the House of Bishops, even though
the current New Hampshire diocesan, Douglas Theuner, and, tacitly,
Frank Griswold, the presiding bishop of ECUSA, were backing him.

Voting in the houses is complicated. Each of the 109 dioceses has eight
votes, four clergy and four lay, and in order to win endorsement, Robinson needed a clear majority of the votes within both groups in each
diocese – a tie was not enough – for it to count towards the simple majorities he required. The bishops would vote separately as individuals on the
following day and there a simple majority on a head count was required.

Frank Griswold's position, even as presiding bishop, was not in doubt.
He had written in the past on something called the Gamaliel Principle,
from the speech to the Sanhedrin in the Acts of the Apostles.[2] This was to
say that if a proposed plan was of human origin it would fail, but if it
came from God it would succeed: sometimes a debate which has become
bogged down could only be advanced by enabling an experience to happen and then afterwards reflecting on it in an attempt to discern the will
of Christ. Thus Robinson's appointment would test the will of God.
Others would say it pre-empted the debate.

The bishops were significantly divided, never more so than when two
with neighbouring dioceses appeared at a press conference. Asked whether
they thought Gene Robinson was suitable to be a bishop and, if not,

whether he was fit to be in holy orders at all, Bishop Wendell Gibbs Jnr of Michigan, young, bright and black, said sure, he had ordained a practising homosexual only recently. Next to him sat Bishop Edward Little II of Northern Indiana, older, white and a little mousy – no surprise really since he proudly admitted that his middle name was Stuart, and Edmund White had written his children's novel for him when he was a boy – and he thought Robinson should be excluded from the priesthood altogether. No question.

All sides came together, however, for a spirited Sunday morning service in one of the aircraft hangars of the convention centre, a vivid demonstration of the difference with the Synod service in York Minster three weeks before. They scarcely seemed to belong within the same church. Where York had been a grave and stately Sunday Eucharist, the sunlight shining in through the medieval stained-glass windows, this was an exuberant display of public worship, with trumpets and banners, vestments for all clerics and a spirited sermon from a Nigerian archbishop. Not Akinola but Josiah Idowu-Fearon, a more intellectual figure who managed to warn the congregation without demonizing them. 'When America sneezes the rest of the world catches cold. ... I want to plead with you not to sneeze too much because if you do we will all catch a very bad cold indeed and I want to avoid that.'[3]

The clergy and lay debate on Robinson's appointment was scheduled for the Sunday afternoon of the Convention. Three-quarters of an hour was allowed for what would be a very brisk debate, with speakers queuing up in long lines at separate microphones, pro and anti, to speak for a few moments each. No time for the waffly sermonizing interspersed with small jokes that characterizes Synod debates: there was time for just one point each. The Minneapolis debate was passionate and very American, much given over to the expression of feelings. Broadly Robinson's supporters argued that his election should be endorsed because he had been elected by the voters of New Hampshire and he was a good man: 'who are we to deny him his calling?' asked one. 'Let us affirm Gene and go on with the work of the church to fight hunger and clothe the naked, so our church will thrive,' said a young woman priest from Tennessee. There were noticeably more young delegates and more women in the pro-queue.

There was a sense, however, in which the debate had already been had over the previous decade or more. Too many people knew gay priests or had heard the arguments too many times before at previous conventions for much that was original or new to be said. Unlike in England, there was very little Biblical outrage and instead, from the pro-ordination side, an impatience to move on. If the rest of the world did not like the decision, they could lump it – America was taking a decision for itself. This was a local, democratic election. It need not affect worshippers anywhere else. And couldn't such a decision be prophetic for the rest of the Communion, just as the ordination of women had been? America, as in so many things, would lead the way: the telephone, the production line, supermarkets, openly gay bishops, all for the greater benefit of mankind.

The opponents were pained and aggravated, adamant that the election breached Holy Scripture and only incidentally that it threatened the unity of the worldwide Communion. This last was an argument that seemed to have very little resonance, as if it belonged to a faraway church in a distant hemisphere. More common was puzzlement: 'My people are not homophobes. They are good, hard-working people and they do not understand why we are having this debate,' said the Rev. James Flowers of Louisiana. Another speaker, from New Jersey, said that they would be removing themselves from the worldwide church 'and aligning ourselves with parts of the Communion which are dying like Great Britain'.

And with that the debate was concluded: 'We are Nicene Christians wrestling to discern the will of Christ,' said the chairman, while calling for no public demonstrations, whatever the outcome. The vote however was clear: 63 dioceses voted yes among the laity and 32 no, with 13 split and so not counted. The figure was almost identical for the clergy: 65 dioceses, yes, 31 no, 12 divided. It was a decisive two-thirds to one-third split.

The following day the bishops were to vote, but before they could do so two allegations suddenly surfaced to challenge Robinson directly and threaten the whole process. The first was produced like a rabbit out of a hat by David Virtue, a portly and red-faced journalist addicted to conspiracy theories and running his own raucously partisan conservative religious website. Sweating profusely and glowing with triumph, Virtue claimed to have unearthed a direct link between Robinson and a pornographic website via an Internet advice line called Outright.org that the canon had helped to set up some years before for youngsters in New Hampshire troubled about their sexual identity. Virtue pranced excitedly around the media centre shouting: 'I have found the smoking gun. We got him!'

Potentially as serious, a man in Manchester, Vermont, called David Lewis, who had been watching on television, sent an email message to friendly bishops saying that Robinson had inappropriately touched him during the course of a meeting some time before. His message added: 'As outstanding as Gene Robinson may have been as a priest ... my personal experience of him is that he does not maintain appropriate boundaries with men. ... He put his hands on me inappropriately every time I engaged him in conversation. No gay man has ever behaved towards me this way.'

It was not quite clear what Mr Lewis, a freelance theatre reviewer for a local free newspaper, hoped to achieve by this. He was certainly taken by surprise when fellow journalists suddenly started descending on his doorstep to ask what it was about Robinson's behaviour that had shocked him. It surprised his wife too, for she had never before heard him mention the allegations.

Both claims together brought the confirmation process shuddering to a halt as Bishop Griswold dispatched one of his colleagues, Bishop Gordon Scruton of West Massachusetts, to investigate. Robinson himself vanished back to his hotel with his entourage.

Opponents knew that if the investigation could be prolonged beyond the end of the Convention later that week, the confirmation would fall. If it lasted three months, the whole process of electing a new bishop of New Hampshire would have to start all over again, with Robinson fatally damaged. The Convention was meanwhile in limbo.

Robinson's supporters were confused and confounded by the sudden turn of events. Bishop Geralyn Wolf of Rhode Island said: 'I am going to contradict my grandmother and say where there's smoke, there's not always fire.'

The American Anglican Council made what it could of the desperate turn of events. Founded in 1996, the AAC, conservative and traditionalist, represented only 260 of the 7,300 Episcopalian parishes, but was increasingly active and vociferous in the campaign against Robinson and the liberal leadership of the church. The council maintains an office in Washington DC next to the similarly right-wing think-tank the Institute on Religion and Democracy (IRD), sharing a politicized social agenda and some key personnel and having links to people such as Marvin Olasky, a key adviser in the early days of the Bush Jnr White House and a man widely regarded as the most influential propagandist for the Christian Right in recent years. Both organizations are reported to have been heavily funded by Howard Ahmanson's Fieldstead Foundation and by a similar trust in the name of Sara, the wife of Richard Mellon Scaife, the oil millionaire who underwrote the campaign against President Bill Clinton in the late 1990s.[4]

In Minneapolis the AAC's chairman, the Rev. David Anderson, the Ahmansons' former minister at St James's Church, Newport Beach, California, haunted the press centre. Had he confronted Robinson personally with the suspicions so that he could respond to them himself? Certainly not. Why, he didn't even know the man, he said. 'I don't know whether Gene knew of the website link, but maybe he ought to have done,' Anderson continued sanctimoniously. 'I really believe the light of

Christ will shine into the dark corners of all our lives. I would like to see Gene Robinson's candidacy defeated but within the Anglican family this is simply not how we do business. We did not create a smear campaign.'

If there were those in Minneapolis who hoped that the light of Christ would expose Robinson as a pornographer, however, they were to be disappointed. In the event, the hiatus lasted less than a day before Scruton was back with his report. Neither charge bore close scrutiny. The website link had been established, apparently accidentally, within the previous three months whereas Robinson had ended his active association with the outreach programme some years before. It was pointed out that many respectable websites can find themselves inadvertently linked to pornography, accessible within a few clicks of a mouse.

David Lewis proved reluctant to pursue his charges. This was hardly surprising since they amounted to a complaint that Robinson had touched him on the forearm and shoulder during the course of a brief conversation at a public meeting in a crowded hall six years previously. The allegation was dismissed with some derision.

The smears had been crude and insubstantial, fuelled by wishful thinking and the sort of innuendo that now accompanies almost every American political appointment. Robinson's opponents were themselves uncertain, for Mr Lewis's intervention came out of the blue and caught them by surprise. The Internet allegation bore all the hallmarks of a desperate smear thought up in the wake of the clergy and laity vote which had suddenly precipitated the likelihood of Robinson's imminent election. It was all rather too convenient. But whoever promoted it had not done his homework properly, as it was easily discredited and had merely contributed to a shabby and demeaning episode.

So, 24 hours late, the bishops finally came to debate with much prayer and deep sighing. The opponents, realizing they were likely to lose, prepared for a dramatic walk-out but were wrong-footed. The vote came at the end of the afternoon's session: 62 bishops for and 43 against (four of the 109 dioceses were vacant), almost identical to the other two houses and a clear majority once more in favour of Robinson's confirmation. Presiding Bishop Griswold himself voted for the new Bishop. There was nothing to stop his consecration now, no archbishop to apply the thumbscrews as Rowan Williams had done to Jeffrey John a month earlier. The people of New Hampshire had spoken and democratic majorities of all three houses of the Episcopal Church's decision-making body had endorsed that decision. Robinson's lifestyle might not stand comparison with Dr John's personal abstinence but he had the weight of election behind him.

A group of the opposing bishops stood up and, led by Bishop Bob Duncan of Pittsburgh, made their pre-arranged announcement: 'This decision has denied the plain teaching of scripture and the moral consensus of the church. ... With grief we bishops must reject this action. May God have mercy on his church.'[5]

They were denied their dramatic walk-out, however, as Bishop Griswold immediately called for prayers and after that the day's session ended too, so everyone was leaving anyway. The opposing bishops already had their strategy all worked out, however: they announced immediately that there would be a meeting in Texas in October to discuss setting up a traditionalist church. There was much talk of lines being drawn in the sand and of the *Titanic* heading for the iceberg.

In England it was after midnight, but the Archbishop of Canterbury immediately issued a statement warning of difficult days ahead and calling for the needs of those who were greatly worried across the Anglican Communion to be 'heard, understood and taken into account'. He summoned the primates of the world to an emergency meeting in London in October to discuss the crisis, a decision taken in such haste that Lambeth had no idea who would pay the tens of thousands of pounds needed to transport the 38 archbishops across the globe and put them up in London. Attempts to persuade the Americans to pay were ignored and the £70,000 bill was to remain unsettled for months.

Almost as quickly English Evangelicals issued a statement, coordinated by Andrew Carey, warning that the election was contrary to the clear teaching of Scripture. 'The church is in a dreadful mess. It's fairly dismaying for many people,' said the son of the man who had led it until nine months previously. There appeared to be a certain degree of schadenfreude. 'The American church seems to have put itself outside the Christian tradition,' he declared.

Reaction from the developing world was uncompromising. Dr Mounir Anis, the Bishop of Egypt, North Africa and the Horn of Africa, said: 'We cannot comprehend a decision to elect as bishop a man who has forsaken his wife and the vows he made to her in order to live in a sexual relationship with another man outside the bonds of his marriage.'[6]

Gene Robinson, on the other hand, looked as pleased as Punch: 'Today is a wonderful day because Jesus is Lord. Yesterday was a terrible day but I am through it because Jesus is Lord,' he told the assembled press.[7]

Bishop Geralyn Wolf said wearily: 'If we could get off sex there are so many other issues that we could consider that would challenge our nation and our government.'

12

PAVED WITH
GOOD INTENTIONS

'By schisms rent asunder,
By heresies distressed.'
('The Church's One Foundation' by Samuel John Stone, sung at the consecration
of Gene Robinson)

Within six months of his enthronement on the uncomfortable and unforgiving stone seat of St Augustine, Rowan Williams found himself presiding over a worldwide church that not only seemed to be falling apart in his hands but positively revelling in doing so. A conjunction of accidental events had caused this: occurrences in the USA and Canada that might well have happened under his predecessor and a near-miss in England which he had partly brought on himself. There was a sense among Evangelicals that the long-awaited Armageddon was at hand. They embraced it only too willingly, their threats of splitting the church made with relish rather than reluctance, their expressions of sadness tinged only too well with righteous satisfaction.

Some of them had warned of the danger of appointing a liberal, unsound, un-Christian archbishop and it had all come to pass just as they had predicted. Williams appeared to be the hapless victim of events – as indeed he was – but he was patronized and imprisoned by the rhetoric of the Right. Forcing Jeffrey John to stand down had done him little good, reneging on an appointment he had earlier approved while winning him little respite from the Evangelicals. The conservatives had had their triumph in demanding the head of Dr John, but they were still nervous that they were losing the cultural war as exemplified by the election of Gene Robinson in America. That would be a harder nut to crack but they could not rest without forcing the issue. What happened in a small, remote corner of New England was held as a personal affront to all Christians everywhere in a way that the appointment of a female bishop in Massachusetts in 1989 somehow had not been.

There was a sense of malign plotting on both sides – a worldwide liberal conspiracy to hustle their gay friends into jobs as suspected by the conservatives on the one hand, or the long-awaited chance to bring down the church by the conservatives as imagined by the liberals on the other. In all this, what suffered was the image of Anglicanism as a broad and tolerant church, rather than one obsessed by the sexual practices of its adherents, and its victims were the gays within its chancels who were despised as sinners and tolerated only on sufferance. The long-standing commitment to listen to their experience was gone. Out of Africa came stories of young ordinands forced out of their theological training colleges for even suggesting that the Americans were entitled to take their own decisions.

In England in August a new group was formed called Inclusive Church, intending to show that not all Anglicans felt the same way as conservative Evangelicals and that the church was a welcoming institution. At its launch at Putney Parish Church, however, Colin Slee of Southwark preached a vehement sermon that did not sound terribly inclusive: 'Moderate and open people are not good at organized lobby groups and funding and that may be a good trait, but moderate people also need to recognize there is a sin called sloth.' Calling on them to rally, Dr Slee said:

> Churches with a sacramental tradition, a high doctrine of the church, have been willing, as for example when Dr Carey became archbishop, to say, 'OK we will work with him, we respect his office, we will do our best and we will co-operate,' and they did. But when Rowan Williams was appointed we see that there is a different definition of a high doctrine of the church whereby an archbishop can be unwelcome if you don't like him, subverted even by diocesan bishops and overseas archbishops. ... Some of the characterisation of the ordination of women, of gay and lesbian people and of broad and tolerant churches as 'failing' or unfaithful' is deeply hurtful.

He described threats to withhold financial contributions from central church funds as an abuse of a proper doctrine of the church. And he attacked the threatening of schism:

> To those who believe that schism is a threat worth making I would say that the boot is altogether on the other foot. Schism may doctrinally occur when the church tells someone they are no longer acceptable as a member, it is not something a member, or a group, can effect: that is different, that is sectarianism.[1]

Not all Evangelicals were comfortable with the idea of an inclusive church organization that insisted on a liberal agenda, just as not all Evangelicals were comfortable with their self-appointed spokesmen insisting that all within it felt the same about either Archbishop Williams or the issue of homosexuality. But its emergence was unsettling to the conservatives: Andrew Carey sneered that the Inclusive Church group had failed because it had only attracted 5,000 supporters within its first fortnight.

In early September Rowan Williams briefly broke free from his minders to write an article for an obscure magazine called *New Directions*, published by Forward in Faith, the Anglican pressure group opposed to the ordination of women. He had apparently promised them an article for some time but its imminent appearance caught his staff off guard. They had no idea he had written it until it appeared at the Palace in proof. In it the Archbishop contemplated for the first time the possibility of the break-up of the Anglican Communion. Not that he said so particularly clearly or decisively:

> Unity becomes finally unintelligible and unworthwhile when it itself ceases to be a theological category. Staying together is pointless unless it is staying together because of the Body of Christ. ... I think it worth working at structures in Anglicanism that don't either commit us to a meaningless structural uniformity or leave us in mutual isolation.

> I suspect that those who speak of new patterns, of the weakening of territorial jurisdiction and the like are seeing the situation pretty accurately. ... I don't expect the next few years to be anything other than messy as far as all this is concerned. The question is not whether we can afford mess, but whether we can hang on to common convictions about divine grace and initiative. ... The danger to avoid is an entirely modern or post-modern map of church identity in which non-communicating and competing entities simply eradicate the very idea of a communion of churches.[2]

Next into the fray was Archbishop Ndungane of southern Africa, who laid into his fellow African primates in an interview for the *Guardian*. His volume increased as he unburdened himself, particularly about Peter Akinola who had supplanted him as leader of the Anglican Communion in Africa, but his points were trenchantly expressed: 'There is an attempt to divert us from the major life and death issues in the world. There is a woman waiting to be stoned to death for adultery in Nigeria and yet we are not hearing any fuss from the leadership of the church there about that.'[3]

The Archbishop insisted that the US Episcopal Church had made its own decision over Robinson's appointment, as it was entitled to do:

> It is very arrogant to assume that the people in America do not know what they are doing. We have got to respect their decision. We have also got to respect the integrity of our provinces as autonomous entities whether we agree

with them or not, or whether they make us uncomfortable or not. ... Some kind of hypocrisy is going on in the church. Gene Robinson and Jeffrey John have been open and honest about their private lives. It is no secret that there are gay clergy and there are gay bishops and the institutional church seems to be turning a blind eye when we should be encouraging honesty. If Gene Robinson had kept quiet there would have been no issue.

I know people who are gay and lesbian who are African. The issue of orientation knows no culture and my fellow bishops are in denial, they have an ostrich mentality on this subject. Our church must learn how to live together as a diverse community. That's what should be on the agenda, not seeking to cast stones or talking about schisms.

Ndungane received a public and highly personal rebuke from Akinola, running throughout a four-page letter, a couple of weeks later. The Archbishop of Nigeria had only heard of the interview when he was sent a copy of the *Guardian* article by the Lesbian and Gay Christian Movement. He wrote:

We are poised using every gift of God available to us to defend orthodoxy, the integrity of the church and banish the erroneous teachings you plan to impose on us. Where the autonomy of any part of our communion becomes a scandal in the entire Christian world, then we must be humble enough to accept rebuke and correction. There is still room for repentance. Amen.[4]

Bishops in the Church of England appeared far more disposed to support Akinola's line than Ndungane's, content to overlook the shortcomings of the church in Africa, arguing instead that the undoubted courage of many of its leaders in the face of threats from militant Islam should be supported and that the West should not attempt to impose its values on a different culture. Articles along these lines by the likes of Durham's Tom Wright and Winchester's Michael Scott-Joynt ignored the fact that, unlike in the Victorian era, no one in the West was attempting to impose their values on the Africans and that indeed the reverse was the case: it was the Africans who were anathematizing the West.

Bishop Wright argued in an article in the *Independent*: 'There is an implicit sense that we in north-west Europe and America actually know how the world works and you poor people have to catch up. Those who enshrine tolerance become extremely intolerant of anyone who disagrees.'[5] This was not the case: no one in the decadent West was attempting to assert that Africans should start electing gay bishops. Nor, in a fit of postcolonial seemliness, were they generally daring to criticize, say, the Zimbabwean Anglican bishop who had supported the Mugabe regime and accepted two confiscated farms from him without apparent sanction or censure from his colleagues across the continent. But Africans like Aki-nola could not refrain from spying out the motes in the eyes of those elsewhere.

In mid-September 2003 English Evangelicals met in conference in Blackpool for the first time since 1987. It was the fourth such meeting of the National Evangelical Anglican Congress (NEAC) since the Keele gathering of 1967 and had been planned since long before the eruption of the gay issue, or indeed the appointment of Rowan Williams. Blackpool was chosen, as opposed to the Congress's previous venue, at a holiday camp at Caistor on the Norfolk coast, in deference to the movement's growing numbers, but it was an incongruous location. Along the wind-swept, rain-spattered front, late-summer holiday makers braced themselves for fun of an entirely different sort. The 'adult' comedians Roy 'Chubby' Brown and Bernard Manning reigned supreme at the promenade theatre, crotchless knickers were dispensed from bubblegum machines and little devils advertising the local Heaven and Hell nightclub glittered from the illuminations. This was Sodom-by-the-Sea, except for the nature of the sex it was advertising. Only the dull, redbrick Victorian chapels in the streets behind the seafront were dark, locked and cheerless as a wet Sunday afternoon.

The NEAC had originally been conceived by conservative Evangelicals as a demonstration of their hegemony, but gradually other groups had exerted themselves to modify the message. Rowan Williams was invited to lead prayers, though not to speak at any length – and was heartily ap-plauded by most of those present – and David Hope, the Archbishop of York, was allowed in too to address the Sunday night congregation. The meeting's motto was: 'Meeting the Challenge of the Gospel in a Changing World' and its watchwords were Bible, Cross and Mission: 'The Bible is our boundary, beyond which we will not stray and up to which we must live. The Cross is our centre, from which everything we believe and do flows. Mission is our task, to which we are all committed.' The latter was only added at a late stage in an attempt to save the Congress from com-plete introspection.

As a representative sample of Evangelicals, those attending were largely middle-aged and almost entirely white. Andrew Goddard, one of the younger participants, would subsequently write in an editorial for *Anvil*: 'It is a shame that a national congress could appear so sociologically unrepre-sentative and dominated by white, middle-class, middle-age and older males. How to avoid repetition of that impression is a crucial question for future Evangelical gatherings.'[6]

While women made their appearances leading some seminars, precious few were in headship on the main conference platform, whose leaders were the conservatives Chris Green of Oak Hill and Paul Gardner of Exeter. Others prominent in the organization were Bishop Wally Benn and Richard Bewes of All Souls, Langham Place. They were not too keen on allowing much dissension, indeed the keynote 'debate' of the gathering, on the issue of homosexuality, was not one at all since the only three speakers were all on the same side of the argument. Broadly, they were agin it. The only openly gay speaker present was Martin Hallett, a celibate himself who runs a counselling group called the True Freedom Trust.[7] His was the only walk on the wild side allowed.

Among the other speakers were Archbishop Jensen, popping up from Sydney, and David Holloway, still vicar of Jesmond, still fulminating about the wickedness of the Church of England just as he had 16 years before during the Higton debate in Synod. They had a fervent, excitable air. Holloway produced a document entitled, some way after Luther, '50 Theses on the Future of the Church of England':

> No solution to the slow death of the Church of England (or to the problems of the Anglican Communion) will come from the centre and the existing leadership. The solution will come – and is coming – informally at first, from a new federal structure of autonomous, local, Anglican churches but united together under members of the historic episcopate who confess the historic doctrines of the Church of England. ... These churches are especially likely to develop in dioceses where there is teaching in support of the homosexual agenda, or where there is support for open homosexual relationships among the clergy. ... There is a clear duty not only on bishops but also on clergy to banish and drive away all erroneous and strange doctrines contrary to God's word.[8]

Holloway was scathing about Archbishop Williams in the document and grew more so as he presented his theses before an enthusiastic audience of several hundred in the incongruously ornate setting of the Blackpool Winter Gardens Theatre. Heard without open dissent or contradiction by an audience which included three bishops – Wright of Durham, Buchanan of Woolwich and Broadbent of Willesden – Holloway implied that liberal bishops were somehow akin to concentration camp guards and compared Rowan Williams to a modern Jezebel for his false teaching:

> Homosexuality is so clearly a scriptural issue. Sexual activity outside marriage is sinful, homosexual practice is especially condemned. Modern Jezebels have to be disciplined. ... If you have a bishop who says on Monday morning that Jews and Muslims should be put into gas chambers, at what point is it right to

toe the line? We have lost our outrage over some things God says are absolutely wrong.[9]

In this fervent atmosphere, Archbishop David Hope's address was a
message of sweet reason. He told the Evangelicals to pipe down and listen
to other sections of Anglicanism, though he did it in such a gentle way
and, cleverly, utilizing Evangelical traditions, that they did not realize they
were being rebuked.

> If people out there - the world beyond the church - are only able to perceive
> the church in terms of politics, controversy, party spirit, then what hope is
> there that the gospel of reconciliation with which we have been entrusted is
> likely to be even heard, let alone taken seriously? ... The truth is that we have
> become altogether too ... noisy. Where is the stillness, the silence, the listen-
> ing - what used to be termed among evangelicals the quiet time? We need to
> be listening to each other and not least those who from the same basis of the
> same God's holy word may differ from us most sharply.[10]

The organizers were furious when they discovered a new moderate
Evangelical group called Fulcrum holding its first meeting during the
conference itself. When they found that John Martin, the former editor of
the *Church of England Newspaper*, who had been called in to act as press
officer for the Congress had actually had the temerity to join the new
organization, he was called in for a dressing-down. For the Congress was
also a launch-pad for another new grouping called Anglican Mainstream, a
name appropriated by conservative Evangelicals to indicate that they really
were representative of the broad body of Anglican opinion. Its figurehead
was Philip Giddings, and also involved were the organizers of the Oxford
Centre for Mission Studies. That two rival pressure groups should set up
at a Congress intended to demonstrate Evangelical unity was not really
what the organizers had been looking for.

Unlike previous NEACs, the organizers did not issue a statement at
the end. What they did instead - and without troubling to put it to a vote
- was to send a letter of support to the minority traditionalists on the
North American continent: 'We weep with you [and] assure you of our
deepest prayers and support. We pray also that He who is our Lord and
Saviour will encourage you all to stand firm.'

After the Congress, the hardliners met to discuss their dissatisfaction.
It had been far too moderate and inclusive for them, they decided. In
minutes from a post-mortem meeting and a further gathering attended by
representatives of the Church Society, Reform and the Fellowship of
Word and Spirit, strong criticisms were voiced particularly by the latter
meeting: the Archbishop of Canterbury was still a 'false teacher' and it

had been wrong for the audience to applaud him because it gave the false impression that he was welcome. The Archbishop of York's invitation was a mistake too since he 'was seen to rebuke us' and even James Jones, the impeccably Evangelical Bishop of Liverpool who had addressed the gathering 'was a complete let-down. Completely failed on the Bible and simpering words [on Dr Williams]. He was seen to be stepping back.'

Both documents criticized 'open' Evangelicals, especially Fulcrum, calling on the new group to apologize for organizing its meetings at the Winter Gardens during the Congress without prior approval. The Reformistas said they should be excluded from future gatherings: NEAC 'must blow out of the water the view that Evangelicalism is made up of three strands: open, mainstream and Charismatic. Open must be excluded.' Instead they wanted 'more repentance and more Biblical exposition', Evangelical bishops must not be feted and liberals must not be allowed on the platform. The organizing committee should only consist of conservatives to ensure there would be 'no Rowan Williams or equivalent problem'.[11]

Pete Broadbent, the Evangelical Bishop of Willesden, a former Islington Labour councillor who had been one of the signatories of the bishops' letter opposing Jeffrey John's appointment, was scathing, describing the conservatives as untrustworthy and two-faced:

> The document is explicit in asserting what Reform et al have always denied – that there was a deliberate attempt by the right wing to take over. ... These are, of course, the same people who write and speak to us telling us how much they respect us when we make a stand for what they believe in. In reality they are two-faced and show themselves to be completely untrustworthy. It would seem to me that there is little to be sanguine about in relation to the climate of Evangelical Anglicanism post NEAC. Whatever sense of unity we may feel across the spectrum, it is clearly not reciprocated.

A fortnight after Blackpool the US traditionalists opposed to Gene Robinson's appointment met in Dallas in surroundings about as far away from the famous seaside resort as could be imagined. But the enormous, ostentatiously plutocratic Wyndham Anatole Hotel was similarly preposterous for a gathering of Episcopalians, even ones as angry as those who gathered in its marble halls. The hotel proclaims itself the largest in the South West and appears to cover the ground area of a small English county. Its atriums, many stories high, could swallow a moderately sized cathedral, spire and all. 'You turn right at the elephants,' the receptionist said as she directed me to the lifts, and indeed she was right. Wandering for some minutes through echoing chambers, past restaurants and cafeterias, meeting rooms and souvenir shops, I eventually encountered the marble statues of two full-sized elephants. And there, round another corner were the elevators, ready to take me to my 17th-floor room, or to the rooftop restaurants a further ten storeys above that.

The Dallas meeting, called 'A Place to Stand', had been organized by the AAC some time before the general convention, but had grown in size since Robinson's endorsement. The gathering of the angry and disorientated from all over the US was large, affluent and almost entirely white. They believed their church was being taken away from them by a liberal conspiracy and they wanted to take it back, or alternatively declare independence, or demand their own bishops, or something – anything – to register their hurt. In this they were encouraged by the revivalist atmosphere of the gathering which had been organized by the Evangelical church in Plano, the comfortable conservative middle-class Dallas suburb which provides George Bush with one of his most solid constituencies. Plano has one of the largest Episcopal congregations in the USA, though not as large as the nearby gay church which has a rather more flamboyant style of Texan worship.

To demonstrate their seriousness, the 2,600 attendees were instructed to undergo a day of fasting in order to 'instead feast on the word and promise of God' before heading for Dallas and its gigantic meals. Clergy were instructed to wear clerical garb, laity to don 'business attire' and bishops to bring their rochets, clerical surplices – all injunctions which would have bemused English Evangelicals – to show just how serious they were.

Representatives of the Episcopal Church were barred, except for its press officer the Rev. Jan Nunley, who came as a journalist ('If you call a meeting, part of what you have to decide then is to invite people who are able to vote on the sort of decisions you wish to take,' David Anderson had said in Minneapolis). Presiding Bishop Griswold had to be content with sending a letter, copied to all bishops, piously hoping that everyone might move beyond the spirit of condemnation and insisting that the election in New Hampshire had not settled the question of human sexuality: 'I hope that in this world, so full of hate and so in need of love, the reconciling energy of the divine compassion may flow.'

That seemed unlikely. The Dallas-ites gathered in another aircraft hangar in the conference centre at the back of the hotel. 'What an incredible event we are about to witness! There's an electricity among us! It's the power of the Holy Spirit renewing His church! Amen!' declared the Rev. David Roseberry, rector of the Plano church, to rapturous applause. 'We are much larger than I had imagined. People are confused, angry, concerned, upset and grieved.' As he led them in a spirited rendition of

'Stand Up, Stand Up for Jesus', a cynical Evangelical voice beside me murmured: 'Are you impressed by the theological depth?'[12]

There was much talk over the next two days about hollow allegiance to a church in which people no longer believed and the immense ramifications of what they were doing, much fervour and proclamation of the salvation of souls, even injunctions for groups that disagreed over such minor matters as the ordination of women to overcome their differences and work together to defeat the elevation of a gay bishop.

But when it came to discussing what to do about it, there was more uncertainty and confusion. Should they leave and set up their own faithful church? No, they weren't going anywhere, it was the church that was leaving them – *they* weren't splitting. Should they seek alternative oversight? Yes, but with whom and would the alternative bishops be recognized? Lambeth had better. Hadn't it? Anyway, who's fault was it? Kendall Harmon, the canon theologian of South Carolina, had a little bit of suffering for them too: they also had sinned in allowing the church to arrive at its present pass. They were guilty as well: 'We have dropped the ball, Lord, give us back the ball by the power of your holy spirit.'[13] This went down well.

The meeting did receive some extraordinary external backing, however, from an unlikely source. The Vatican chose this moment to meddle in the internal affairs of another denomination by sending a letter of support to the Dallas meeting. Cardinal Joseph Ratzinger, the Roman Catholic Church's enforcer of doctrinal purity, wrote to the organizers praising their stand:

> I hasten to assure you of my heartfelt prayers for all those taking part in this convocation. The significance of your meeting is sensed far beyond [Dallas] and even in this city, from which St Augustine of Canterbury was sent to confirm and strengthen the preaching of Christ's Gospel in England. ... I pray God's will may be done by all those who seek that unity in the truth, the gift of Christ himself.[14]

The Vatican, which earlier in the summer had issued a document condemning homosexuality as evil and disordered, clearly thought it was winning. Maybe it would eventually even gain converts. There had been much gossip about the ailing Pope's conservative advisers circling round him, jockeying for position and influence, making policy behind his chair without his full knowledge or assent. There had been examples of doctrinally rigid and more than usually reactionary statements on matters such as the taking of communion in other churches, even the use of girls and women in church choirs, wording that had had to be explained away or softened after giving offence. But this was not one of those occasions. The 83-year-old Pope, third longest-reigning pontiff, was clearly weakening and shortly there would be whispering about his impending demise, but his mind remained acute even as his body faltered. He had focused his beady eye well enough on Rowan Williams the previous week when the Arch-bishop of Canterbury had paid his first formal visit to the Vatican and the one thing that came across loud and clear through John Paul II's wheez-ing, whispered discourse had been a warning against any softening of the line on gays. They remained anathema in Rome even as its training col-leges and those of the church across the Western world filled up with, camp young men preparing for ordination.

In Dallas, the cardinal's letter, written a couple of weeks before, was read out to wild applause, eclipsing even that accorded to a similarly supportive message from the Evangelical 'pope' John Stott. One wonders whether Ratzinger's words would have been received quite so rapturously by the low church Evangelicals in other parts of the Anglican Commun-ion, so suspicious of Rome's intentions and rapacity and so hostile to its pretensions. What would Peter Jensen, the Archbishop of Sydney, a man who found it difficult to imagine sitting through a Mass, have thought? Or those like Reform who saw interfaith services as their next target following the battle over homosexuality?

Two days into the Dallas meeting came the most sobering session, from church lawyers, brought in because of their sympathy for the cause. Theirs was an unwelcome message: it was not going to be easy to leave and take their churches with them. Twenty-five years before, the Episcopal Church had had the foresight to adopt the Dennis Canon, which shrewdly vested all church property in the national church. There was a question mark over clergy pensions too. The nine-step process to be considered by each dissident parish, as promulgated by the lawyers, had as its first injunction that they should get a good lawyer. Only ninth was it suggested that prayer might be adopted. 'This is no time for Lone-Rangerism,' one of the lawyers told the congregation. Separating could take years, would have to be formally endorsed at the next meeting of the general convention in 2006 and would almost certainly involve litigation to gain control of church buildings. It might be possible for a whole diocese to opt out if everyone agreed and Pittsburgh seemed likeliest to lead the way, under Bishop Duncan. But even there, Episcopalians loyal to the national church warned they would launch their own legal action if he tried it.

The meeting did at least adopt a resolution on its final day, repudiating the election of Canon Robinson and calling on the US Church's leaders to repent and reverse their schismatic actions: 'We declare our commitment to the Lord's life-giving teaching about sexuality and marriage embraced by Christians throughout all ages. ... We celebrate God's unconditional love for all people and we proclaim God's transforming power for everyone seeking sexual purity and wholeness.' The statement was ceremonially signed by everyone and the copies were borne to the front of the hall as the congregation sang: 'Oh God our help in ages past'.

It was all very cathartic, but was it more? Jan Nunley did not think so. 'I think people will go away from this conference feeling rather confused, expecting to see action for their money and not getting any for quite a while. You could say it was a case of the old Texas saying: All hat and no cattle,' she said.[15]

On the bus back to the airport, reality was dawning on two young curates from Colorado Springs. 'It's easy if your church is only 40 years old but ours is ancient – over 100 years – and it's valued at 16 million dollars. What about the people buried in the graveyard? It's all going to be very difficult,' said one, shaking his head. The Ethiopian minibus driver grew impatient: 'It breaks my heart,' he shot back over his shoulder. 'The church is fighting for sin. It is saying sin is OK. I'm from Africa. This thing for us is very annoying.'

The following week, 37 of the Anglican Communion's 38 primates gathered in London for their emergency crisis summit. Only the Archbishop of the Philippines was missing. Most were put up in an £84-a-night south London hotel, just down the road from the Palace and, incidentally, just a stone's throw from where Canon Jeffrey John still lived, though none chose to wander the 200 yards to meet him.

The day before the meeting, 18 of the primates gathered in some secrecy in a safely Evangelical central London church to discuss tactics for the following two days. Attempts by the *Church of England Newspaper* to infiltrate the meeting were not entirely resisted: Andrew Carey was allowed to attend because of his role as press spokesman for Anglican Mainstream.

Eighteen was slightly short of the number that Evangelicals had supposed would be on their side and indeed was just short of a majority for the coming meeting. The rhetoric which had previously been of threats and splits was also softening. The Evangelicals did not wish to be seen to be the ones splitting the Communion. Theirs was to be the voice of sweet reasonableness, placing the onus for anything they did on the liberals. It was *their* recalcitrance in electing a gay bishop that was forcing the issue.

What the traditionalists now wanted was some sort of disciplining of the US Church, at least a rebuke and a call for repentance. There was not much more they could do. They could not call for ECUSA's expulsion from the Communion and were anyway divided over whether that was the best strategy to adopt, not least because it would have left the American traditionalists in limbo and would probably not have troubled the Episcopal Church too much. It was also too soon to sustain a call for the Anglican Communion to recognize the American opponents of Gene Robinson in preference to the national church headed by Frank Griswold. What would they be recognizing? There was nothing there.

Indeed expulsion or any disciplining at all was constitutionally impossible since there was no mechanism to chastise an errant province in the way the Evangelicals would have liked. The provinces were autonomous and ECUSA had followed its own procedures in electing Robinson. Evangelicals might mutter about the election somehow having been rigged, or the Convention packed with unrepresentative liberals, but the argument could not be sustained that the Americans had not acted within their own rights. They had not denied any of the central tenets of Christian or Anglican tradition, unless you elevated homosexuality to that level. They had not been schismatic.

To attempt to discipline them on such grounds would undermine the autonomy of the provinces of a church that cherished its broad and tolerant traditions. The primates were not a curia, the Archbishop of Canterbury was not a pope, Anglicanism could not enforce its will, even if it knew what that will was. To go down that route was fraught with difficulties. Evangelicals might assume that their theology would always in future prevail but what if it didn't? What if the tide turned? What if his fellow primates ganged up against Akinola and denounced him for some future unspecified crime against the Communion? The way would be open for heresy trials, splits and realignments on a political whim. The most that could be hoped for was moral suasion. The traditionalists were in the unfortunate position of having to rely on the Episcopal Church to find a way out of the dilemma that it had insouciantly caused them. The trouble was, the Americans did not see what they had done in the same light at all. That is why they had elected Gene Robinson in the first place.

Part of what may also have caused the softening of the line for some developing-world archbishops was the fear of losing American financial backing, however often the Americans denied that they would take such action. The developing-world bishops were only too conscious that their missions and sometimes their dioceses were sustained by subventions from the Episcopalians. Some were very poor indeed. At least one Central-African bishop was worried about his clergy's pension fund. The Africans resented the Americans' largesse, saw it as post-colonial imperialism, but knew they couldn't do without it. Where would their paid-for jaunts around the world be without it?

On the first morning of the meeting, the caucus of archbishops met David Anderson of the American Anglican Council over breakfast in their hotel for further briefings before clambering aboard the bus to Lambeth Palace where each was greeted with a fraternal kiss and embrace by Rowan Williams.

Inside, the meeting commenced in the Palace's medieval guardroom, where in the Middle Ages troops had whiled away the days in readiness to protect archbishops from the London mobs. Now the archbishops only had themselves for company. Seated around a large square table, over-looked by stern glares from the portraits of past archbishops adorning the walls, they launched into long résumés of the reactions in their provinces to the election of the hitherto obscure New Hampshire canon. It took up much of the first day.

Outside, Inclusive Church had organized services at the three nearest parish churches to the Palace 'to surround the meeting with prayer'. Across the river at St Matthew's, Westminster, Walter Makhulu, the former Archbishop of Central Africa, whose successor was one of those most vehement against Robinson, could barely contain his impatience, describing the Evangelical primates as Taliban zealots. Makhulu, who had lived for many years in England and retired to London, had spent his primacy campaigning on the issue of Third-World debt and African poverty. He was hugely frustrated that homosexuality had assumed such importance among his fellow bishops. He was also deeply suspicious of American influence over the Africans on the issue, remembering clearly the attempts made on him in the past to soften his criticisms of the apart-heid regime in South Africa with offers of money and travel. His deep voice rang out through the golden gilt and scarlet Victorian splendour of St Matthew's: 'The notion of an exclusive church is totally abhorrent to me. It is a heresy in the same way as apartheid was. ... The Bible should not be used as a whip to beat those regarded as sinners.'[16]

From the first day's meeting there was only the briefest of commu-niqués. Mindful of the need to give the waiting media something to write about, the avuncular figure of Robin Eames, the Primate of All Ireland, was dispatched outside to speak. He was also the man who had presided over the Lambeth Conference debate five years earlier. Everything was going smoothly he told us now, just as he had said then that the debate had shown how Anglicans could disagree and yet still love each other:

I have never attended a meeting where there is such openness, frankness and honesty, where each and every primate has been given the opportunity to respond in his own way to the question that has brought us together. There is a tremendous anxiety to maintain the Anglican Communion on the basis of collegiality, co-operation and common faith. ... If I were to hazard a guess, it's moving towards a consensus situation. In Northern Ireland I am known as the divine optimist, but I would say that the Anglican Communion will emerge stronger than it has ever been.

On the second day, the primates moved on to agree a statement and adopt a strategy. There would be a commission to discuss not homosexuality but how best the Communion might tackle 'grave difficulties' when they arose in future. It would be required to report by September 2004 – a date which later slipped into early 2005 – and (it was eventually announced) it would be headed by the divine optimist himself, Archbishop Eames. Supposedly there was a year's breathing space in which to devise a policy for the future. This was action, but it was pretty tenuous stuff, inadequate to damp down a raging crisis, but the best that Anglicanism could manage.

The rest of the agreed statement, taken at face value, was a triumph of hope over experience. It had been reached, it was said, following a struggle, at great cost and with profound pain and uncertainty. It was bluntly critical of ECUSA, warning that if the consecration of Gene Robinson a fortnight later proceeded 'a crucial and critical point' in the life of the Anglican Communion would have been reached and its future would be put in jeopardy.

In this case, the ministry of this one bishop will not be recognised by most of the Anglican world and many provinces are likely to consider themselves to be out of communion with the Episcopal Church. This will tear the fabric of our Communion at its deepest level and may lead to further division on this and further issues as provinces have to decide whether they can remain in communion with provinces that choose not to break communion with the Episcopal church.[17]

The statement was handed out at Church House a few minutes before Dr Williams led Archbishop Eames and Drexel Gomez of the West Indies, representing the traditionalists, and presiding Bishop Griswold on to the platform of a press conference. Griswold sat smiling gently, in an otherworldly fashion. He had agreed the statement but immediately undermined it by making clear that in his view Robinson's consecration in New Hampshire would be going ahead as planned on 2 November. 'All ordinations are in some sense provisional but I stand behind the election process in New Hampshire and I fully respect the decision of the general convention,' he said.

Griswold even ventured a little joke when asked whether he would be attending: 'The second coming could occur but I am scheduled to be in New Hampshire ... something could happen to me but I hope it will not.' The presiding bishop's rationale for his stance was that his role was to uphold the decisions made formally and officially by the Episcopal Church – a statement denounced as 'dishonest, false and a great betrayal' by the primate of Central Africa.

Rowan Williams sighed:

> It has been a very remarkable couple of days. ... It has been honest and open and I hope we have grown in some real, shared understanding as a result. Such understanding as we have achieved has been very hard won. It could not have been otherwise given the widely differing positions ... talk of winners and losers is irrelevant.

On BBC Radio the following morning the archbishop was less sanguine, talking of a huge crisis looming in the Anglican Communion – 'it leaves the church with a huge challenge about coordinating its discipline and its legal systems across the world, which we have never had to do before' – and insisting that any change of policy would have to be talked through by the whole church. A measure of his distraction was a highly unusual spat with the interviewer, John Humphrys, who had slipped in a question at the end on the seemingly much less contentious issue of the immorality of the recent war in Iraq. It nevertheless threw the Archbishop. There was a 12-second pause while he collected his thoughts. 'Immoral is a short word for a very, very long discussion,' he said eventually. Williams was clearly caught off-guard and unprepared and, following representations by Jonathan Jennings, his press officer, who had been present, that section of the interview was cut, much to Humphrys' annoyance. It did the Archbishop little good since the incident – and a transcript of the expurgated version – was immediately leaked, leaving Williams appearing suddenly less sure-footed and more compromised than ever.[18]

In far-off New Hampshire a statement by Gene Robinson's diocese made clear that there was no chance of his consecration being abandoned – 'We warmly invite the primates and anyone else in the Anglican Communion to come to New Hampshire and experience our shared communion here' – and the AAC's David Anderson went for overkill in the opposite direction by claiming that people could die because of the service. 'When one gets a reckless disregard for the values and life and freedom of others, it goes on the internet within minutes and mullahs download the messages and read them out at Friday prayers and Christians may die ... apparently the church does not feel guilt about this because it shows no sign of repenting and changing its ways,' he said, without indicating whether this was a reasonable thing for mullahs to do, or whether the people of New Hampshire should take into account the bigotry of fanatics of different religions in far-off places before making the choice of their own bishop. Even when New Hampshire had had a heterosexual bishop, that had not stopped people killing Christians, nor had the fanatics felt they needed any excuse to do so. There subsequently appeared to be no killings attributable to the consecration of Gene Robinson.

It was time for the other side to speak, and the following weekend in Manchester the Lesbian and Gay Christian Movement had organized a conference. A year earlier they had expected Rowan Williams to attend but that had ceased to be a possibility some months before. But such was the nervousness of the Church of England that Nigel McCulloch, the Bishop of Manchester, had cancelled the Sunday morning service that the LGCM had been told it could have in his cathedral. His pusillanimity was compounded by a statement insisting that he was not being homophobic but merely acting in the light of current 'sensitivities'.

The conference went ahead without McCulloch's blessing but with several other bishops and retired bishops - including David Jenkins - in attendance. It even had the ethereal presence of Gene Robinson himself, beamed in and beaming, on a fuzzy satellite link from Manchester, New Hampshire, to Manchester, old Lancashire, to warm applause. More striking was the appearance in person of Michael Ingham, the Canadian Bishop of New Westminster:

> We believe that God is calling the church to end discrimination and prejudice based on sexual orientation. We believe that the continued exclusion of people through the misuse of scripture and the repetition of inherited and unexamined prejudices against minorities is a sin against the love of God.
>
> Our actions in Canada and the US have been guided by the Holy Spirit, which is the Spirit of freedom and of truth. They were taken in response to changes in the sciences and social sciences that affect our understanding of human sexuality. They were not taken in rebellion against scripture but in faithfulness to its constant and greater witness that God does not deny his own children the bread of compassion and justice. ... Some of the solutions being proposed today by proponents of so-called orthodoxy - solutions which would impose for the first time the necessity of a universal consensus on the church - are the same arguments that were made by the opponents of the very English Reformation they claim to represent.[19]

Ingham argued that homosexuals were the only members on whom the church sought to impose celibacy. It was a cruel double standard that denied and diminished the humanity of gay and lesbian people, denying them the legitimate yearnings for stable, faithful and lifelong intimacy:

> Will the church continue to call for costly sacrifice by its gay and lesbian members through the renunciation of their full humanity but not take upon itself the costly sacrifice of witnessing to God's love in homophobic societies or to other world religions? Why are we accused of conformity with secular trends in western society while conformity with inherited prejudice and the standards of other religions goes unchallenged?

It was a powerful address, understandably well received by the audience.

A week later still and, with the first wintry winds blowing through the fall foliage of New England, it was time for Gene Robinson's consecration as bishop coadjutor, ready to succeed Douglas Theuner as ninth Episcopal Diocesan Bishop of New Hampshire when he retired the following spring.

Despite the primates' call, there was never any question of Bishop Griswold asking Robinson to stand down. He did not even try. Nor did Rowan Williams. Robinson himself had barely considered it: 'The only thing that would keep this from going forward is if I cannot be there for some reason,' he said. 'This has strengthened my faith. God seems so very close now that prayer almost seems redundant. I feel absolutely surrounded by his love and his presence is almost palpable to me. I am calm and at peace and I am prepared to move forward. To raise the issue of homosexuality above the Nicene Creed and belief in the Trinity seems to me to border on idolatry.'[20]

The ceremony itself was to be held in the largest indoor arena in the state: the ice hockey stadium of the University of New Hampshire on the outskirts of the small town of Durham, about 30 miles east of the state capital Concord. Ecclesiastically the Whittemore Centre, with its banks of concrete steps, its motifs of the hockey team and the long flat tundra of its central arena, lacked something of the ambience of the cathedral at Durham, England. Robinson had received a picture postcard of the beautiful, high altar in that great cathedral from an anonymous correspondent in England a short time before. On the back, it bore the inspiring message: 'You fornicating lecherous pig'.

Robinson had by this stage given up reading, or attempting to reply to, the more obscene messages he had received. Like the Bishop of Oxford, he too claimed that the thousands of communications ran two-to-one in his favour. But the messages of hate were sufficiently serious for him to be given police protection – one reason he had not travelled to the LGCM conference in Manchester – and for the ceremony itself he and his partner Mark Andrew wore bullet-proof vests under their outer garments. Presiding Bishop Griswold wore one too. It may have been the first time in the developed world in modern times that a bishop had needed such protection under his vestments at a religious ceremony.

On the rainy Sunday afternoon, there was a heavy police presence, some mounted on horseback, and the congregation had to undergo electronic searches to get inside. Penned in a small corral behind crash barriers the Rev. Fred Phelps had shown up with no more than about half-a-dozen bedraggled fellow protestors, though there was no sign of his large wife. Perhaps she had better things to do. Phelps and his cohort held up banners depicting their normal messages: 'Fags Doom Nations', 'AIDS is God's Curse', 'Fag Church, Fag Gospel' and 'Thank God for September 11', together with depictions of little matchstick men bending over.

Opposite his group was a rather larger gathering of university students from the campus, calling in a friendly fashion for peace, love and tolerance for gays. Down the pathway between them strode the hundreds attending the service. They were old and young, white and black, middle-aged and affluent. There were many clergy in dog collars and young people from parish choirs and youth groups across the state.

Inside they had covered over the floor of the arena (this was not going to be a Consecration on Ice), a silver band played, a group of children rang handbells and a massed choir sang. The stadium was far from full, but about 3,000 people finally filtered in. As a result of the security the service started late but it was preceded by a colourful procession of banners from local churches, the massed ranks of more than 50 bishops and an altar server bearing a large white paper dove, bobbing and fluttering on the end of a long pole. Among them were Robinson, Mark Andrew, Robinson's former wife Isabella McDaniel and their daughters Ella and Jamee with their families. Robinson's sister and his aged parents had flown in from their old Kentucky home. Mrs Imogene Robinson had told her local paper proudly the week before: 'To me he's always been a wonderful boy. We've been proud of him all his life.' The Kentucky *Lexington Herald-Leader* with a touch of pride referred to the local boy-made-good as the most controversial Anglican leader since Henry VIII.

The bishops had certainly turned out in force. Griswold was indeed present, as was his predecessor, Edmond Browning. Barbara Harris, the first woman bishop, was there as was the president of the New England Episcopalian province, Chilton Knudsen, and Krister Stendhal, the Lutheran former Bishop of Stockholm. There were Canadian bishops, including Michael Ingham, and an Irish bishop, but none from the

Church of England. Barbara Harris had already given her opinion of the furore: 'This is a power struggle as to who is going to run the church, the white boys who have always run it, or some different kinds of people.'[21]

The congregation sang 'The Church's One Foundation', with its splendid warnings against schism. This was originally written by the young English curate Samuel Stone in 1866 to counter the heresy of Bishop Colenso of Natal because of his questioning of the doctrine of eternal punishment – the same event that led to the summoning of the first Lambeth Conference. In England the third verse, with its warnings against heresy and schism ('Though with a scornful wonder, men see her sore oppressed ...'), is normally omitted these days, but it was defiantly sung at Gene Robinson's consecration.[22]

At the start of the service came the traditional moment for opponents to protest against the appointment – usually a formality but not of course on this occasion. Griswold asked: 'If any of you know any reason why we should not proceed, let it now be made known.' A small delegation, nestling together at the foot of one of the aisles, stepped forward, but they were beaten to the microphone by the cadaverous and black-clad figure of the Rev. Earle Fox of Pittsburgh, emerging like the bad fairy at Sleeping Beauty's christening from an entirely different part of the congregation.

This was a man whose early promise as a theologian had been warped and worn away by his gathering demons and vehement obsessions. He moved with alacrity to denounce the proceedings. 'It breaks my heart to do this,' he said before starting with some relish and a flurry of statistics to describe what homosexual men do to each other: 99 per cent engaging in anal sex and so forth. As he reached the 70 per cent who he said engaged in rimming, a practice he began to elucidate, Bishop Griswold blanched and said: 'Please spare us the details.' 'You understand what I am talking about?' said Fox. 'Yes, I think we do,' said Griswold weakly.

After such a virtuoso performance the other, more dignified protests could only be an anticlimax. Mrs Meredith Harwood of a church in New Hampshire described the consecration as the 'defiant and divisive act of a deaf church' leading down the path of unrighteousness. Then the Suffragan Bishop of Albany, David Bena, read a statement of behalf of 19 serving and seven retired bishops: 'The consecration poses a dramatic contradiction to the historic faith and discipline of the church. We join with the majority of the bishops in the Communion and will not recognize it. We also declare our grief at the actions of those who are engaging in this schismatic act.' With that, the protesters left to join a congregation at a church two miles away holding a sorrowful service of their own.

There were no further disruptions. The bishops crowded round Robinson to lay their hands on him at the consecration and, in all other respects, the ceremony was entirely traditional. Hymns such as 'Amazing Grace' and 'For All the Saints' and the great psalm 100, 'All People that on Earth Do Dwell', were sung. Bishop Theuner gave a notably pugnacious address:

> Gene, you will be asked to acknowledge that you are persuaded that 'God has called you to the office of bishop.' The emphasis is on God, not on you. Today we honour not you, but God and God's call through God's church as our church understands it.

> I am not talking about quoting; I am talking about comprehending. Our Lord's attention was directed to the outcast and the marginalized. ... His wrath was reserved for the members of the religious establishment of his own faith community. ... O to be sure, the Pharisees and Sadducees were generally fine people. And yet we are told by our Lord, they went down from the temple condemned because they 'bind heavy burdens, hard to bear, and lay them on men's shoulders'. They were chastised by our Lord because they thought people were made for their religious establishment; not their religious establishment for people.[23]

With heavy irony, he quoted an earlier South Carolina divine who thundered from his pulpit before the Civil War: 'If the scriptures do not justify slavery, I know not what they do justify. If we err in maintaining this relation, I know not when we are right – truth then has parted her usual moorings and floated off into an ocean of uncertainty.' Theuner added: 'Sound familiar?'

Towards the end of the three-hour ceremony, Robinson himself, now dressed in his gold robes and mitre, stepped forward. There were tears in his eyes. Acknowledging the 'faithful and wonderful people' who might leave the church and who would be welcomed back, he added:

> This occasion is not about me, but a God who loves us beyond our wildest imagination. It's about so many other people who find themselves at the margins and for whatever reason have not known the ear of the Lord's favour. ... He is a God of unimaginable compassion and love. We couldn't buy this kind of publicity. Let us use it for God, for the Good News ... to reach out to all those in the world who so desperately hunger for it.[24]

As the procession of bishops moved off at the end, the small figure of the new bishop looked up. He had one of the broadest grins imaginable. It was not just a look of triumph but of simple happiness. The congregation burst into applause and for the first time in my professional life at a meeting, I did the same.

Outside in the dark and rain, the small band of Phelps's followers had diminished while the group of student supporters of Gene Robinson had grown to several hundred. They were singing genially. The congregation smiled as it walked past them.

In London, late at night, Rowan Williams issued a statement, resigned in tone: 'The divisions that are arising are a matter of deep regret. They will be all too visible in the fact that it will not be possible for Gene Robinson's ministry as a bishop to be accepted in every province in the Communion.'

Elsewhere the traditionalists had their condemnation already prepared. Greg Venables, the primate of the scattered Anglicans of the pampas, had prematurely declared the church already split a fortnight earlier. 'The breaking has already happened; we can't wait for the break. ... We said way back that if anybody goes ahead and does this then there will be impaired Communion,' he had announced then with an air of satisfaction.[25] Now he had to row back a bit, saying that the consecration had robbed the church of a dialogue it could have had to find a way forward.

The American Anglican Council called the consecration 'a grievous day in the history of our Church'. Uganda severed its ties with the Episcopal Church and the Primate of Kenya, the Most Rev. Benjamin Nzimbi, announced: 'The devil has entered our church.' In Sydney, Archbishop Jensen denounced Robinson as a bishop of disunity: 'I myself would have preferred if the Archbishop of Canterbury had spoken more clearly ... about the fact that this is against the Bible and should not have gone ahead because it is against God's word.'[26]

In the weeks to come 13 provinces of the developing world declared themselves out of communion with the American church and issued critical statements. The Ugandan church withdrew invitations to representatives of ECUSA to the enthronement of its new archbishop in the most insulting terms it could summon up in its self-righteousness. Canon Stanley Ntagali, the church's provincial secretary, wrote:

> If we fall silent about what you have done promoting unbiblical sexual immorality and we overturn or ignore the decision to declare a severing of relationship with ECUSA, poor, displaced persons will receive aid. ... The Gospel of Jesus Christ is not for sale, even among the poorest of us, who have no money, Eternal life, obedience to Jesus Christ and conforming to His Word are more important.[27]

The Ugandans decided to invite a delegation from the American Anglican Council instead. The bishops of the Congo condemned the US and Canadian churches in a statement of their own, evidently believing that homosexuality was akin to a noxious gas: 'In its position of moral keeper, the Church must do all in its power to prevent immorality and itself avoid being corrupted and in turn corrupting the whole world.'[28]

However, the Africans and others did not start refusing aid from the devil-possessed US church. No American missionaries were dismissed. The Council of Anglican Provinces in Africa, chaired by Archbishop Akinola, not only accepted $80,000 for its new headquarters building, but also sent a representative to Washington DC's diocesan convention in early 2004. The diocese of Honduras, whose bishop, Lloyd Bishop, had called on Americans to financially starve the US church, happily accepted renewed aid for a further three years from the Washington diocese, one of the most liberal in the Episcopal Church. A diocesan spokesman said: 'My feeling is that these guys are grandstanding. They keep vilifying us but they keep seeking the benefits of an ongoing relationship. It's a great gig: you get money from us; you curry favour with homophobes at home and abroad and you get to look courageous without taking any sort of risk.'

In the USA itself, Bob Duncan, the Bishop of Pittsburgh, announced the formation of a new network of Anglican Communion dioceses and parishes under his own supervision and that 13 of the Episcopal Church's 98 dioceses would be joining it and seeking recognition from overseas. The announcement, however, was premature and went off at half-cock – within days several bishops of those dioceses had said they would not be joining. Nevertheless, the network announced that it would be holding its first 'organizing convention' back at Christ Church, Plano, in late January 2004, claiming they were being backed by Rowan Williams in doing so.

The Americans' touching faith in the Archbishop of Canterbury intervening – a strikingly different attitude towards him than that of their English conservative Evangelical allies – had no basis. 'I have no authority to determine what happens in other provinces,' Williams told me.

That was not quite how it appeared a few weeks later at the Church of England Synod in February 2004, however. The Archbishop gave a brief statement about the situation in the United States but failed to follow his text, instead talking loosely round it, as clever men are prone to do. He said that he was committed to searching for a place for all Episcopalians to remain within the church and had been involved in working towards 'some sort of shared future and common witness so far as is possible'. But he then went on to add: 'I've been following sympathetically the discussions around the setting up of a network within the Episcopal Church ... engaged in negotiating some of these questions of Episcopal oversight.' The word 'network' was heavily loaded because that was the way the conservative Episcopalians were describing themselves. They immediately claimed that this showed they had the Archbishop's explicit support, whereas all Williams was trying to do was to explain that he hoped everyone could be kept together. It was pretty close to intervention in another province.

Since Dallas in October, the AAC's tactic had been to insist that the traditionalists were not leaving the church and that their goal was to seek alternative oversight from like-minded bishops. This strategy was dented when a letter was leaked in January 2004. It was written by the Rev. Geoff Chapman, rector of St Stephen's, Sewickley, the largest church in the Pittsburgh diocese, and outlined in some detail for similarly minded congregations how to go about splitting the church. It made clear that while adequate Episcopal oversight was the immediate aim, 'our ultimate goal is a realignment of Anglicanism on North American soil committed to faith values and driven by Gospel mission' – a replacement jurisdiction which would seek to achieve a split while enabling the parishes to take their churches with them. It added that the task would be difficult, urged parishes to gather together in clusters and make 'ready for a season of conflict if necessary'. It advised them how to withhold money from their dioceses and then added: 'We think that the political realities are such that American revisionist bishops will be reticent to play hardball for a while. They have just handed the gay lobby a stunning victory but are being forced to pay a fearsome price for it. ... Read your Bible. Pray lots. Be aware of Satan's opposition and resist him.'

So sensitive was the issue and so blatant Mr Chapman's strategy letter that the AAC's leadership immediately issued a statement insisting that alternative oversight was indeed the limit of its ambition. But when Don Johnson, the conservative Bishop of West Tennessee, who had voted against Robinson's confirmation, issued a diocesan letter condemning Chapman's splitting tactics, he was petulantly condemned by the AAC, without apparent irony, for having the temerity to exceed his Episcopal authority.

A meeting of British Evangelicals and Americans in Charleston, South Carolina, in early January saw splitting as the only way. Men such as Kendall Harmon believed that the Archbishop of Canterbury would have to choose, between them and perdition. Peter Walker of Wycliffe Hall, the Evangelical training college in Oxford, told the meeting that there was a growing archway of interest between the Anglicans of the global south and conservatives of the north, which was becoming daily stronger, regardless of any future involvement by the Archbishop: 'The question is whether Canterbury will be the keystone of the arch or will it be left out.

... We must take the high ground and not give in. We must not get off the ship. This is a very difficult time.'

The Rev. Ephraim Radner, a former African missionary now ministering to the heathen in Pueblo, Colorado, said: 'By the end of 2004 there may be a situation on the ground of provinces terminating communion with ECUSA that is so extensive that Dr Williams will have no choice but to deal with it.'

Chris Green, vice-principal of Oak Hill, the Evangelical college in north London – the man who had organized the separate prayer room when Rowan Williams attended the Blackpool Congress – added: 'There are very senior figures among Evangelical circles in Great Britain who would like to say to you: "Elect your own presiding bishop and force Rowan Williams to choose".'

Drexel Gomez, the Archbishop of the West Indies, declared: 'The battle is on and we must not allow ignorance to prevail. ... My own opinion is that discipline should be applied to all bishops who voted aye on Gene Robinson and all who co-consecrated him.' He told the gathering that the bishops of the developing world wanted to attend no more meetings about sex. 'The Anglican Communion stated its position on sex at the Lambeth Conference. ... I don't believe that our brethren in the global south will just break camp and leave but they are not prepared to compromise. After September [we] will want some definite action.'

But it was by no means certain how far the internal sundering was reaching in the USA. Many resented the partition of their church, the denomination they had chosen. The New York Times reported that while some lifelong Episcopalians were leaving in alarm over its alleged headlong rush to humanism, mainly to join the Catholic Church, others were coming in – some of them Catholics in quiet rebellion against the Vatican's conservatism and in disgust over the church's paedophile scandals.[29]

During a trip to Florida, George Carey lamented: 'The Anglican Communion [does not have] elastic boundaries. It is the same with sexuality. We can't start reinventing the wheel and say that there are actually three sexes now: men, women and homosexuals. We are bound by what Scripture says. I don't think we have any grounds whatsoever to make these changes that we are doing. This is the most critical issue since the Reformation. It affects the unity of the Communion.'[30]

In December, to keep the pot boiling, Anglican Mainstream devised an Internet petition appealing to the Archbishop to provide alternative oversight for congregations whose members could not stomach the idea of Gene Robinson's consecration. They wanted a million signatures by Christmas, describing the petition as 'your chance to make the Anglican

Communion as God intends it to be'. The numbers were fairly slow in coming but jumped suddenly when archbishops from Uganda, South East Asia, the Congo, Central Africa, Kenya, the Indian Ocean and South America signed up every member of their archdioceses. This suddenly produced 13 million supporters, which Mainstream blandly announced represented 'a majority' of the 70-million-strong Anglican Communion – shaky maths and shakier polling practice. For good measure, the petition announced that Robinson had only been endorsed by 'a minority group' in the American church. In the small print, the petition appeared to have been signed by only 4,013 individuals, 3,192 families, 249 parishes and eight dioceses out of 500.

Out in the world such disingenuous nonsense passed most people by. In June 2003 the US Supreme Court overturned Texas's anti-sodomy laws, removing the state police's right to prosecute couples they found privately in bed together. And in November the Massachusetts Supreme Court ruled that the state's constitution entitled gay couples to all the rights of marriage. President George W. Bush vowed to overturn the ruling, or to legislate against it by introducing a constitutional amendment, for the prospect it opened up was ghastly. As spring 2004 advanced, however, mayors all over the USA were starting to conduct civil wedding ceremonies for gay couples. Gene Robinson himself said he would marry his partner Mark at a minute's notice, given the chance. In Britain too, the government promised legislation to formalize the civil rights of cohabiting partners, so that they could receive benefits, have hospital visiting rights and inherit property. It wouldn't be a marriage but it would be a civil contract. George Carey popped up on the David Frost programme to say that he could not see any problem with this, just so long as it wasn't a marriage. But when the government initiated legislation enabling the transgendered to marry, the Church of England again reacted with alarm, even though clergy would have a conscience clause allowing them to refuse to conduct such ceremonies. Why, it said, such clergy might even conduct such services not realizing whom they were marrying.

These were developments potentially much more far reaching for gays and their societies than the consecration of a gay bishop in a faraway state of which Africa knew little. Gene Robinson continued to conduct services, Africans continued to worship, the weather continued cold, but the sky didn't fall in. At its General Synod in May 2004 the Canadian Anglican Church decided it would consider allowing all its dioceses to follow New Westminster's lead and authorize the blessing of same-sex partnerships. Now there was a whole province going out on a limb. Predictable outrage followed. In leisurely fashion, the commission intended to save the Anglican Communion decided it couldn't meet until February 2004, four months after Lambeth's emergency summit.

In the same week that the commission met for the first time at Windsor, the Church of England's General Synod in London at last discussed the gay issue in a debate on the bishops' recently published *Some Issues in Human Sexuality*, discussed in Chapter 3 of this book. The tone was surprisingly liberal, the conservative Evangelicals seemingly demoralized or unable to muster their previous moral indignation or even marshal their arguments coherently. It was almost as if they had nothing new or challenging to say.

Brian McHenry, one of the senior lay members of the Synod, warned: 'There is increasing evidence that we are not in tune with public opinion. It is uncomfortable to be a member of a church which is perceived to be homophobic, hypocritical and discriminatory.' The RAF's chaplain-in-chief, Ronald Hesketh, told the assembly how easily the armed services had accepted homosexuality in the ranks once it was no longer prohibited: 'One day homosexuality was banned; the next it was not an issue. ... My adult son tells me to get a life. This is a non-issue to many in his generation.' Even an elderly, celibate, nun, Sister Rosemary, from a religious community in Nottingham, told the Synod that close companionship with another loved person was the best environment in which the majority of people could flourish: 'Forced celibacy is as abhorrent as forced marriage,' she said vehemently.

But the most arresting speech was by Paul Collier, pony-tailed, thin and nervous, a vicar from south London. He was gay, living with a partner, he said. Abstinence was very different for heterosexual people who lived in the hope and expectation of marriage. For gays it could only be sterile and hopeless. 'I continue to trust God utterly to lead us as Christians into all truth.'[31]

He was warmly applauded, with even Rowan Williams joining in. The debate did not change church policy but it did give rise to some hope for the future.

In March 2004, the first meeting of US Episcopalian bishops since Robinson's appointment came up with a possible compromise for dissident parishes. This would allow them to apply to their dioceses for oversight by a conservative bishop rather than their own diocesan, though it did not allow them to leave and set up their own separate jurisdictions. It was immediately and contemptuously rejected by the American Anglican Council as 'woefully and undeniably inadequate'. So much for conciliation.

13

WHO BEARS
THE COST?

*'We are now ready to start on our way down the Great Unknown. ... What falls
there are, we know not; what rocks beset the channel, we know not; what walls rise
over the river, we know not. Ah well! We may conjecture many things. The men
talk as cheerfully as ever ... but to me the cheer is sombre and the jests are ghastly.'
(John Wesley Powell, 13 August 1869, on the first white expedition down the
Grand Canyon)*

On the morning of Tuesday 11 September 2001, a young man – a
committed Christian Evangelical, former assistant to John Stott
and, as it happens, a friend of mine – set out on a routine business trip from his home in Manhattan. He was late for his flight to San
Francisco from Newark Airport and as his taxi speeded down the New
Jersey turnpike he looked across at the twin towers of the World Trade
Centre looming above the New York skyline. They were gleaming in the
early morning sun and he thought how beautiful they looked. At the
airport he checked in and made it to the departure gate just in time. They
were closing it and told him that he could take the next flight out, which
was leaving only a few minutes later; but, as he had a reservation and was
already there, they finally let him board. It was a routine thing and he
made it to his seat just as the aircraft started moving.

A couple of hours later, high above the Mid-West, the pilot announced
that the flight was being aborted as all planes in the country were being
grounded. It wasn't until they had landed in Nebraska that the passengers
learned the reason why. All the airport televisions were switched to pictures of the twin towers and the Pentagon in Washington, ablaze. The
passengers debated what to do and eventually a group of them, including
my friend, decided to hire a car together and head home as fast as they
could. As they drove back to Manhattan, listening to the growing disaster
on the car radio, it dawned on him that the flight he had nearly caught –
and would have done had he been only a couple of minutes later – was

the one that had crashed with the loss of all souls on board in a field in Pennsylvania as hijackers tried to turn it towards Washington. Much worse than that realization though was the sickening knowledge that his former companion had a job at the top of the World Trade Centre. His mobile phone did not answer.

This was a relationship that had now ended but which my friend had kept deeply to himself. His homosexuality was hidden from all but the closest of his acquaintances. Although his parents knew, they were deeply unhappy about it, to such an extent that his father had refused ever to discuss the issue. He had only come out to John Stott after stopping working for him. Stotty said very little, for there was little they could discuss. 'Well, you know what I think about that,' he said. It was not a dismissal and was respectful, but nevertheless their friendship was at an end.

My friend was distraught about the loss of his former partner. He knew now that he must be more open, that he could not keep such a loss bottled up within himself and that he would have to come out. It was not until several days later, after he finally arrived back in New York, that he discovered that his friend had after all survived, saved by being late for work.

This may sound like one of those anonymous little stories that some vicars tell to illuminate an otherwise trite and unconvincing sermon, but it happens to be true. My friend remains anonymous, though Mr Stott will undoubtedly know who he is, because he has not fully come out and has still not told his relatives his secret.

✠　✠　✠　✠　✠

In Tonbridge, a commuter town in Kent, in a neat little semi on a housing estate, lives Angela Widdicombe. She is a devout Christian. On her bookshelves sit religious books and on her upright piano the music was open on the day that I went to see her at the old nineteenth-century hymn 'Brightest and Best of the Sons of the Morning'. She works part-time as a volunteer at the local Christian hospital, Burrswood, which is how I have come to meet her because my wife works there too. Angela's late husband was organist at their local church for many years and she herself organized the choir for eight years after his death until a new conservative Evangelical vicar arrived and decided he did not want to be bothered with traditional hymn singing any more.

In the last year Angela has stopped going to the church she has attended for decades because of her vicar's obsession with homosexuality. He is a member of Reform and she showed me recent parish magazines.

In one edition of *Contact*, the Rev. Stephen Seamer, the vicar of the parish of St Peter and Paul, with St Andrew, St Philip and St Saviour, fulminates against the appointment of Rowan Williams:

> The only conclusion which I can currently draw is that we appear to now have an archbishop who will not recognise the authority of scripture in *all* matters. ... My second concern ... is that he could become the darling of the gay lobby, whether by default or intention. ... There is a difficult line to be drawn some-times between generosity of heart and wisdom and foolishness. ... Public popularity is immaterial, faithfulness to Almighty God is essential.[1]

In the August issue there was a report from Jon Cox, a young curate now returned with his family to New South Wales. He cheerfully wrote about his new parish:

> It is a very low church with no robes, no liturgy and loads of young people. ... The regional bishop is a strong Evangelical who was concerned that I hold to the Bible as God's inspired and inscripturated [sic] word and that I see the gay debate as being an unbiblical non-starter. There are no women ordained in the diocese apart from one chaplain. So all in all it looks a good fit.

Well, all according to taste, but what upset Angela were the frequent assaults on homosexuality from the pulpit and the pressure to sign protest petitions, such as when the Children's Society decided that it would consider same-sex couples for fostering. You see, one of her sons is gay.

> They kept on and on about it, how wicked it was. It was put up on a board in the church as one of a list of sins. I was horrified by it all and gradually felt I could not go any more. It was my son they were talking about and I felt I was being made to feel guilty about it. I didn't tell anyone at the church because I felt I could not trust them. It was dreadful really.

Angela now attends another local church, a few miles away, with a woman vicar in headship, in whom she has confided. She did not feel she could ever do that with 'your friend and pastor' Stephen Seamer.

In a letter published in the local paper last July, Angela wrote:

> I long to see the whole Anglican church showing ... love and acceptance to homosexuals both inside and outside the church and trying to acknowledge the fact that homosexuality is not a choice but inborn. Coming to terms with it is often painful and bewildering. What is so badly needed from both clergy and laity is a realistic and understanding attitude as opposed to one of rejec-tion and dismissal.[2]

✠　✠　✠　✠　✠

Or take Bishop Peter Lee of Virginia. His story was told in the *New York Times* in early January 2004. In his 19 years in charge of the largest diocese in the Episcopal Church he has held the state's diverse congregations together, largely through taking a middle-of-the-road line. He had always resolutely refused to ordain non-celibate gay or lesbian clergy or to authorize same-sex blessings. Last summer as he pondered on how he should vote over Gene Robinson's nomination, he thought of the 200 bishops for whom he had voted over the years. Some had divorced and remarried, some did not share his theological views or opposed the ordination of women, but he had voted for them all because they had been legitimately chosen. He decided to vote for Robinson for the same reason, even though the Canon could not have been ordained in Virginia, still less become a bishop.

Lee told his diocese what he was doing. The result has been a torrent of abuse, 'You have betrayed the calling of Christ to be faithful' being one of the milder rebukes. Four of the largest, most conservative churches have told him that he is no longer welcome and they want to find another bishop. Parents have told him they do not want him to touch their children at confirmation. 'Psychological studies of clergy show that we are people who like to be liked. It's painful that there are churches where I am not welcome – that there are people who feel I have betrayed them,' the Bishop told the paper.[3]

Lee certainly did not take his decision lightly. He had read his Bible and been struck in the 15th chapter of the Acts of the Apostles by the way that the early leaders of the church had adapted Jewish law to the Gentile world. He had also read Martin Luther King's famous letter from Birmingham Jail, stating that significant change, especially if it creates a new understanding of justice, often starts in a disruptive or disturbing manner.

He took his case to a series of meetings across the diocese, to explain himself to congregations, telling the first of them that Robinson's consecration represented 'a conflict between hope and fear. Hope for God's grace versus fear of change. I chose hope'. He was met with silence and rebuke. At one meeting he was publicly told he would not be welcome at a forthcoming confirmation – a gratuitous insult, since he had already privately told the church concerned that he would stay away and yet they chose to publicize and make an issue of their demand, though not his acceptance of it.

Or what of the parish church of St Luke with Holy Trinity in Charlton, the south London suburb? It has been holding blessing services for same-sex couples since 1978. It has hardly been a secret: the national newspapers reported earlier services in their normal sensitive way ('Rumpus as Gay Couple are Blessed', *Sun*, 17 May 1985) and the current vicar has even written a book on the subject.[4]

Any one of four archbishops could by now have diverted their chauffeur-driven cars a few minutes off the direct route between Lambeth Palace and Canterbury to visit the church and anathematize the practice, but none has done so. Donald Coggan wrote to the diocesan bishop, Mervyn Stockwood of Southwark, when he first read about what was going on in the *Kentish Times* in the 1970s and the Bishop (who was himself gay) wrote to the then rector mildly to chastise him: 'It is true we have a duty as priests towards homosexuals, but we also have a duty to those who sincerely take a different point of view.'[5] Later, in retirement, Stockwood wrote again: 'I hope you did not find me too unsympathetic ... as you know, I did a lot to help in this matter during my episcopate, but I never appeared in print or joined a campaign.' No wonder: Stockwood's biography makes clear that he himself conducted at least one such service himself, for a headmaster and an Anglican priest.[6]

None of these events shattered the Anglican Communion or even rattled the windows of the Rev. Wynne-Jones, pillar of the Church of England Evangelical Council, in nearby Beckenham. The Church of St Luke is not alone in offering such services. Nor was Stockwood the first, or last, gay bishop. If they conform to the rest of the population, there are at least half a dozen within the Church of England now who are quietly, discreetly, homosexual. They haven't come out publicly, as is their right and choice, nor are they likely to do so, given what happened to Canon Jeffrey John. Perhaps they have all always lived celibate lives, but given that Canon John's assurance that he had not sinned for years was insufficient to appease the avenging angels on the bench of bishops and that only a public recantation and repentance would have satisfied them, no closeted cleric in future is likely to risk the wrath of the Evangelical community if he is at all ambitious. Hypocrisy, it appears, is preferable to honesty.

✠   ✠   ✠   ✠   ✠

Towards the end of the writing of this book, Rowan Williams agreed to see me at Lambeth Palace. We met in his study on a dark winter's afternoon to discuss the project and I asked him why he thought homosexuality had become the issue on which the church was dividing and why now.

> I think it is about a cultural challenge to the whole view of Scripture. This is
> an issue which allows a clear line to be drawn in the sand. It's not something
> that affects many people, unlike divorce. It's a good rallying point at a time of

cultural flux. If you are a Catholic there are other issues you can find as a marker – divorce, contraception – but Anglicanism does not have these.

The powerful politicization around the issue makes it very much harder to have a discussion and I don't think we are going to get a balanced debate going in the near future. There will not be a rapid reconciliation, especially in the US. Do we want some endless fragmentation of the kind traditionalist groups are prone to, or some coherent strategy which will enable us to work cooperatively together?

I think we need rather more attention to what really are church-dividing issues. Many of us thought we knew what those were – things like the divinity of Christ – not splinters of interpretation. It seems curious to me that at a time when we need quite a lot of attention and understanding to be given to the big central shape of the story, border skirmishing like this is taking up so much of our energy.

The Archbishop spoke of his pain about the campaign of the conservative Evangelicals – 'some spokesmen for the solidly conservative constituency have not done themselves justice. ... Sometimes it is hard to see the broad lines of Christian theology' – but he accepted that they had been influential in setting the pace for Evangelical opinion. 'What upsets me most is the idea that if you disagree on one issue, you are thought to be unsound on all the rest. ... If the Church of England can't make a model of sensible pluralism work, who can?'

I asked him what he would say to a gay priest, or ordinand and he sighed. 'Objectively the position of the Church of England has not changed, but, yes, I do recognize the perception and hear it directly. For some ordinands it is a headache. You have to make calculations as to what you can with honesty live with. ... It depends how much somebody feels this is a huge cost and yet it is worth doing. You need quite a lot of maturity to think it through in this climate. It is very difficult ...' His voice trailed away.

And how would it be worked out? He thought, maybe, by bringing in an outside expert on conflict resolution: 'When the dust has settled, it may be time to think about a facilitated conversation. Somebody coming in to structure discussions, who is an outsider and so does not threaten or bully. ... That might bring the two sides together.'

The lights were going on across London. Outside it was getting dark. And one of the leaders of the Christian Church was saying that he and his co-religionists could not resolve an internal conflict among themselves.

But maybe he has a point. The Evangelical community sees homosexuality as the last great taboo and has determined to fight it tooth and nail. If they give way now, the whole authority of the Bible, on which they base

their belief, must crumble, just as their ancestors thought it would disintegrate if slavery was deemed un-Christian or women were ordained or
divorce was permitted or shellfish was eaten. It is the issue that they have
chosen. It has not been thrust upon them – they spotted it as the rallying
point more than a decade ago and have been waiting for their opportunity
to strike. They see it as a useful way to unite their constituency in opposition to the shifting sands of belief and secular culture. The banks of the
broad river of belief have their limits, they say, without apparently notic-
ing that rivers change their course and occasionally overrun their channels
or that lines in the sand get washed away by the tide.

What precipitates the split now is that a section of conservative Evangelicals, with a militant and exclusivist philosophy and a taste for
confrontation, has organized an attempted coup to seize the old church
for its own agenda. Theirs is a sectarian, congregationalist church that can
tolerate only one sort of Christian and only the authority of those bishops
who agree with them. There is no room for dialogue, doubt or debate –
and maybe not for so many of the things many Anglicans still value:
ancient music, historic buildings, formal worship, hallowed prayers, the
Authorized Version or a sense of stillness and spirituality. The militants
hold these things in contempt as outdated painted vanities and they think
everyone else· should believe the same. This is a small faction within
Evangelicalism – though it claims itself to be the largest grouping – but it
is certainly a noisy and rancorous one.

In the USA, and to a lesser extent in England, this movement is bol-
stered by financial support from very wealthy men with a very reactionary
political agenda and a Fundamentalist theology: men who want to change
society, not just the church, and are prepared to pay to do it. In America
the likes of Howard Ahmanson and Richard Mellon Scaife have been
relatively successful in changing the country's political agenda. In Britain
religious pressure groups with a similar programme have been less successful but they have had more subtle triumphs, in the long campaigns against
the repeal of the otiose Section 28 and to win exemption for religious
institutions from equality legislation.

This has become in some ways an institution that is rather the reverse
of the traditional, bumbling, avuncular, wishy-washy Church of England.
Just as the Militant Tendency tried to subvert the old Labour Party in the
1980s, so the Church of England is being invaded by a Taliban Tendency
with its own agenda and a strong determination to win. This is a takeover
bid, to create a pure church of only one sort of believer. And it has found
allies in the USA and the developing world.

Some of these people complain, in similar terms, of a liberal plot and a gay conspiracy. But these are figments or excuses. In Britain the Lesbian and Gay Christian Movement has been active for a quarter of a century and has watched the church become more hostile to its members, not less. Similarly the liberals have been so successful that they have become an enclave, not a movement. It is not the liberal faction that has originated hate mail and vituperative abuse of a most un-Christian and even disgusting kind during the current row. There have been precious few on the Evangelical wing of the argument who have publicly deprecated such behaviour.

The truth is – as thoughtful Evangelicals acknowledge – that Christianity, particularly its Anglican strand, has changed its mind or argued its way around many of the things that are forbidden in the Biblical texts without the sky falling in on belief or worship. It has even half done so over homosexuality, accepting gay partnerships for lay members. True Christians, secure in their own beliefs, need no longer fear that their own faith will be undermined if others do things slightly differently from themselves. No one, after all, is demanding the compulsory ordination of gay bishops or the obligatory blessing of same-sex couples.

But this is dangerous ground for a Bible-believing Evangelical. When I suggested to Philip Giddings that Christians had changed their minds on other things, he suddenly became quite vehement and pink in the face. 'So what is your point? What is your point?' he bellowed. 'What's the logic? It is simply inapplicable. Homosexuality is a sin. It is different. No one has ever suggested that being a woman is sinful, or being a slave is sinful.' Well, yes, actually they have, right from the days of Eve – and, anyway, aren't we all sinners? Or does Dr Giddings have a unique dispensation?

The Bible is hostile to homosexuality but there are legitimate questions to be asked about how its scattered phrases on the subject should be interpreted for today's society and whether its concept of sexuality could encompass modern Christian homosexuals in permanent loving relationships. Evangelicals tend not to consider these questions.

There is an accompanying argument that needs addressing: how can the church come to terms with the realities of cultural diversity in the modern world and yet stick rigidly to Biblical coherence? Diarmaid MacCulloch, Professor of the History of the Church at Oxford University, in his magisterial recent work *Reformation*, suggests a choice has to be made: 'The only alternatives are either to try to cleave to patterns of life and assumptions set out in the Bible, or to say that in this, as in much else, the Bible is simply wrong.'[7]

For if the Bible offers a certain defence, traditionalists are also aware that it may not be convincing enough, which is why they cast around for other reasons to endorse the views of the writers of Genesis and Leviticus and argue that homosexuality is also medically or socially dangerous or subversive. In this, they have a very narrow view of the homosexual and his activities. Like the Rev. Earle Fox, they are seduced by the disgusting practice and recognize only one lifestyle choice of behaviour, lumping faithful gay couples together with promiscuous, faithless ones – in a way that they would not do with heterosexual couples – and supposing that homosexuals somehow choose their condition. They also tend to group homosexuals with paedophiles and other sexual perverts, being unable to recognize or acknowledge the essential difference between a consensual relationship and a coercive, abusive one.

No one seriously argues that the church should be prepared to bless all gay relationships, any more than it should bless all heterosexual ones – though many vicars appear perfectly willing to marry men and women who are in the most fleeting, promiscuous and vestigial, even adulterous, relationships. What will happen if Prince Charles, the future supreme governor of their church, wants to marry Camilla Parker Bowles? Will the bishops reject him? Or will they find some way to do it, even knowing what the whole world knows about the couple's past behaviour?

The Anglican Church already does bless certain homosexual relation-ships and has done for many years without provoking threats of schism. It does so quietly and furtively. Why should it not offer blessings to couples who have proved their commitment to each other? These would be a minority of an already small minority and it would not be a marriage. It would not be a service offered to everyone who came along or offered compulsorily by every priest regardless of personal conscience. But it would be a recognition of a faithful and loving friendship, which may – who knows and who has the right to inquire? – have a sexual expression.

Already the hurdles would be higher than for a heterosexual couple because a much higher degree of commitment would inevitably be de-manded. Surely such a service would not undermine the nature or practice of heterosexual marriage – how could it, any more than the church has already done by sanctioning non-procreative sex through contraception and remarriage for divorcees? The church has expressed a number of definitions of marriage in its rites over the years, including the avoidance of fornication, but it is only recently that the procreation of children has come to be seen as its paramount and sole-defining purpose. What of heterosexual couples who have no intention of having children, or who are unable to conceive them, or are too old or infirm to do so? Are their unions somehow incomplete or irregular?

This is the problem with thinking of gays in only one way, as people who are not quite human, referring to them as deviants and inverts as rather too many otherwise loving Christians often do. It is a consequence of talking *at* them, not listening *to* them, as the church does too frequently. What is the point of listening to gays and lesbians, as clergy are supposed to do, if their minds are already made up and can never be altered because of what was written several thousand years ago?

Ultimately any organization can impose on its members such rules as it wishes, but the church purports to have a more serious purpose than a golf club. It wants, it says, to welcome all souls and to share the Good News of a loving and inclusive God with them. And yet the message it conveys is usually one of disapproval, of rejection and contempt. Why has no one told Peter Akinola that he is a bigot? Is it just because he is black? Why does no one point out that Gregory Venables speaks for an archdiocese with a congregation the size of a small parish? If the church wishes to be an exclusive sect then that is its right, but Evangelicals of all people claim not to believe that. And there is another point: the Church of England is more than just another denomination: it is the established church of the country, available to all but in practice excluding by its language and actions one section of the community to which it is supposed to minister.

That the church is out of step with civil law and social attitudes may serve only to confirm to conservative Evangelicals that they are right, but a state institution cannot step too far away from the mainstream of public opinion. The monarchy and the Conservative Party have learned this and so, in the past, has the Church of England. It will continue to receive a battering on this issue while it is perceived to be hypocritical in its actions and judgemental of the private behaviour of people whose loving relationships affect no one but themselves. This is a church coming down hard on a group of people because of who they are as much as what they do, to the exclusion – for it can talk of little else – of other much more critical issues affecting many more people, such as family breakdown, poverty, promiscuity, illegitimacy and divorce. These are social problems on which moral stances should be taken, not on what men do privately in bed with other men, or women with other women.

The author Monica Furlong died shortly before the controversies of 2003, but she wrote perceptively in her last book:

Gayness arouses deep feelings among some Christians. ... Yet more and more in Britain it is being taken for granted; it is being understood not as something wicked or sinful or a sign of depravity but simply as how some people are and there seems no good reason not to trust their account of the way love and sex seems to them, even if it is different from the way George Carey or anyone else happens to experience it. ... Part of loving one's neighbour is allowing him or her to be different from oneself – if one cannot fully understand them or imagine how their taste can be so different from one's own, at least one can try to give them the benefit of the doubt.[8]

The commission, appointed by Rowan Williams following the primates' meeting, is now in occasional session. It will probably choose uniformity of practice over diversity, and prize unity above pearls such as truth and justice. It now has precedents in the establishment of alternative oversight for congregations unable to conceive of the idea that a woman is capable of priesthood, let alone episcopacy, and so it may seek to hold together the different provinces of its communion by a plurality of primates, a burgeoning of bishops, a diversity of deans and competing cliques of clergy, all believing everybody else to be in Fundamental Error. This will be an evasion. The old church's broad foundations will be placed under intolerable strain, but everyone will have their own doctrinal purity and be able to look down on everyone else: each flying buttress with a different gargoyle, spouting a variety of creeds. Whatever else it is, it won't be a broad church. How will that profit a man? And in what sense will it be a communion?

Or the church could grow up, challenge the bigots in its midst and allow perhaps for a degree of prophetic vision. No one need be forced to do anything, least of all leave, but nor would they be required to ram their own narrow interpretations of belief and ideological purity down the throats of anyone else. They could live together in mutual tolerance and harmony and so demonstrate an example to a world that has suffered too much from religious persecution and sectarianism over the past 2,000 years. The choice needs to be made, otherwise the church will decline and die in the West and wither in the developing world. But the problem is, some of these people have got Religion.

My suspicion is that the vehemence of the current debate is partly caused because Evangelicals fear that, while they are winning the church, they are losing the argument. The tide of history is against them. Philip Giddings at the end of our discussion fell to musing how God might have to resort to miracles to get His church back on track and force the US Episcopalians to retreat. 'It will need a miracle. I know one should not talk of classes of miracles, but a very visible miracle. That is what it will need – direct, divine intervention. But I don't think that's unusual.'

This was a couple of weeks after Gene Robinson's consecration, so I asked what he meant – something like a heart attack? 'Well, God is pretty active in His world,' Giddings said without a smile. 'God is in control of all this, He works graciously, for better or for worse.' He added:

> There are puzzling questions about why God is allowing this. From time to time He exposes His people to severe trial. The Bible talks of pruning, purging and so on and the church always grows under persecution. If the church disintegrates, maybe that is because God discerns a better means for the building of His Kingdom. God sometimes allows things to go in very strange directions.

NOTES

CHAPTER 1. THE SORROW AND THE PITY

[1] Penry Williams, *The Later Tudors* (OUP, 1998) p 458.
[2] *Church Times*, 6 November 2003.
[3] Donald Cozzens, *The Changing Face of the Priesthood* (Liturgical Press, 2000), pp 20-1.
[4] Noel Annan, *Our Age* (Fontana, 1991), p 144.
[5] *Guardian*, 14 July 2003. (Articles cited as appearing in the *Guardian* and *Tablet* since 2000 were written by the author of this book.)

CHAPTER 2. THE WORD MADE FLESH

[1] John Stott, *Same Sex Partnerships? A Christian Perspective* (Fleming H. Revell, 1998).
[2] Interview, Bishop W. Benn, September 2003. All the interviews in this chapter were conducted in September and October 2003.
[3] Bishop of Chester, reported in the *Guardian*, 8 November 2003.
[4] Paul Gardner, et al, *Fanning the Flame: Bible, Cross and Mission: Resource Materials for NEAC 2003* (Zondervan, Michigan, 2003), p 7.
[5] *Church of England Newspaper*, HTB/Alpha insert, 13 November 2003.
[6] *Baptist Times* on Clements (23 September 1999).

CHAPTER 3. IN THE BEGINNING WAS THE WORD

[1] Recent articles in *Nucleus*, journal of the Christian Medical Fellowship, 1999–2001.
[2] Colin Slee, address to Inclusive Church service, Putney, 11 August 2003.
[3] Peter Akinola, *Church Times*, 3 July 2003.
[4] *Church of England Newspaper*, 9 October 2003.
[5] Gareth Moore, *A Question of Truth: Christianity and Homosexuality* (Continuum, 2003), p 147.

[6]   Martyn Percy, *Intimate Affairs: Sexuality and Spirituality in Perspective* (Darton, Longman and Todd, 1997), appendix.

[7]   Reay Tannahill, *Sex in History* (Abacus, 1980), p 146.

[8]   Stott, *Same Sex Partnerships?*, p 21.

[9]   *Some Issues in Human Sexuality: A Guide to the Debate* (Church House Publishing, November 2003), p 122.

[10] John Richardson, *What God Has Made Clean ... If We Can Eat Prawns, Why Is Gay Sex Wrong?* (The Good Book Company, 2003), p 21.

[11] *Ibid.*, p 17.

[12] *Ibid.*, p 28.

[13] *Ibid.*, p 29.

[14] *Some Issues in Human Sexuality*, pp 125–6.

[15] *Ibid.*, pp 127–9.

[16] 'Homosexuality and the Bible', in Tony Higton (ed), *Sexuality and the Church: A Way Forward* (ABWON, 1987).

[17] Percy, *Intimate Affairs*, p 112.

[18] Michael Vasey, *Strangers and Friends: A New Exploration of Homosexuality and the Bible* (Hodder and Stoughton, 1995), pp 133–4.

[19] Timothy Bradshaw, *The Way Forward? Christian Voices on Homosexuality and the Church* (SCM Press, 2003): Jeffrey John, p 50.

[20] *Ibid.*, pp 52–3.

[21] *Some Issues in Human Sexuality*, p 138.

[22] Vasey, *Strangers and Friends*, pp 135–6.

[23] *Some Issues in Human Sexuality*, p 140.

[24] Peter Coleman, *Christian Attitudes to Homosexuality* (SPCK, 1980), quoted in *Some Issues in Human Sexuality*, p 143.

[25] *Guardian*, 4 October 2003.

[26] Vasey, *Strangers and Friends*, p 137.

[27] Quoted in Frederick Clarkson, 'Christian Reconstructionism: Theocratic Dominionism Gains Influence', *Public Eye*, vol. VIII, March 1994.

[28] *Ibid.*

[29] Stott, *Same Sex Partnerships?*, p 24.

[30] *Washington Post*, 24 October 2003; *Pittsburgh Post-Gazette*, 17 May 2004.

[31] Salon.com news feature: 'Avenging Angel of the Religious Right', by Max Blumenthal, January 2004.

[32] *Guardian*, 30 December 2003.

[33] G. Wenham, address on Old Testament and Homosexuality, NEAC Conference, 21 September 2003.

CHAPTER 4. QUEER AS FOLK

[1]   Diane Knippers, address to 'A Place to Stand' Conference, Dallas, reported in the *Guardian*, 8 October 2003.

[2]   *Guardian*, 19 July 2003.

CHAPTER 5. OLD AS THE HILLS

[1]   Tannahill, *Sex in History*, p 337.
[2]   Annan, *Our Age*, p 168.
[3]   Graham Robb, *Strangers: Homosexual Love in the 19th Century* (Picador, 2003), p 7.
[4]   Tannahill, *Sex in History*, p 70.
[5]   *Ibid.*, p 81; cf. Plato's *Symposium*, 178E–179.
[6]   Robb, *Strangers*, p 235.
[7]   *Ibid.*, pp 240–1.
[8]   Tannahill, *Sex in History*, p 130.
[9]   *Ibid.*, p 133.
[10] *Ibid.*, p 143.
[11] John Boswell, *Christianity, Social Tolerance and Homosexuality* (University of Chicago Press, 1980), p 180.
[12] Tannahill, *Sex in History*, pp 148–52.
[13] William Naphy, *Sex Crimes: From Renaissance to Enlightenment* (Tempus, 2002), p 90.
[14] Robb, *Strangers*, p 26.
[15] *Ibid.*, pp 22–31.
[16] Diarmaid MacCulloch, *Reformation* (Allen Lane, 2003), pp 209, 517.
[17] Robb, *Strangers*, pp 101–4.
[18] Curt Gentry, *J. Edgar Hoover* (Norton, 1991), pp 307–10.
[19] John Boswell, *Same-Sex Unions in Pre-Modern Europe* (Random House, 1995), p 232.
[20] Stott, *Same Sex Partnerships?*, p 37.
[21] Alan Bray, *The Friend* (University of Chicago Press, 2003), pp 78–83, 140–2.
[22] Noel Annan, *The Dons* (University of Chicago Press, 1999), p 65.
[23] *Manchester Union Leader*, New Hampshire, 1 November 2003.
[24] Naphy, *Sex Crimes*, p 102.
[25] Robb, *Strangers*, p 158.
[26] *Ibid.*, pp 20–1.
[27] Richard Ellmann, *Oscar Wilde* (Penguin, 1988), p 450.
[28] Tannahill, *Sex in History*, p 378, quoting W.T. Stead in *Review of Reviews*, 15 June 1895.
[29] Roy Jenkins, *A Life at the Centre* (Macmillan, 1991), p 209.
[30] Tannahill, *Sex in History*, p 435.
[31] *Church Times*, 14 July 1967, and following weeks.

CHAPTER 6. THE DAY BEFORE YESTERDAY

[1] Monica Furlong, *C of E: The State It's In* (Hodder and Stoughton, 2000), p 117.
[2] *Church Times*, 4 August 1967, and following weeks.
[3] Sean Gill, *The Lesbian and Gay Christian Movement* (Cassell, 1998), p 9.
[4] *Ibid.*, p 11.
[5] *Independent*, 18 March 1995.
[6] *Guardian*, 16 May 1996.
[7] Furlong, *C of E: The State It's In*, p 140.
[8] *Church Times* and *Guardian* reports, 12 and 13 November 1987.
[9] *Daily Mail*, 22 October 1987.
[10] Jeffrey Heskins, *Unheard Voices* (Darton, Longman and Todd, 2001), p 38.
[11] National press reports, 14 March 1995.
[12] Stott, *Same Sex Partnerships?*, p 40.
[13] BBC *Breakfast with Frost* programme, 24 November 2003.
[14] Gill, *The Lesbian and Gay Christian Movement*, p 66.
[15] *Ibid.*, p 68.
[16] *Church Times*, 20 May 1988.
[17] *Church Times*, 16 February 1990.
[18] *Some Issues in Human Sexuality*, p 45.
[19] *Guardian*, 29 April 1997.

CHAPTER 7. THE DIGNITY OF DIFFERENCE

[1] David Bebbington, *Evangelicalism in Modern Britain* (UnwinHyman, 1989), p 187.
[2] See Edward J. Larson, *Summer for the Gods* (Harvard University Press, 1997) for an account of the Scopes trial and the rise of American Fundamentalism.
[3] Bebbington, *Evangelicalism*, p 259.
[4] *Church Times*, 19 September 2003.
[5] Furlong, *C of E: The State It's In*, pp 331–3.
[6] *Church Times*, 19 September 2003.
[7] Graham Cray et al, *Mission-Shaped Church: Church Planting and Fresh Expressions of Church in a Changing Context* (Church House Publishing, 2004).
[8] Furlong, *C of E: The State It's In*, p 337.
[9] Martyn Percy: 'A Blessed Rage for Order: The Rise of Reform in the Church of England', *Journal of Anglican Studies* (forthcoming, 2004).
[10] *Crossway*, Autumn 2003, p 90.
[11] Gill, *The Lesbian and Gay Christian Movement*, p 22.
[12] *Ibid.*, p 77.
[13] *Ibid.*, p 27.
[14] *Ibid.*, p 195.

[15] *Guardian*, 12 December 2003.
[16] Martyn Percy (ed), *Modern Believing*, article: 'A Matter of Attitude, Homosexuality and Divisions in the Church' (Ashgate, forthcoming 2004).

CHAPTER 8. DOING THE LAMBETH WALK

[1] James E. Solheim, *Diversity or Disunity? Reflections on Lambeth 1998* (Church Publishing Incorporated, New York, 1999), p 24. Much of the information in this chapter is taken from this book by the US Episcopal Church's director of communications.
[2] Bradshaw, *The Way Forward?*, pp 5–11.
[3] Drexel Gomez and Maurice Sinclair, *To Mend the Net* (Carrollton, 2001).
[4] *Church Times*, 17 July 1998.
[5] Solheim, *Diversity or Disunity?*, pp 52–3.
[6] Heskins, *Unheard Voices*, p 32.
[7] *Church Times*, 17 July 1998.
[8] Solheim, *Diversity or Disunity?*, pp 95–6.
[9] *Ibid.*, p 94.
[10] *Ibid.*, pp 63–6.
[11] *Church Times*, 14 August 1998
[12] *Church Times*, 21 July 2000.

CHAPTER 9. THEN CAME ROWAN

[1] 'The Body's Grace', republished by LGCM, 2003.
[2] Bradshaw, *The Way Forward?*, p 12.
[3] *Ibid.*, pp 17–18.
[4] *Anvil*, vol. 20, no. 4, November 2003.
[5] Rupert Shortt, *Rowan Williams: An Introduction* (Darton, Longman and Todd, 2003), p 51.
[6] *Guardian*, 24 July 2002.
[7] *Sunday Times*, 6 July 2003.
[8] *Anvil*, vol. 20, no. 4, November 2003.
[9] *Churchman*, Winter 2003, p 291.
[10] *English Churchman*, 14 June 2003.
[11] *English Churchman*, 21 September 2002.
[12] *Guardian*, 26 September 2002.
[13] *Guardian*, 11 December 2002.
[14] *Church Times*, 29 November 2002.
[15] *Guardian*, 16 May 2003.
[16] *Guardian*, 23 December 2002.
[17] *Guardian*, 17 December 2002.
[18] Rowan Williams, enthronement sermon, Canterbury, 27 February 2003.

CHAPTER 10. DOCTOR JOHN

[1] National newspapers, 18 April 2003.

[2] *Guardian*, 28 May 2003.

[3] *Guardian*, 31 May 2003.

[4] *Daily Telegraph*, 29 May 2003.

[5] Bradshaw, *The Way Forward?*, p 56.

[6] *Daily Telegraph*, 6 June 2003.

[7] Graham Dow, *Explaining Deliverance* (Sovereign World Ltd, 1991), pp 37, 44.

[8] *Guardian*, 17 June 2003.

[9] *The Times*, 19 June 2003.

[10] BBC2 *Newsnight*, 16 June 2003.

[11] *Guardian*, 21 June 2003.

[12] Diocese of Oxford figures, November 2003.

[13] *Guardian*, 23 June 2003.

[14] *Sunday Times*, 22 June 2003.

[15] *Guardian*, 24 June 2003.

[16] *Church Times*, 20 June 2003.

[17] *Guardian*, 7 July 2003.

[18] *Reading Chronicle*, 17 July 2003.

[19] *Guardian*, 15 July 2003.

CHAPTER 11. GENE GENIE

[1] *Observer*, 19 October 2003.

[2] Statement by Isabella (Boo) McDaniel M.Ed, to Minneapolis Convention, quoted in the *Guardian*, 2 August 2003.

[3] Heskins, *Unheard Voices*, p 120.

[4] *Institute for Democracy Studies*, vol. 2, issue 2, December 2001: 'A Church at Risk: The Episcopal Renewal Movement' and Salon.com news feature: 'Avenging Angel of the Religious Right' by Max Blumenthal, January 2004. See also *Washington Post*, 24 October 2003 and *Pittsburgh Post-Gazette*, 21 September 2003.

[5] *Guardian*, 4 August 2003.

[6] *Guardian*, 6 August 2003.

[7] *Tablet*, 9 August 2003.

CHAPTER 12. PAVED WITH GOOD INTENTIONS

[1] Slee, sermon, 11 August 2003.

[2] *New Directions*, Autumn 2003.

[3] *Guardian*, 8 September 2003.

[4] *Guardian*, 27 September 2003.

5   *Independent*, 29 December 2003.
6   *Anvil*, vol. 20, no. 4, November 2003.
7   True Freedom Trust, PO Box 13, Prenton, Wirral, CH43 6YB.
8   David Holloway, '50 Theses on the Future of the Church of England', 20 September 2003.
9   *Guardian*, 22 September 2003.
10   *Ibid.*
11   *Church Times*, 9 January 2004.
12   *Guardian*, 8 October 2003.
13   Kendall Harmon, 'Anglican Essentials and Our Future Call', tape published by Manna Conference Taping Inc, New Mexico.
14   Vatican letter, published 9 October 2003.
15   *Guardian*, 10 October 2003.
16   *Guardian*, 16 October 2003.
17   Primates' statement, 16 October 2003.
18   *Guardian*, 18 October 2003.
19   Michael Ingham, 'Reclaiming Christian Orthodoxy', address to LGCM Conference, Manchester, 25 October 2003.
20   *Guardian*, 31 October 2003.
21   *Boston Globe*, 31 October 2003.
22   Ian Bradley (ed), *Penguin Book of Hymns* (Penguin, 1989), p 386.
23   Douglas Theuner, sermon at consecration of Gene Robinson, Durham, New Hampshire, 2 November 2003.
24   *Guardian*, 3 November 2003.
25   Statement to Christian Challenge, Washington DC, 19 October 2003.
26   *Church Times*, 6 November 2003.
27   *Church of England Newspaper*, 2 January 2004.
28   Congo bishops' statement, 5 January 2004.
29   *New York Times*, 29 December 2003.
30   Episcopal News Service, 17 December 2003.
31   *Guardian*, 12 February 2004; *Church Times*, 13 February 2004.

CHAPTER 13. WHO BEARS THE COST?

1   *Contact* parish magazine, Tonbridge, February 2003.
2   *Kent and Sussex Courier*, 4 July 2003.
3   *New York Times*, 4 January 2004.
4   Heskins, *Unheard Voices*.
5   *Ibid.*, p 199.
6   Michael de la Noy, *A Lonely Life* (Mowbray, 1996), p 186.
7   MacCulloch, *Reformation*, p 705.
8   Furlong, *C of E: The State It's In*, p 364.

BIBLIOGRAPHY

Books

Annan, Noel, *Our Age* (Fontana, 1991)
—, *The Dons* (University of Chicago Press, 1999)
Bartley, Jonathan, *The Subversive Manifesto* (Bible Reading Fellowship, 2003)
Bebbington, David, *Evangelicalism in Modern Britain* (UnwinHyman, 1989)
Betteridge, Tom, *Sodomy in Early Modern Europe* (Manchester University Press, 2002)
The Bible: Authorized King James Version (Oxford World's Classics, 1997)
Boswell, John, *Christianity, Social Tolerance and Homosexuality* (University of Chicago Press 1980)
—, *Same-Sex Unions in Pre-Modern Europe* (Random House, 1995)
Bradley, Ian (ed), *The Penguin Book of Hymns* (Penguin, 1989)
Bradshaw, Timothy (ed), *The Way Forward? Christian Voices on Homosexuality and the Church* (SCM Press, 2003)
Bray, Alan, *Homosexuality in Renaissance England* (Columbia University Press, 1995)
—, *The Friend* (University of Chicago Press, 2003)
Chadwick, Henry, *The Early Church* (Penguin, 1967)
Church of England: The Power and the Glory (BBC Four, 2003, transcript)
Countryman, L. William, *Dirt, Greed and Sex: Sexual Ethics in the New Testament and Their Implications for Today* (Fortress Press, 1990)
Cozzens, Donald B., *The Changing Face of the Priesthood* (Liturgical Press, 2000)
Cray, Graham et al, *Mission-Shaped Church: Church Planting and Fresh Expressions of Church in a Changing Context* (Church House Publishing, 2004)
de la Noy, Michael, *A Lonely Life* (Mowbray, 1996)
Dow, Graham, *Explaining Deliverance* (Sovereign World Ltd, 1991)
Ellmann, Richard, *Oscar Wilde* (Penguin, 1988)
Furlong, Monica, *C of E: The State It's In* (Hodder and Stoughton, 2000)
Gardner, Paul, Chris Wright and Chris Green, *Fanning the Flame: Bible, Cross and Mission: Resource Materials for NEAC 2003* (Zondervan, Michigan, 2003)

Gentry, Curt, *J. Edgar Hoover* (Norton, 1991)

Gill, Sean, *The Lesbian and Gay Christian Movement* (Cassell, 1998)

Gomez, Drexel and Maurice Sinclair, *To Mend the Net* (Carrollton, 2001)

Hallett, Martin, *Sexuality and the Church – A Problem and a Gift?* (True Freedom Trust)

Hastins, Adrian, *A History of English Christianity 1920–2000* (SCM Press, 2001)

Heskins, Jeffrey, *Unheard Voices* (Darton, Longman and Todd, 2001)

Higton, Tony, *Sexuality and the Church: A Way Forward* (ABWON, 1987)

Holloway, David, *Church and State in the New Millennium* (HarperCollins, 2000)

Ind, Jo, *Memories of Bliss: God, Sex and Us* (SCM Press, 2003)

Ingham, Michael, *Reclaiming Christian Orthodoxy* (address to LGCM Conference, 2003)

Issues in Human Sexuality: A Statement by the House of Bishops (Church House Publishing, 1991)

Jenkins, Roy, *A Life at the Centre* (Macmillan, 1991)

Larson, Edward J, *Summer for the Gods* (Harvard University Press, 1997)

Le Goff, Jacques, *The Medieval World* (Collins and Brown, 1990)

Louden, Stephen H. and Leslie J. Francis, *The Naked Parish Priest* (Continuum, 2003)

MacCulloch, Diarmaid, *Reformation* (Allen Lane, 2003)

McNeill, John J., *The Church and the Homosexual* (Beacon Press, Boston, 1993)

Moore, Gareth, *A Question of Truth: Christianity and Homosexuality* (Continuum, 2003)

Naphy, William, *Sex Crimes: From Renaissance to Enlightenment* (Tempus, 2002)

Oddie, William, *The Crockford's File* (Hamish Hamilton, 1989)

Percy, Martyn, *Intimate Affairs: Sexuality and Spirituality in Perspective* (Darton, Longman and Todd, 1997)

—, 'A Blessed Rage for Order: The Rise of Reform in the Church of England', *Journal of Anglican Studies* (forthcoming, 2004)

— (ed), *Modern Believing* (Ashgate, forthcoming, 2004)

Reid, Gavin, *To Canterbury with Love* (Kingsway, 2002)

Richardson, John, *What God Has Made Clean ... If We Can Eat Prawns, Why is Gay Sex Wrong?* (The Good Book Company, 2003)

Robb, Graham, *Strangers: Homosexual Love in the 19th Century* (Picador, 2003)

Russell, Conrad, *The Crisis of Parliaments* (OUP, 1971)

Schluter, Michael, *Christianity in a Changing World* (Marshall Pickering, 2000)

Shortt, Rupert, *Rowan Williams: An Introduction* (Darton, Longman and Todd, 2003)

Solheim, James E., *Diversity or Disunity? Reflections on Lambeth 1998* (Church Publishing Incorporated, New York, 1999)

Some Issues in Human Sexuality: A Guide to the Debate (Church House Publishing, 2003)

Stott, John, *Same Sex Partnerships? A Christian Perspective* (Fleming H. Revell, 1998)

——, *Human Rights and Human Wrongs* (Baker Books, 1999)

Stuart, Elizabeth, *Gay and Lesbian Theologies: Repetitions with Critical Difference* (Ashgate, 2003)

Tannahill, Reay, *Sex in History* (Abacus, 1980)

Vasey, Michael, *Strangers and Friends: A New Exploration of Homosexuality and the Bible* (Hodder and Stoughton, 1995)

Walker, Peter and Andrew Goddard, *True Union in the Body?* (Grove Books, 2003)

Williams, Penry, *The Later Tudors* (OUP, 1998)

Williams, Rowan, *The Body's Grace* (LGCM, reprinted 2003)

Wilson, A.N., *God's Funeral* (Abacus, 1999)

Newspapers and periodicals

Anglican Communion News Service; Anglican Mainstream; Anvil: An Anglican Evangelical Journal; Baptist Times; Boston Globe; Church of England Newspaper; Church of England Yearbook 2003; Church Times; Churchman (journal of the Church Society); Concord Monitor, New Hampshire; Contact (magazine of St Peter and Paul, Tonbridge); Crucible; Daily Telegraph; English Churchman; Guardian; Lexington Herald Leader, Kentucky; New York Times; Sunday Times; Tablet; The Times; Union Leader, New Hampshire

Interviews

Anderson, Rev. David, President, American Anglican Council

Banting, Rev. David, Chairman of Reform, Vicar of St Peter's, Harold Wood, Essex

Benn, Rt. Rev. Wallace, Bishop of Lewes

Brierley, Rev. Michael, Bishop's Chaplain, Diocese of Oxford

Clements, Dr Roy

Coward, Rev. Colin, Director, Changing Attitudes pressure group

Fisher, Rev. George, Vicar of St Thomas's Church, Blackpool

Fraser, Rev. Giles, Vicar of Putney and lecturer in philosophy, Wadham College Oxford

Gerken, Mr Richard, New Hampshire

Giddings, Dr Philip, Diocese of Oxford and lay member of General Synod

Green, Rev. Chris, Vice Principal, Oak Hill Theological College, London

Griswold, Most Rev. Frank Tracy, Presiding Bishop, US Episcopal Church

Gumbel, Rev. Nicky, Curate, Holy Trinity, Brompton, London

Harmon, Rev. Dr Kendall, Canon Theologian, Diocese of South Carolina

Harries, Rt. Rev. Richard, Bishop of Oxford

Higton, Rev. Tony, General Director, Church's Mission Amongst Jewish People

Holloway, Rt. Rev. Richard, former Primus, Scottish Episcopal Church

Ingham, Rt. Rev. Michael, Bishop of New Westminster, Canada

Jennings, Rev. Jonathan, Lambeth Palace

Junkin, Rev. Hayes, Diocese of New Hampshire

Kirker, Rev. Richard, Director, Lesbian and Gay Christian Movement

Millar, Rev. Sandy, Vicar of Holy Trinity, Brompton

Nesbitt, Rev. Pat, Curate, St Thomas's Church, Blackpool

Newton, Dr Robert, Diocese of New Hampshire

Nunley, Rev. Jan, Press Officer, US Episcopal Church

Percy, Canon Dr Martyn, Director, Lincoln Theological Institute, Manchester University

Phelps, Mrs Abigail, Topeka, Kansas

Rees, Mrs Christina, former member Archbishop's Council, lay member of General Synod

Reid, Rt. Rev. Gavin, former Bishop of Maidstone

Reynolds, Rev. Martin, Lesbian and Gay Christian Movement

Robinson, Rt. Rev. Gene, Bishop-Coadjutor, New Hampshire

Rosenthal, Canon Jim, Director Anglican Communion News Service

Slee, Very Rev. Colin, Dean of Southwark

Sugden, Rev. Chris, Oxford Centre for Mission Studies

Taylor, Rev. William, Vicar of St. Helen's Bishopsgate, London

Thomas, Rev. Richard, Diocese of Oxford

Widdicombe, Mrs Angela

Williams, Most Rev. Rowan, Archbishop of Canterbury

Wright, Rt. Rev. Tom, Bishop of Durham

And others.

INDEX